Psychologist at Large

EDWIN G. BORING

Psychologist at Large

An Autobiography
and
Selected Essays

BASIC BOOKS · NEW YORK

Contents

77702

Illustrations

Psychologist at Large

Psychologist at Large
1960

Introduction

Every psychologist who was trained for the doctorate in E. B. Titchener's Psychological Laboratory at Cornell in the first two decades of this century knew—or at least believed—that the historical approach to the understanding of scientific fact is what differentiates the scholar in science from the mere experimenter. That conviction was a product of the magic of Titchener's infectious faith, and in 1912, when Titchener suddenly turned over the advanced systematic courses in psychology at Cornell to his very junior staff, we four youngsters—for that is what we were—proceeded in after-midnight endeavor to discover for ourselves psychology's facts, to prepare them for promulgation, and then to dig out the history of research that provided them with their present status in the body scientific.

Out of my participation in these lectures at Cornell and then the giving of them by myself at Clark and later at Harvard grew my book in 1929, *A History of Experimental Psychology*, which in a second edition is still alive after more than thirty years. In this volume I tried to go into such biographical detail as might connect the convictions of important men with those events in their lives which helped to form their personalities, but there

Expanded, updated, and reoriented from the 1950 sketch in *A History of Psychology in Autobiography*, 1952, vol. IV, 27–52, by permission of the Clark University Press.

3

was not enough information of this sort available. Why not, I thought, make an effort to get these data? So I suggested to Carl Murchison that the Clark University Press might undertake a series of the intellectual histories of important psychologists as each man analyzed the sources of his own achievement. The project succeeded in that the autobiographies were written. There were three volumes in 1930–1936 and then a fourth in 1952 to which I contributed. I wrote at length, trying hard to achieve the goal which I myself had set twenty years before, endeavoring to penetrate to the springs of my own motivation and to see why my values were as they were and why they are now as they are. Success in such an undertaking can only be relative. Comment has led me to believe that I dug somewhat deeper in self-analysis than most of the fifty-seven others who contributed to these four volumes. One good friend advised me not to publish what I had written because "it is too frank; your graduate students will never again respect you." I treated his advice with a proper contempt and found that respect for the maturity of graduate students wins their respect in return.

I had written at length in order to be free and unconstrained— 28,000 words. I was supposed to keep down to 12,000. I cut to 14,000 and that is what was printed. I had to rewrite completely, of course. Now, ten years later, the project of this present volume arises, and my publishers have asked for the old long version, plus a new introduction, the addition of the new decade of professional activity, and a new kind of summary at the end. Here it is. Up to 1950 this account is an intellectual history written mostly in 1950 when I thought the theme of my life had been the search for maturity. The most recent decade is described in 1960, when I had decided that I had by 1950 achieved enough maturity to get along with and when I was beginning to find life richer, less frustrating, more rewarding, and in general happier than the Philadelphia boy with the lonely childhood expected it to be. And that brings us to the story itself.

The Background

Ancestors. Do autobiographies properly mention them? Yes, if the ancestors were known and talked about in the autobiographer's youth and so affected him by social and cultural means. I know the names of ten of my one hundred twenty-eight great-great-great-great-great-grandparents (five men and their wives), and I know only a little more about two of the men, John Boreing and Jean Garrigues. I know nothing at all about the five million genes of these one hundred twenty-eight grandparents, nor anything about the forty thousand of them that I got. Not blood nor genes, but tradition and lore tell of ancestors.

It seems proper to mention the patronymic line first. In the summer of 1670 John Boreing emigrated from England to Maryland and presented his claim as a settler for land. The claim was granted, and before he died in 1690 he had become a holder of considerable property in Maryland, near the site of Baltimore. He was my grandfather with five greats.

We have never been able to find any connection in England. We have no knowledge of Boreings or Borings there. There are, of course, the English Bowrings who trace their ancestry back to a Bouryng of 1303 and of whom the best known person is Sir John Bowring, diplomat, linguist, and Jeremy Bentham's literary executor. Twice a *w* has been inserted into the name in America, but both instances were capricious. My grandfather, a contractor and carpenter, put in the *w* for a while because my Uncle John had his eye on the famous Sir John Bowring; later my grandfather took the *w* out again because his Irish workmen pronounced the name like the forward end of a boat instead of like what propels an arrow.

John (d. 1690), the Maryland planter, had a son Thomas, who had a son Thomas, who had a son Ezekiel, who had a son Ezekiel. The first Thomas held land near Baltimore. The second Thomas

moved away from the bay, and the first Ezekiel Boreing continued to live inland. The second Ezekiel (1780–1861) dropped
the *e* from his name to make it *Boring*, as did practically all the
other Borings who were proliferating exponentially from the original immigrant John. This Ezekiel was a minister of the Church
of the United Brethren in Manchester, Maryland. His son, John
Dobbins Boring (1811–1884), was my grandfather, the contractor who put the *w* into the name and took it out again. He
lived in Lancaster, Pennsylvania, where my father was born.
That family belonged to the Moravian Church, an ancient Bo-
hemian church with bishops who had the episcopal succession
from Peter through the Waldenses, followers of the martyred
John Huss, vigorous educators and missionaries who mixed their
liturgical forms with Bach music and quaint communal customs.
I was brought up in that church in Philadelphia.

It was in his Lancaster home that my father, Edwin McCurdy
Boring (1839–1920), acquired his belief in the value of education. He worked for his father, went to high school, used to
study with his book set up at the far end of the table with the
candle in between (until he picked up some spectacles with
convex lenses at the drugstore and suddenly saw revealed a new
world of detail), and could quote Virgil to his children thirty
years later in spite of the forgetting that should have been
induced by four years of active service for the Union in the
Civil War. That war was his college experience and there never
was a more loyal alumnus than he at the reunions of the "Green
River mess" which had marched with Sherman from Atlanta to
the sea. To us children that "mess" of five veterans was an honorary society whose annual meetings rivaled birthdays and the
Fourth of July in importance.

After the war in 1865 my father went to Philadelphia, learned
the drug business from great-grandfather Edward B. Garrigues,
married the boss' granddaughter in 1873, became first his partner
and then his successor. My father was much more interested in
pharmacy than in soda-water, and eventually it came to be
known that his clerks received especially competent training in

his store while they were attending the Philadelphia College of Pharmacy, of which my father presently became a trustee. This drug business, founded by my great-grandfather in 1843, is still extant, with THE BORING DRUGSTORE lettered on its windows. There a third idealist, Abraham Rabinowitz, and later his son Howard, have for forty more years compounded prescriptions for the neighbors who now occupy a housing project for Negroes. It is rumored that this project was planned so as not to require the demolition of the ancestral home because it seemed desirable to preserve such an ancient and respectable business, now nearly 120 years old. Indeed it was respectable. I can still hear my father lecturing Sunday morning customers who wanted to buy Jamaica ginger because the saloons were closed—lecturing them and refusing to sell.

The important descent, however, as it was genealogized and advertised by my great-great-aunt in my early childhood, was the maternal Garrigues line. That goes back to Jean de Garrigues, a Huguenot, who fled from Périgord, France, at the revocation of the Edict of Nantes in 1685. (*Les Garrigues* are mountains in the southern valley of the Rhône.) Jean went to The Hague, where his son Matthieu was born. Then with Matthieu he came, via the West Indies, to Philadelphia. Matthieu Garrigues became an Episcopalian and an innkeeper. His son Samuel readily turned Quaker in William Penn's city, and the descent passed first to William Garrigues (1746–1831) and then to his son, Edward Briggs Garrigues (1795–1889), whose nurse held him up to see George Washington and whom I remember on the momentous occasion when I first saw him without his wig. He was, of course, my great-grandfather, who taught my father the drug business and then took my father as a partner and son-in-law.

There was also the Truman line which was genealogically self-conscious and is traced back to early eighteenth-century Trumans, Llewellyns, Moores, Smedleys, and Pratts. This line too was Quaker, but in my day the Trumans were Hicksite Quakers, the liberal branch of the Society of Friends, which dates back to Elias Hicks' resistance in 1828 to the pedantic doctrines of the English Orthodox Friends. There came to be great feelings in America between the Orthodox and the Hicksite Quakers, and my grandmother used to tell a story about the Orthodox Quakers' slamming the shutters on the fingers of the Hicksites. (She must have meant the shutters used to divide the women from the men in the center of the meeting house, but I did not know that then.) When Alexander Shaw Truman (1822–1894), my Hicksite grandfather, fell in love with and married Lydia Smith Garrigues (1824–1901), my Orthodox grandmother, the Orthodox Friends disowned my grandmother from meeting and she went with my grandfather to the Hicksite meeting. Thus, my mother was not a birth-right member of any meeting. When my father, a Moravian from Lancaster, turned up, my mother joined the Moravian Church; later, after my grandfather's death, my grandmother joined.

There was, then, this odd mixture of Moravian and Quaker in my youth. I was brought up in the Moravian Church, with its simple customs and its music and its bishops and liturgy; my sisters went to a Quaker Hicksite school; I went to a Quaker Orthodox school. We always used the plain language (*thee*, not *thou*) in the family; my wife and I still use it now to each other and to our children, who do not, however, use it to each other. Strangers who hear us talk think we are Quakers, unless I am telling how the chorales which the trombone choir plays from the church tower indicate who has died in the congregation— whether a man, a woman, or a child, and whether widowed, married, or unmarried. Then they do not know what to think, for few people know about the Moravian customs.

Childhood

On 23 October 1886, I was born in Philadelphia into an Orthodox-Hicksite-Quaker-Moravian family living in two juxtaposed houses which connected inside for some communal living. The drugstore was on the corner. In the three stories above it lived my grandmother and my Hicksite grandfather, who had by then gone blind, my parents, my three sisters, and now I. Next door were my great-grandfather and my great-great-aunt and a great-aunt, both unmarried. The great-great-aunt dominated the household; the great-aunt was always kind to little children. The group was a matriarchy. My great-grandfather Garrigues had been an important person and once a man of means. Then he failed in business and was put out of meeting until he had paid his creditors in full. After that he founded the drug business, but now he was old. My grandfather Truman was blind. My father was an outsider. He was, for one thing, a Moravian and not a Quaker. Moreover, he lacked the cultural background of the Garrigueses; worst of all, in the eyes of my grandmother when she came to dominate the household, he was responsible for my mother's having children—four of them! At first my great-great-aunt dominated; then, when she died, my grandmother. Soon after my grandmother died I went away to college and family atmosphere no longer influenced me much. The matriarchal pattern was always there, however. My oldest sister used to think of our sister's children as "Borings," although they have not that name, and of my own sons as "Days," which is my wife's maiden name.

It is my impression that my birth was a shock, at least to my mother and grandmother, who had never supposed they would have to cope with a boy in the family. I had a lonely childhood. In 1843, when the drug business was begun, the neighborhood was good. Fifty years later, when I was seven, it was not, and I was forbidden to play in the street or on the sidewalk with the naughty little boys and girls who were our neighbors' children. Once I got an offer to join the "Mt. Vernon Street gang," but Father and Mother both said an emphatic No. We had a yard, brick paved, shaped like a T, about six feet across and each arm of it about twenty-five feet long. It had in it two semicircular patches of bare earth, each less than a square foot, one of them with a frustrated trumpet creeper growing in it, the other nourishing a successful ivy which spread all over the side of the brick house. I used to try to grow corn and wheat in a small packing box. I put a grill over it to keep out the cat, but the cat ate the wheat as soon as it grew up through the grill. There was also the "flat" for drying clothes on top of the house, where I built a private castle of packing boxes and named it "Tectidomus." Indoors I played with my youngest sister, four years older than I, until, at the age of twelve, she found outside friends.

My father always managed to get the family away to a long summer vacation. He would rent a house in the country. There would be a few days of exciting turmoil when my father, my mother, and my grandmother packed pots, dishes, clothes, and many other things in boxes and trunks, and then we all moved, two Trumans and six Borings. Each year of my youth is labeled by that year's summer place, but I was still lonely, for there was never anyone to play with even then.

Why I did not start school until I was nine I do not know. I was thought to be delicate, nervous, easily excited. At home my oldest sister taught me to read. Then my parents, after much study of the problem, took me to the primary grade of an Orthodox Quaker school (Friends' Select School), where they had found an understanding teacher. I was nine and my classmates were, on the average, six, but I did not realize that I was too old. Soon I was demonstrating, however, that the brain can develop without practice to make learning easy. I became too good for the first grade and was promoted to the second. Then, hearing that the third grade had long division whereas the second had only short, I asked my mother to show me how to do long division, learned the art in one trial, demonstrated my new skill the next day, and at once was promoted again. Thus, by doing three years' work in one, I moved up until I was only one year behind my proper place, a decrement which I made up later by skipping the sixth grade and mensuration. I still do not know what mensuration is.

At school I turned out to be somewhat of a sissy. I was good in my lessons and I soon took it for granted that I should be at the top or near the top of my class in everything except drawing and gymnasium. But I had no athletic skill and for twenty years I lived in terror of a ball's falling near me so that I would have to throw it back and be laughed at for throwing like a girl. Once I paid a boy the great sum of twenty-five cents to teach me how to kick a football so that I might dare to go out of doors at recess, only to find that paid-up tuitions do not guarantee learning.

At that school I stayed until I was ready for college in 1904. The school was coeducational and, as the classes at the higher levels got smaller, the number of boys diminished more rapidly than the number of girls. I was graduated with two other boys in a class of about twenty. As the boys disappeared, brains became more important than muscle. In my junior year the school, with only eleven boys, including me, in the upper classes, did try to have a football team. Thus I was compelled to play—left end. We had one practice game with a small school. During it I heard the enemy captain tell his backs to go around my end. They won, 57 to 0. We never played the next game. Intramurally I led a revolt against the Literary Society to found the rival Abraham Lincoln Debating Club, of which I became the first president. We even had log-cabin pins. I also discovered girls and suffered acutely because I could not dance. One other boy and I took secretly the kind of dancing lessons where they teach you in three lessons. He tried it out first and hurried in with the bad news in the morning. "We can't dance after all," he warned.

Atmosphere and Personality

Let me try to recreate the atmosphere of that Philadelphia home. When the old people died, the Borings moved in next door to the store. There we were in contact with many objects from the cultivated Garrigues past—furniture, dishes, heirlooms.

Later Truman heirlooms were added to the household. There were none such from the Boring past. Nowadays we still eat Christmas dinner from the Staffordshire china that my great-great-grandfather William Garrigues bought in 1831 ($26 for 124 pieces!), eat as I ate from it on Christmas seventy years ago.

My father brought no furniture to Philadelphia, but he brought his belief in education and in that he matched the Garrigueses, who boasted one Ph.D. from Göttingen in 1848, twenty years before there were any such degrees in America. My father offered college to all his children, and they all became educators. My oldest sister was of the class of 1896 at Bryn Mawr, when not many women went to college, and she taught in high school all her life. My next sister chose music instead of college, and then married a minister-professor in the Moravian Church. For forty years she was wife of the President of Salem College in North Carolina, an unofficial dean, vice-president, and housemother. My third sister had her A.B. and her Ph.D. from Bryn Mawr and some European study, and my father helped her for at least six of these years. Her main contribution was teaching biology at Yenching University, in Peking, China, for twenty-seven years before the People's Republic took over. And I—we are coming to me.

I have said how wonderfully my father managed the summer vacations for us—at least for his children, since it was heavy housework for my grandmother and my mother; but both college and vacation were achieved against a background of financial worry and insecurity. Money was constantly talked about. My father's favorite phrase was, "When we go over the hill to the poorhouse." There never seemed enough money to do what we wanted to do, or what father wanted to do. Mother and Father had agreed when they married that they could not afford to entertain, so we had few guests and went out little. I do not think I thought of this scarcity of money as strange, but I did form the opinion that the talk of "happy childhood" was bunk, and said so. (When I was about six I had a repeated paranoic fantasy: I would walk into the dining room with all the family assembled and shout, "I have found you out!" and they, all conspiring against me, would pale and blanch. But I never could get them, in my fantasy, to go down on their knees and ask my mercy.) I have the impression that my father carried this pattern of financial insecurity from his youth, and I kept finding myself reestablishing it in my children. I too, as a parent, used always to worry about money—at least until I grew up at the age of fifty-six, say. Never did there seem to be enough for what seemed reasonable. And every child of mine has been thrifty, too thrifty, the kind of thrift that stems from fear and insecurity.

In this description of the atmosphere in which I grew up I am seeking at least a partial explanation of what finally became my temperament for half a century. Perhaps these social forces are not enough; perhaps the genes really should come in here. Yet it is interesting to examine the psychological dynamics that may have operated.

It is clear, in the terms of W. H. Sheldon's psychosomatics, that I am a 4-5-2 in body type and temperament. That is to say, for body type, I am a 4 of rotund, soft "endomorphy," just topped by a 5 of tough, rugged, muscular "mesomorphy," with only a next-to-minimal 2 of slim and wiry "ectomorphy." That seems right to me too. I have muscle and strength to go with my energy in mesomorphy. Tending to gain weight in the direction of sphericity, I starved my 227 pounds down to a vigorous 198 twenty years ago, and that is my weight now. For the twenty years after college I weighed a steady 133 and sometimes I refer wistfully to those old "ectomorphic days," but Sheldon declares that those ancient photographs of me, fragile and skinny, still look to him like a 4-5-2.

In temperament this formula becomes a 4 of friendly, compassionate, love-seeking "viscerotonia," combined and conflicting with a 5 of tough, energetic, hard-working, power-loving, ambitious "somatotonia," with just a soupçon of intellectual, self-assured "cerebrotonia" to season the whole. That all makes sense. I have always wanted power and always wanted love, and what a time I used to have resolving those two perpetually contradictory needs! It is different now, though.

The psychosomatic way to describe me is to say that I have the ulcer personality, and that is not all nonsense since I really have had a duodenal ulcer since the Clark controversy of 1922, one that used to break out into disabling hemorrhage at some, but not all, times of great stress. A book on the ulcer personality says that the patient has great drive (he must always be doing something and cannot enjoy relaxation or loafing); he is versatile (undertaking many things, holding many jobs); he is emotionally responsive (wants love); he is self-reliant (was early free of dependence on his parents); he is responsible (assumes responsibility readily and is conscientious); he has determination (persists against opposition, drives ahead to long-range goals); he craves superiority (wants power and success and is not content with attainment of false prestige). If this be I, the authors of that book did a fairly good job of description. I am not synchronously versatile: I find myself getting into many things and then getting out, to drive ahead with a one-track mind. I recognize the basic cravings for love and for superiority and the recurrent fear that my successes may turn out to be based on veneered ability. I do drive perpetually for long-range goals, and my friends, my children, and my students know how I have talked about the eighty-hour week in the fifty-week year (the 4000-hour working year) and I have scorned those forty-hour academicians who take long summers off from work. I have no hobbies, except for a shop in my cellar. My vacations were never successful until I got a little study with a typewriter in it and could answer eight letters a day and write up the waiting papers. I wanted love and for the first twenty-five years of my life I thought it was something I might never command—for that verb is true: I did want it to command.

In brief, then, I wanted affection and I wanted success. I wanted not merely a satisfactory love-life, but the affection and admiration of many men and women. I wanted success, but I never wanted it without work. Work was what one lived for, and my inability to distinguish between work and play has always been with me a matter of pride. Nearly always I have been doubtful of the validity of my successes, have sought a reassurance that they were genuine, and then, with hope happily ratified, found myself doubting the validity of the ratification. That boils down to the statement that, until recently, I always felt insecure and inferior, although the persons who have experienced my somatotonia did not realize this fact. My felt insecurity has been both financial and intellectual. Even when, in 1950, I had just published what was clearly a good revision of my twenty-one-year-old still much used *History of Experimental Psychology*, my pet paranoia would have me wondering whether people were saying, "But anyone can write history. Can he not do research?"

Here I may say a little about my ruthlessness, for I had that reputation when I was Director of the Harvard Psychological Laboratory in 1925–1949. I would make tough judgments that hurt people, that interfered with their careers. I never felt, though, that I was cruel; I had too much desire for affection and admiration for that. Sometimes I was called legalistic, and that word shows me what was going on. I stuck to principle. When the psychologists were combined with the philosophers, I had two very distinguished colleagues, both philosophers, who would listen to special pleading. This man was late with his thesis, but his wife was ill and he was poor and distracted with outside work. Should we not extend his time? I never said Yes. I had visions of the good sports caught in the same dilemma who never made a special plea. I would be loyal to them. Should we let this chap slide by though he was deficient in his German? Then I would be loyal to the University and its standards, and also try to avoid future trouble that arises from past laxity. I have a very good psychologist friend, not at Harvard, who believes in doing favors for his friends. "What is friendship for?" he asks. Friendships are for favors if what you give is your own, but not if you are giving away something that belongs to another —the standards of a university, equal justice to all for whom you assume a judicial role. Indeed I was tough and ruthless. I did hurt people, but I always believed that I was refusing a smaller loyalty to maintain a larger one.

Now how much of this conflicting personality of mine did the Philadelphia family generate? No sure answer to that question is possible. Certainly I thought at ages four, six, eight, ten, and twelve that I lacked love and security. Was I, in my drive toward success, compensating for this lack? I have thought so. The Adlerian conception generates both of these conflicting needs from the same cause. It may be too simple a view, but it seems to me to make fundamental sense, at least for fifty years of my life. After I turned sixty I felt less inferior, and so far the seventies have been a wonderful decade. My daughter says she remembers my announcing my achievement of maturity at age fifty-six. That just could be right.

Another way to look at this matter is that a lonely child, a boy born unwanted into a matriarchy, a boy who never found playmates until he was adolescent, would already have achieved the beginnings of neurosis. My excitability, my fear of ridicule, my lack of athletic skill, my enuresis, may have been symptoms or causes, or more likely they may have been both in the vicious circle of neurosis. How destiny took this neurosis and used it to bring me success and even love, and to translate me to the level at which I could be asked to write an autobiography for others to read, that is one of those natural paradoxes which warn the philosopher not to distinguish too rashly between good and evil. The frustrations of youth can yield the rewards of age.

Engineering

In 1904 I went to Cornell to study electrical engineering and in 1908 I received from Cornell the M.E. degree. I have no A.B.

Later, when I got into graduate work in psychology, I was labelled an "uncultured engineer," then a common phrase at Cornell for its engineers. What got me into engineering?

Action at a distance. When I was quite young, I discovered electricity—with a dry cell, an electric door-bell, and some wire. It seemed a marvellous thing to be able to ring the bell at will away off at the far end of a wire. Soon I could ring the house door-bell from many strange parts of our house. Magnetism seemed just as wonderful. I could penetrate almost anything. And there were electromagnets. I began to play with motors and electric machines. I had, of course, to prepare in some way to make my living; the family's sense of financial insecurity made that clear for my sisters as well as for me. So, knowing but little what I was doing, I chose electrical engineering. I know now that my father would have liked to have me want to carry on his drug business, but, if he hinted at that hope then, I did not perceive his wish. For a college I chose Cornell from vague hearsay that its work in engineering was exceptionally good. I could have gone more cheaply to the University of Pennsylvania, but my father said nothing about that. He supported me at fifty dollars a month all through my four years.

I never liked engineering. I know now that what I wanted was science, but there was no one to tell me then the difference between science and engineering. The engineer—so I was convinced after I was graduated and was working for the Bethlehem Steel Company—had to get effects that would yield an industrial profit. A scientist could be concerned with basic principles having regard neither to costs nor to the human factor in production. At Cornell I did not do very well. I had to work very hard with a stiff schedule and many laboratories to make my average B, and in integral calculus I almost failed, the lowest grade of my academic history. I got through to an uninspired but not discreditable M.E. in 1908, ready to start to make my living.

My undergraduate social life was meager. I was not asked to join a fraternity and could not have afforded to live in one had

I been. I fell in with a group of four other men and we had joint rooming arrangements and did many things together. I tried distance running as a freshman but was not good enough. I made the class debating club but not any important team. I knew almost no girls all through the four years. And I worked very hard indeed to prepare the many laboratory reports that were required.

In this rigid engineering schedule there were a few electives. For two of them I chose telephone engineering and alternating generator design, but for two others I did a very queer thing. I chose English composition and elementary psychology. No engineer ever made such choices. There had been a girl in high school who had warned me against taking psychology. "It will make you morbid," she had said; so I judge that there must quite early have been some clear danger that I might want to take psychology. In the registration room at Cornell the professor of mechanical engineering, a great big burly man, looked me up and down in astonishment and then shouted across the room to the professor of electrical engineering, "Hell, here's a damned engineer wants to take psychology!" Little he knew about Titchener.

So I turned up in E. B. Titchener's course in elementary psychology in the fall of 1905, when Titchener must have been near his prime in the showmanship of lecturing. His lectures were in the old laboratory on the top floor of Cornell's oldest building. The room was crammed with students, and the long desk was jammed with apparatus set up for demonstration. Titchener lectured in his Master's gown. "It gives me," he said, "the right to be dogmatic," fitting his talk to the gown. The lectures were magic, so potent that even my roommates demanded, each lecture-day, to be told what had been said. And what had been said? I do not know now. I remember that the lecture on tonal beats sent me excitedly away bubbling over to tell the latest in psychic truth to those who would hear. I remember how the first examination was followed by a fascinating discourse on the one gift for which we do not have to work. That free gift turned out to be the English language, a gift of which so many of us had failed to avail ourselves in the written test. But I had done well, and Titchener himself, in gown, at the door handed me my paper with a 90-something on it and said, "*You* have the psychological point of view!" That remark was to me the accolade it was meant to be. Of course, it was not true, but as a motivator it proved in the long run to have been effective.

After Cornell came my year with the Bethlehem Steel Company in Bethlehem, Pennsylvania. I was interviewed and hired by Eugene G. Grace himself, who was afterwards president of the Corporation. Once, as I worked at a lathe on a Sunday morning, Charles M. Schwab, then president, inspecting the plant and wearing a white vest, stood close behind me and watched me work. Grace's plan was to hire college men and let them learn the business from the bottom up, allowing the advantages of having had a college training to prove themselves. For this purpose I was provided with a running start: I was given eighteen cents an hour for work for which others got only sixteen cents. Already college was being worth two cents more an hour in an eighty-four-hour week. Yes, it was an eighty-four-hour week, for this was the old system of the steel plants, the system with the twenty-four-hour shift. You had a buddy. You and your buddy ran one job continuously. You worked days one week and he nights, and then you reversed the next week. To change over you worked for twenty-four hours straight one Sunday before he relieved you, and then the next week you had a continuous twenty-four-hour Sunday off. Eighteen cents an hour may seem small now, but it came to $65 a month, all my own money, and that seemed large after I had depended on my father for $50 a month, with tuitions to pay from that sum. I even bought a standard typewriter, and presently a canoe.

This after-college year was fun. Half the time I was making money, being called "Eddie, the electrician," and learned at close range why labor does not like capital. In the other half, I got a little sleep and had, for the first time, an exciting social life. Bethlehem, Pennsylvania, was the chief center for the

Moravian Church in the North, with its candle service on Christmas Eve, its tromboned chorales on early Easter morning, the Home Church, the *Gemeinhaus,* the Single Sisters' House, the graveyard—and young people. There were parties, a dancing class, canoeing on the Lehigh River. It was the first time I had ever belonged to a young group and I loved it.

Still, I did not like engineering, and the event that drove me out of the field was the offer of a promotion. He would make me, said the new superintendent, assistant night foreman of the Gray Mill, which rolled a special section of steel beam. It meant more money and a start in the steel business with knowledge of a special process. And I found that I loved electricity still and did not want to scrap my training or to identify myself with steel. So, instead of accepting, I astonished the superintendent by quitting entirely, leaving with a recommendation that said: "This is to certify that Mr. E. G. Boring has been in my employ for the past year and take great pleasure in recommending him to any one in need of a first class electrician. I have found him to be sober, industrious and attentive to his work at all times." The commendation seemed somewhat less than Titchener's accolade.

Teaching

The next year I taught science in the Moravian Parochial School in Bethlehem. I had a large class of boys and girls in physical geography and we started the custom of displaying weather flags from the school's flagpole which was visible far over the town. Also I taught physics, chemistry, higher algebra, and solid-geometry-and-trigonometry to five senior boys who were preparing for Lehigh University. None of them ever went to Lehigh. I was then in my slight 133-pound phase, feeling insignificant, and I had disciplinary trouble. These boys put shellac on my chair at one time, painted my derby hat white at another. By June I was ready to escape and return to college. I needed an A.M. if I were to teach—that was my rationalization. My principal urged me to stay another year, said that it was important for my record that I should not have seemed to quit after only one year; but I stuck to my plan of returning to Cornell for an A.M.

At this time I was clearly the family failure. I had not stuck to engineering and had wasted all the money spent on that training. I had not made a go of high-school teaching. All that was needed to confirm the misgivings of the family was that I should shift my interest in graduate work from physics, at which I might make a living, to psychology, in which the family could see no future. I made the shift. Why?

In the summer of 1909, in the interlude between the Bethlehem Steel Company and the Moravian Parochial School, I had gone to Cornell to better my preparation for teaching, meaning to take work in physical geography. The magic of Titchener's lectures four years before was, however, still working, and I found myself in the elementary laboratory course in psychology. Madison Bentley, Titchener's animal psychologist, also caught my interest in his special field and led me to keep a bucket of once-alive earthworms behind my bureau all the next year. I was to give them burrows between glass panes and to study their behavior, but I never got to the burrows. Now I was back at Cornell again, and the physicists gave me less encouragement than did Bentley. So it was he who landed me in psychology in the fall of 1910, and, when in February 1911 I won an assistantship at $500 a year, I saw that I was now fixed for life, independent of my father and able to do what I wanted, for a man could live on $500 a year. I struck out for the Ph.D.

Cornell and Psychology

Psychology at Cornell—at least the orthodox psychology that centered in the laboratory—revolved around and was almost bounded by the personality of E. B. Titchener, a staunch Briton, educated at Oxford but trained at Leipzig with Wilhelm Wundt, who often is said to be the founder of the new experimental psychology and who certainly did organize at Leipzig the world's first formal psychological laboratory for experimental research. For thirty-five years (1892–1927) Titchener maintained at Cornell the German tradition that the proper method of psychology is introspection upon consciousness, that the description of the contents of consciousness is the sole business of psychology, and that psychologists do not—should not—study the behavior of men and animals. Thus Titchener served American psychology by furnishing it with a background against which it could become clear, for the typical American was first a functional psychologist (like William James and his successors) and later a behaviorist (John B. Watson and his successors). No intellectual movement can get moving without something to push against, and American psychology had Titchener.

And what a man Titchener was! He always seemed to me the nearest approach to genius of anyone with whom I have been closely associated. I used to watch my conversations with him, hoping I might gain an insight into why his thought was so much better than mine. I decided that it was no different per second or even per minute, and that its superiority per day and per lifetime lay in the much greater availability of memories to Titchener's mind, its ready entertainment of novel relationships, its equally ready abandonment of hypotheses which proved unprofitable, and its avidity in the pursuit of goals, a drive which permitted no wool-gathering and which never twice tried the same blind alley in the maze of thinking. Titchener loved to solve puzzles, and his skill in numismatics was developed over the problems posed by Mohammedan coins. To obtain this skill he had to learn some Arabic, but he was competent with languages, and could ab lib in Latin when the occasion required it. If you had mushrooms, he would tell you at once how they should be cooked. If you were buying oak for a new floor, he would at once

The Clark Psychologists
1921
STANDING: Matsusaburo Yokoyama (left), E.G.B., Carroll C. Pratt, Samuel W. Fernberger. SEATED: Mrs. E.G.B. (left), Marjorie Bates (Pratt). E.G.B.'s three Clark Ph.D.'s were Yokoyama, Pratt, and Marjorie Bates, who later married Pratt.

The Boring Family
1935
E.G.B. and Mrs. E.G.B. (seated), and then, in descending order of height, Edwin, Frank, Mollie, and Barbara.

The Moon Illusion
1939
E.G.B. faces the apparatus for mirrored moons with the biting board in front of him. The mirrors are out on the ends of the two long arms, 5 m. away.

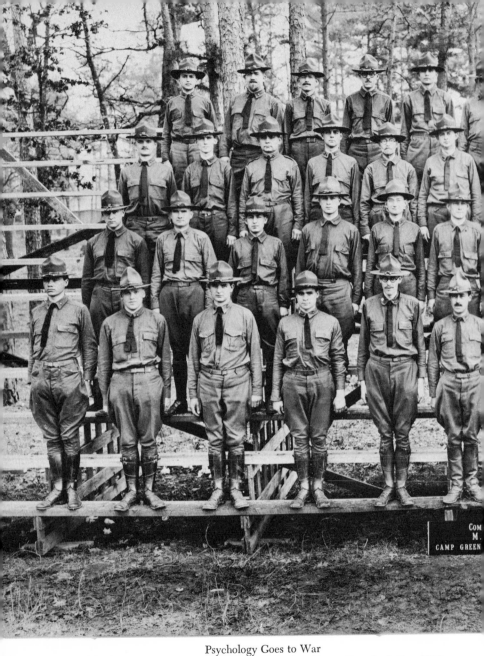

Psychology Goes to War
First Company of Commissioned Psychologists, Camp Greenleaf, Ga., 1918

LEFT TO RIGHT, BACK ROW: D. G. Paterson, K. M. Dallenbach, B. F. Pittenger,
E. G. Boring, H. H. Wylie, J. W. Bare, H. B. English, R. H. Sylvester, J. J. B.
Morgan, J. E. Anderson, J. D. Houser.
SECOND ROW: H. T. Manuel, R. L. Bates, W. S. Miller, E. M. Chamberlain,
G. C. Basset, A. H. Estabrook, A. T. Poffenberger, C. E. Benson, M. R. Trabue,
E. A. Doll, E. C. Rowe, R. M. Elliott.

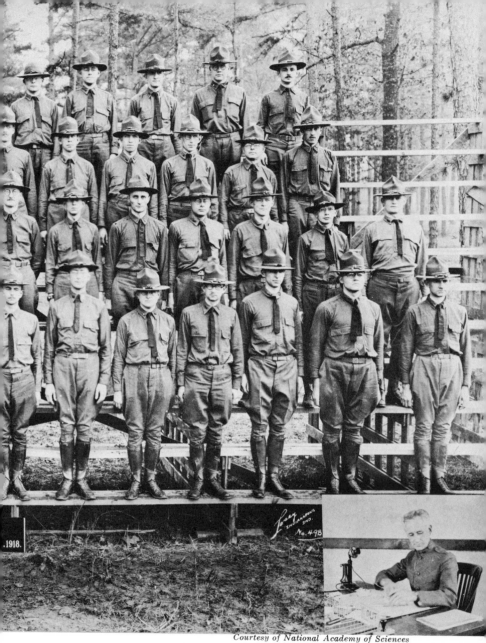

THIRD ROW: ———*, ———*, C. F. Malmberg, H. T. Moore, J. K. Norton, H. P. Shumway, G. F. Arps, ———*, ———*, T. M. Stokes, E. S. Jones, L. D. Pedrick, C. H. Toll.

FRONT ROW: B. D. Wood, R. S. Roberts, L. J. Brueckner, C. P. Stone, W. S. Foster, Major Tyng*, W. S. Hunter, J. W. Hayes, ———*, ———*, A. S. Edwards, C. C. Stech, D. W. LaRue.

CORNER: Major R. M. Yerkes, in charge of psychological examining.

* Not a psychologist.

At the National Academy of Sciences
1950
Clarence H. Graham (left), E.G.B.,
Karl S. Lashley.

As Harvard Lowell Television Lecturer
1957
In "Psychology One" on Educational Television, E.G.B. demonstrates a chart before the camera.

Courtesy of Harvard Alumni Bulletin

As Phi Beta Kappa Visiting Scholar, 1959
E.G.B. in informal conference with students at Franklin and Marshall College.

come forward with all the advantages of ash. If you were engaged to be married, he would have his certain and insistent advice about the most unexpected aspects of your problems, and, if you were honeymooning, he would write to remind you, as he did me, on what day you ought to be back at work. Seldom did he distinguish between his wisdom and his convictions, and he never hid either.

Along with Titchener's vivid and indefatigable intellectual activity went his immutable beliefs about decorum, good and bad manners, deference, and loyalty. He expected both the deference and the loyalty from the juniors of his immediate circle. He had in my day few older associates, for he had been so precocious that nearly all of his contemporaries in intellectual status were already dead, but to the few who remained and to other older men who strayed temporarily within his circle, like my father, he willingly gave the deference which he knew to be due to age. Those who broke the code of manners, however, he ostracized at least temporarily and often permanently. It took over a year before Titchener's loyal adjutant, H. P. Weld, was received back into the communion. What had Weld done? Titchener had called his partner's ball in tennis good, and Weld, in a better position to see but not, under British custom, the person to make the decision, called, "No, it was out! I saw it strike right here!" So Titchener's integrity was impugned and Weld—the charming, honest, affable, generous Weld—was excluded, though not for life.

The Hollingworth story shows best how this code of the English gentleman got mixed with experimental science. Titchener, sweating over his *Text-book of Psychology*, got the first half finished in June 1909 and had it published for use in the fall. The second half was added for full publication in 1910. In the first half Titchener expounded the two-level theory of attention. Then in the fall of 1909 an experiment in Titchener's own laboratory found that some persons have more than two levels, and Titchener, the sheets for the first half of the book already printed, put in the correction on a blank half-page in the second half. H. L. Hollingworth of Columbia, reviewing the book, remarked that "the two-level theory is deliberately expounded in the text, although hidden away in the references for further reading is the confession" that the multilevel theory had been discovered in the author's laboratory, an explanation which gave, Hollingworth added, "hardly sufficient justification for concealing [the facts] from the student." Hollingworth was young in 1910 and he thought he saw a spade and named it. Titchener, replying, quoted the offending paragraph, explained just what had happened, and ended with: "Meantime, Dr. Hollingworth has offered me a public insult. I expect a no less public apology."

Then began ten or a dozen years of difficulty in the Society of Experimental Psychologists, an informal group which Titchener had organized in 1904, which met annually, and which was dominated by Titchener, who asserted a prerogative of inspecting the invitation lists of every host. It was recognized that Hollingworth must never enter a room in which there was the L.G.A. (as the slightly blasphemous title for Titchener had become), lest the latter walk out and the Society be broken up. We may have been wrong in this fear, for the final resolution of the schism between Titchener with honor impugned and the well-intentioned Hollingworth was engineered quite simply by K. M. Dallenbach when Hollingworth was in Ithaca, perhaps along toward 1923. Dallenbach told Titchener by telephone that Hollingworth was in town, that he was thus in a sense Titchener's unexpected guest, and that he would like to call. So Titchener, who knew his duty by a guest quite as well as his duty by his honor, said *Yes*, and stretched out his hand at the threshold exclaiming: "Well, Hollingworth, who would ever have supposed that *I* would be shaking hands with *you!*" Then he had him in and the other mores of the host prevailed.

The stories about Titchener are legion and this is not his biography. One may properly ask here, however, how it came about that Titchener could dominate and control the conduct of his in-group. He did it by the magic of his personality, by his social charm, by his identification of himself with all those others, mostly his juniors, within the circle. You decided eventually from his brilliance, his erudition, and his long list of honors that he was a Great Man, and then you found him always saying *we* to you when he planned to achieve a goal or chanced upon some important new idea about research. You found him concerned over the small details of your life and your family's. You might resent his interference and control, and many of his more able graduate students eventually did and rebelled. Then suddenly they found themselves on the outside, excommunicated and bitter, and usually there was for them no return. Quite early in my married life my wife and I decided that we would accept "insults" and arbitrary control from Titchener in order to retain the stimulus and charm of his sometimes paternal and sometimes patronizing friendship. I never broke with the master and I still feel that the credit balance remained on my side; nor does my wife, with a less aggressive soul than mine, feel differently.

After Titchener's death I went over the 212 letters I had had from him since I left Ithaca to see what there was in them worth publishing; there was a little, but not much. All the rest was this magic personalized glue that held the in-group together, was Titchener's interest in my personal affairs, or his plan that "we" should promote an appointment that would add another laboratory to "our" group of loyal institutions. Freud required loyalty from his in-group and held it together in a similar way. With James the in-group was formed through the democratic charm of friendship, but with Titchener and Freud the friendships were authoritarian and paternal. Both men needed to play the father role, dispensing much real kindness to those disciples who avoided transgression.

I never broke with Titchener, but neither did I follow blindly. On theoretical issues I differed vehemently in the privacy of the laboratory and recognized the importance of Titchener's views by calling myself a "heretic." Others seemed to me to accept unquestioningly the pronouncements of this oracle, and often I found myself arguing hotly against deference to authority in matters of fact or logic.

Since I was required to take two minor subjects for the doctorate, Titchener could not complain of my going too far afield in pursuing them, but actually I had four possible minors and Titchener did not approve of such catholicity. I offered finally animal psychology, a field in which I did research on the behavior of flat-worms, and physiology, where I was doing my four-year-long experiment on returning sensibility after cutting a small nerve in my forearm. In educational psychology I had, in addition, finished a study of fidelity of report on moving picture incidents. In the summer of 1912 I went to work with S. I. Franz at the Government Hospital for the Insane (St. Elizabeths) in Washington and got out a monograph on learning in schizophrenics. It was an invaluable summer in broadening my experience and in establishing a close professional friendship with Franz, but Titchener looked solemn as he perceived me straying so far from the straight and narrow path. I believed, however, that I must get breadth into my training in spite of Titchener, and I got it.

In the Cornell laboratory, fixed for life with a stipend of $500 a year, I became a member of the community, Titchener's in-group. There were many of us, men and women, and we lived in the laboratory from 8 A.M. to midnight. There was some social life and I had my canoe on Lake Cayuga. Presently I was falling in love with Lucy M. Day, who had got her start in psychology at Mt. Holyoke College. We became engaged in October 1911, to be married two and a half years later, the day after I got my Ph.D. In those days graduate students in the east got the Ph.D. first and married later when their earning power for two was supposed to have begun, and we looked askance at the western graduate students who reversed this proper order.

In 1912, when Madison Bentley went to Illinois, Titchener undertook to reestablish the old courses in systematic psychology, the courses which he once gave himself and which covered the entire range of orthodox psychology in three lectures a week spread over two years—a two-hundred-lecture course already referred to. W. S. Foster, who, as Titchener's personal assistant, was the only one of us with direct access to the Chief, delivered the fiat: the lectures were to be given by H. P. Weld, Foster, C. A. Ruckmick, and me. Weld was an assistant professor, but we three were only graduate student assistants. We were to lecture to each other and to the other graduate students. Our motivation was maximal, for we had to save face with one another. Most of the scientific literature was in German, and none of us was very adept with that basic psychological language.

This training in thoroughness and scholarship was magnificent. How in the world could Titchener do that for all of us merely by a fiat transmitted by an underling like an order from a commander? Perhaps he had set the standard in his seminar, which met on Monday evenings in the second semester, the only time during the year that Titchener ever came in person to the Laboratory (for his elementary lectures in the first semester were in another building). You came to this seminar only by invitation. All the staff, being invited, were there as a matter of course, and everyone read a paper. I remember that I had to give a paper on Husserl, the philosopher whom Titchener much later spent a whole year understanding—so he said. I managed something short of reading all the basic volumes in German, getting aid from a German paper on Husserl. The effort to which I went served to make me feel that scholarship had not been unreasonably debased by my performance.

It must have been late in 1911 that Titchener set me a thesis on visceral sensibility, telling me what to read—all of it in German—and then to go on from there. My next conference with him about the thesis was early in 1914, when he told me to hurry up and to try to take my degree in June. Then I had a third conference about the results of the thesis in May. I finished it in time and was recommended for the degree, after an examination which disappointed me because it did not test my knowledge. For two years I had worked on the esophagus as the most approachable of the viscera, learning to swallow stomach-tubes so as to make my own insides more accessible. I got to the stage where I could go downstairs and answer the telephone without removing the tube.

Lucy Day, my fiancée, had taken her doctorate in 1912 and so we had to get along by correspondence during the two years before my Ph.D. One of those years she was instructor in psychology at Vassar. In my last year I was an instructor with a salary of $800 with a routine increase to $1000 due the next year. On that I could marry. I can see now that there was in this marriage some history repeating itself. My father, the carpenter's son, had ventured to enter the well-poised, ancestor-conscious Garrigues family. Now I, the son of a druggist, who had been poor in cash though not in ideals, was marrying a niece of R. L. Day & Co., Bankers, who were not Boston Brahmins but of sound New England Republican conservative business sense. (*My* father had been a Philadelphia mugwump, but it is true that I had never seen a Democrat until I went to college.) The Days appreciated education and at that time I never realized how gauche I must have seemed to them. We had a wonderful wedding in a house with an organ halfway up the huge staircase, and my best man and I discussed Moravian funeral customs with the minister (afterwards the president of Wheaton College) while we waited for the bride to be ready. Then came the honeymoon which ended with Titchener's unyielding call for us to return to duty.

So graduate work expanded imperceptibly into an instructor's job. I kept on with research in both the psychological and physiological laboratories. I found other papers to publish and began to have students who undertook minor problems under my direction. I would write up the papers and publish them over the students' names. During our first year my wife taught at Wells College, twenty-five miles from Ithaca down Lake Cayuga, but then we decided we wanted a family. My son was born on 11 January 1916, Titchener's birthday. We could hardly, my wife and I, have paid him a greater tribute, nor one that would have more certainly secured forgiveness for my being late to his all-male birthday party featuring a filet of beef imported from Rochester. (It was also Ezra Cornell's and William James's birthday.)

In 1917 came Titchener's call to Harvard and America's entry into the First World War. The two were inextricably mixed up, because the Society of Experimental Psychologists was meeting at Harvard on the day when war was declared. Titchener was having conversations with President Lowell about the Harvard post, left vacant by Münsterberg's sudden death on Radcliffe's lecture platform in December 1916. Titchener mistrusted the Harvard situation. If he went he needed to dominate it, and to help with that he wished to bring me along as his adjutant to implement his biddings. He also wanted compressed air led to the lecture room, and Mr. Lowell must have thought that he was debasing the offer by making his acceptance depend on forty feet of two-inch pipe. At any rate the negotiations presently fell through and Harvard asked McDougall, who came.

When war was declared, the "Experimentalists" were meeting in Harvard's Emerson Hall and they turned to a discussion of how psychologists could aid in the war effort. Titchener, a British subject, always conscious of the proprieties, withdrew from the room, sitting outside beyond the threshold, while R. M. Yerkes, a local host and then president of the American Psychological Association, took charge. That was the beginning of Yerkes' leadership which ended in the two million intelligence-test records of American soldiers.

(For more about Titchener, see the biographical sketch of him elsewhere in this volume, pp. 246–265.)

The First World War

The war and the draft for men under thirty-one made all the young psychologists restless. The birth of my second son caused the draft to pass me over at age 30.8, but still I wanted to serve.

R. M. Yerkes had said he wanted me in the Army work on intelligence testing, so I volunteered and was appointed, because of my age and status, a captain in the Sanitary Corps, which was the only branch of the Medical Department of the Army in which they could put us. We tried to minister to sanity, leaving sanitation to others. In February 1918 I reported to Camp Greenleaf, Georgia, for training. We lived in barracks, piled out for reveillé, stood inspection, drilled and were drilled, studied testing procedures, and were ordered to many irrelevant lectures. As soon as I discovered that everyone else resembled me in never accomplishing the impossible, my neuroses left me and I had a grand time, with new health created by new exercise and many good friendships formed with colleagues under these intimate conditions of living.

Then I went to Camp Upton on Long Island where Joseph W. Hayes was Chief Psychological Examiner. I was second in command, succeeding to his post later when he was ordered away. It was an interesting experience, giving group tests to four hundred men who had arrived during the night, reporting intelligence scores for them within twenty-four hours. They were mostly from the New York City draft, and you went down the line saying "You read American newspaper? No read American newspaper?" —separating them in that crude manner into those who could read English and take the Alpha examination and those who must rely for instructions on the pantomime of the Beta examination. Since the Medical Department was a mounted service and I could wear boots and spurs, I could also have a horse, and I asked for one and got him. That was fun, to ride around and hitch my horse outside while I did business inside. I declared that after the war I would become an equestrian professor, but that never happened. When it comes to such a basic decision, the culture cushions impetuosity.

Then came the Armistice in November 1918, and Yerkes wanted me in Washington to work on the big report of the tests. I have never known why either Franz or Yerkes liked me or believed in me, why they reached into Titchener's in-group to take me afield to strange work, but they did and I profited immensely. Yerkes made me his immediate subordinate on the editorial job of organizing and writing the big report, and then he left me free. I carried through the Hollerith sorting of results and the composition of Part III, the section on the analysis of results, which had in it, besides 439 tables, fifteen good chapters by nine different psychologist-authors, and five scanty chapters which I wrote because no proper author was available.

Titchener's in-group at Cornell had appreciated mental testers in much the same way that the Crusaders, gathered around Richard Coeur-de-Lion, appreciated Moslems, but this First World War gave me a respect for the testers. I saw clearly that good, honest, intelligent work in any field merits respect and that testers closely resemble the pure experimentalists in habits of work, in enthusiasm, and in thoroughness. There was indeed a contrast between these research-minded academics and the medical men in uniform who occupied the Surgeon General's Office in Washington. The windows of the psychologists were blotches of light until late every night in an otherwise dark building, wherein general excitement had lagged after the Armistice. Not all these psychologists had peptic ulcers, but they all worked the seven-day, eighty-hour week just as if they had.

This war did me another service. It taught me to disbelieve in randomness as a property of nature, to disbelieve that, when you find variability in nature and you do not know the causes of variability, the differences will be distributed so as to accord with what is called the bell-shaped normal law of error, the "Gaussian law." Long ago (1869) Sir Francis Galton had ventured to scale human genius in accordance with the frequencies represented by this normal probability distribution, and psychologists with their tests were still using the principle in 1919. The law, when applied to nature, is equivalent to saying that tossed pennies in the long run come equally often heads and tails *because* you do not know why a throw should be one or other. If there were no reason why the coin should come down heads or tails it would stay on edge or else not come down. Ignorance, I felt sure, can never be a reason for any natural event. I went to the Congressional Library and read Todhunter's *History of the Mathematical Theory of Probability,* and Laplace and Gauss, and then more recent men on the logic of probabilities. I picked up the cliché that chance is "the equal distribution of ignorance" and used it to ridicule the current conventions. This problem has troubled me greatly for forty years and I have published on it twice, first in 1920 and then in 1941. I have always believed that approval of the first of these two papers by R. B. Perry, the Harvard philosopher, helped to get me asked to Harvard in 1922. My voice has, however, never been effective, although the changing stream of scientific opinion has continued to flow in what I regard as the right direction. No statistician nowadays assumes that ignorance determines frequency, as some seemed to believe in 1919. Now the problem has become the question as to when the degree of fit of generalized empirical data to the model of the probability curve with its infinite dimensions can be conclusively tested. This paper of 1920 is reprinted elsewhere in this book (pp. 143–179).

Clark

Yerkes, my boss in Washington, was all signed up to go to Minnesota and develop a department of psychology there. K. S. Lashley, not yet famous for his neuropsychology, was already there, but Yerkes wanted R. M. Elliott, two others, and me to add to the staff. Later Yerkes withdrew from this undertaking in order to work for the new National Research Council, and Elliott became his substitute—a very successful substitute, as three decades were to show. Elliott would have been glad to have me at Minnesota with the others, but Harvard wanted me as a Lecturer for a term, while William McDougall, due at Harvard from Eng-

land in the fall of 1920, looked me over and decided whether
to keep me or to get somebody better.

Harvard commanded my imagination. I do not fully know
why. I had been involved in Titchener's affair with Harvard in
1917, and I had from long indoctrination by Titchener gained the
conviction that Harvard was potentially the strongest place in
America, that Hugo Münsterberg had debased psychology there,
and that psychology needed to be brought clearly into the scientific circle and rescued from the philosophers who still dominated it. Harvard was opportunity, challenge, insecurity, and
probable loneliness. Minnesota was security, promise, facilities,
and friendliness. Which does one choose in such a case, difficulties or security? Obviously difficulties. It was the right choice for
a man with a peptic ulcer. Yerkes forgave me, but he could
not fully understand why I should prefer the garlic of Harvard
from which he had just escaped.

In the summer of 1919 my family and I moved into an apartment in Cambridge. My wife's family, the Days, proud that their
now slightly less gauche nephew-in-law had been called to
Harvard (which they thought was second only to Yale), found
an apartment and got it fixed up for us. No sooner were we in
it than there came a letter from G. Stanley Hall, then the psychologist-president of Clark University, inviting me to become
Professor of Experimental Psychology at Clark for three years
and saying that at the end of the term my appointment would be
made permanent *if* my work had been satisfactory. What a decision! J. W. Baird had died in 1917 and I was being offered his
post. I was not so charmed by Harvard that I did not believe that
America's two best positions in psychology were Titchener's and
Baird's, since they were both graduate-school research appointments. Usually you do not resign a job before you have filled it
for a year, but this choice seemed to be a case of life versus a
brief inspection by McDougall. I put the matter up to President
Lowell and he said he thought Harvard could not afford to keep
me in these circumstances. My in-laws felt differently and were

scarcely convinced of my rectitude until Harvard called me back three years later.

At Clark I found a laboratory, a big laboratory of a few big rooms. S. W. Fernberger was there as assistant professor, and I had been put "over" him by Hall's whim, as it were. That Fernberger supported me enthusiastically and that our life-long friendship grew out of this relation is a tribute to the generosity all his friends knew so well. Carroll C. Pratt was there as a graduate student, and Marjorie Bates, whom he married later, and M. Yokoyama from Japan. Those persons were my three Clark Ph.D.'s. Fernberger went back to his beloved Pennsylvania in 1920. Pratt was given his doctorate in 1921 and became instructor.

There were never, I think, more than eight of us, counting the secretary and my wife, who had been made an Honorary Fellow, in the intimate laboratory group. We had lunch together in the laboratory every day, although I held my seminar at my house. The laboratory was on top of the huge, factory-like building that Jonas Clark had built for this university when Stanley Hall convinced him that a university on the German model was what the youth of Worcester, Massachusetts, needed. Clark had died later, founding Clark College for Worcester youth and specifying that Hall should never hold a position in it. So we had no undergraduates. Clark College was downstairs, but the College was another institution.

Our little group worked together at scholarship and research. There was a rumor that a professor in the University was supposed to lecture at least twice a week, but actually we knew no rules. I undertook to give the Cornell systematic course, the "two-hundred-lecture" one, by myself, and everyone but the secretary came and listened to me. It was largely a matter of reviewing the literature, giving the references, and translating German for those even less adept in the language than I. Such a situation is ideal for productivity. We all lived together, working the eighty-hour week in the laboratory, lunching together, being democratic.

At the end of three years we had thirty-six published papers to show for our work. Fourteen of them were mine, but they were not all important.

When Stanley Hall had asked me to come to Clark in the summer of 1919 I had asked him to wait a year until I could have fulfilled my obligation to Harvard. He refused, and soon after I had arrived in Worcester I knew why. Hall was retiring in 1920 and wanted to fill the laboratory position before he left. Titchener had been asked to succeed him as psychologist-president and had refused, so now it was settled that Clark was to have a geographer-president, Wallace Walter Atwood from Harvard. It was Atwood's business to displace psychology by geography, and I suppose that included either putting or keeping me in my place. I was astonished and hurt by his coolness when I first offered him my support. He put in a telephone switchboard, which meant that we eighty-hour-week persons had no communication with the outside world after five o'clock. My wife had to stay at home in the evenings with our young sons, and I went to the President to ask to have one of the trunk lines plugged into the laboratory phone, since there were enough trunks and it would inconvenience no one else. He reproved me saying that my place in the evening was with my family and not at the laboratory. Nor did I get the use of the trunk line.

What has been called the Clark controversy occurred for the most part in 1921–22. This controversy consisted of a difference of opinion between the administration and those who came to be called "the disaffected professors" about certain matters of fundamental policy. The administration was President Atwood, who had the consistent support of his trustees (whatever some few of them may have thought in private) and of a minority of the Faculty. The four chief disaffected professors were the sociologist, Frank B. Hankins; the historian, Harry Elmer Barnes; the physical chemist, Charles A. Kraus; and I. Also, Carroll Pratt counted on our side, for he was a disaffected instructor. We had the support of most of the student body, including most certainly the undergraduates in Clark College, and I think of a majority of the Faculty, or at least of the Faculty of the University, although perhaps not of the College.

Back of this controversy there were two quite different issues which reinforced each other. The first was the debasing of the graduate and research character of the University by combining it with Clark College, a change which had become possible under Clark's will now that Stanley Hall had retired. Kraus and I were worried about this change. A special phase of this matter was the substitution of geography for psychology as the chief subject in the university, and that worried me — especially since Clark had for thirty years been internationally famous for its psychology. The second difficulty lay in the red hysteria which was current after World War I, much as it recurred after World War II. It is clear that President Atwood believed that there were subversive influences at work in his Faculty, and that he blamed Barnes, Hankins, and, absurd as it seemed to me both then and now, me.

The *casus belli* was a lecture by Scott Nearing, which was given with previous Faculty permission under the auspices of the Liberal Club of Clark College. Nearing was a radical, and his invitation was based on the argument that the students must hear all sides. This side was reddish. I did not attend the lecture, for I had little time for such things, but Mr. Atwood did. He stopped the lecture in midcourse, asking the audience to go home and emphasizing his wish by flickering the lights. As the story circulated, the details altered; the final version had it that the President had turned out the lights at the lecture in order to stop it. That report was coupled with the motto of Clark University, which is *Fiat lux*.

The students were up in arms. They stormed the library to find quotations from John Stuart Mill and Thomas Jefferson (but not from Karl Marx), posting them on the bulletin board. The local papers took up the fuss. Bruce Bliven covered the matter for the *New Republic* and I lent him the hospitality of our laboratory. It was he who, after talking to the President, warned me that my reappointment might be in jeopardy. The dispute was carried by the press over the country and I still have a scrapbook of 160 pages of clippings—a book which the President had obtained after it had come back from the bindery and which he handed me personally after he had called me over for that purpose.

These pages are no place to discuss fully the Clark controversy. The disaffected professors all left presently—Kraus to Brown, Hankins and Barnes to Smith, Pratt and I to Harvard. Later we asked the Association of University Professors to investigate and their Committee A did an excellent job under the leadership of the philosopher, Arthur O. Lovejoy. I will mention but one informative incident and then tell how I came to leave Clark for Harvard.

This incident illustrates the sincerity of President Atwood's fear of the red underground; it also shows how fear influences judgment. Atwood told Lovejoy that he had in the safe at Clark letters from these professors which showed such a bad situation in the academic ranks that he doubted that he ought to release them. Lovejoy urged him to show the letters to the committee. Finally Atwood sent the committee a copy of one letter. It was a letter from me to Barnes. (The janitor had found it abandoned in Barnes' desk when Barnes went to Smith and had turned it over to the President as possibly sinister.) The letter read: "Dear Barnes: I am glad the high position is yours. May you hold it with a high hand." It is my belief that President Atwood (and perhaps the janitor too) thought that here was direct evidence that Barnes had been given new authority in the red underground. Lovejoy showed me the letter. I recognized my own silly humor and then verified it from a carbon in my files, but I could not recall what I had meant. Then, in looking through my scrapbook of clippings, I discovered a clipping from a Worcester paper, one that Barnes had sent me in the fall of 1922, a clipping that announced the fact that Clark (mind you; *not* the red underground) had given Barnes a promotion. The headline read: DR.

BARNES GIVEN HIGH POSITION. It was, I suppose, a reasonable mis-interpretation for a man so sure that there was a red underground and that some of his Faculty were in it. Neither Lovejoy nor I ever could get to see the other letters documenting our guilt, and President Atwood's successor, when I begged him twenty-five years later to take a look, assured me that any such letters were no longer in the office safe.

In 1922 my three-year term of appointment was running out. Hall's letter of 1919 had said that I would be reappointed if my work were satisfactory, and I did not think anyone would claim that my work had been unsatisfactory. I wanted the reappointment as justification, although Harvard was now interested in me again, since McDougall had arrived and approved me and the philosophers liked me better than any other young experimental psychologist they knew about. I let Harvard recommend me, but I hoped that I might have reappointment at Clark—and the right to resign. Harvard warned me that the matter could not be settled until its Overseers had acted after letting my appointment lie on the table for a month. Pratt was to come along to Harvard with me, and Harvard broke its own rule by printing our names in its announcement of courses before its Overseers had acted. Atwood's attention was called to the announcement. The morning paper in Worcester had the headline, BORING QUITS AS RESULT OF NEARING CASE, with the information that both Pratt and I would transfer to Harvard. The afternoon paper said, BORING AND PRATT NOT WANTED SAYS ATWOOD. It was a wonderful week for peptic ulcers.

Actually, I became somewhat paranoic. I hesitated to be seen talking pleasantly with a friend lest I should jeopardize his status. Nevertheless, departure was ameliorated by much expressed good will. Clark's distinguished physicist, Arthur Gordon Webster, arranged a Faculty dinner in my honor. All my university colleagues came, excepting only the inveterate diplomat of the group, who pleaded a previous engagement. I did not doubt his engagement, but the psychologist of 1960 would say something about engagements that come to those who need them.

Thirty-five years later, in 1956, Clark invited me to come back to receive an honorary degree. I had already had friendly exchanges with the new president, Atwood's successor, and now I was greeted with the utmost cordiality. Only two of us, however, heard what seemed to me the very best words spoken. Hardly any of Clark's 1922 Faculty were left in 1956. But one member who had lived through that storm came to me after the award and said, a twinkle in his eye and gruffness in his voice, "I am glad to see justice done at last!"

It was easy enough in 1922 to wish to leave Clark, but less easy to decide on Harvard, for that offer was complicated by President Wilbur's suggestion that I come to Stanford. I had spent the summer of 1921 at Stanford and loved the place. For years I continued to feel as if I belonged there and to exercise a gratuitous loyalty toward the university. Harvard offered only an associate professorship, a demotion in rank but an increase of $2000 above Clark. Stanford offered a full professorship and $1000 more than Harvard. I think now that I would have decided for Harvard on the same grounds as before: Harvard offered more difficulty and challenge, though less security. Actually, however, President Wilbur of Stanford took the decision out of my hands. He lost patience with my indecision when the Stanford offer was to him obviously so much better, and he withdrew the offer. So I had Harvard's opportunity and difficulty put firmly before me and was presently to find them both fully up to my expectations.

Harvard 1922–1929

In the fall of 1922 I came to Harvard and began my new life by allowing a strange automobile, on a misty, rainy night, to fracture my skull and send me to the hospital for six weeks with a concussion. This event was tough on H. S. Langfeld who had to take over all my work, distressing to my wife who had all the worrying to do, and alarming to Harvard, which now wondered whether it might have given a precious professorship to a future idiot. I have no proof that the accident did not make me brighter. (How would I ever know?) But the consequences were interesting, and, as usual, I was able to reap some profit from disaster.

I had a retroactive amnesia. That was an experience more vivid in the living than it had ever been in the reading. There was also progressive amnesia; that is to say, I chatted with everyone and forgot what I had said in a matter of minutes or even seconds. Was I unconscious, being able to respond specifically and yet not to recall my response? In 1933 this experience helped me to express my sincere doubt that I am ever conscious—conscious in the sense of being immediately aware of my awareness. Thirdly, the accident removed most of my fear of death, for here was I, like Lazarus, dead and later alive again, and the occurrence had not even been unpleasant. It is those who are left who suffer from death, when death is sudden or when it is accompanied with lethargy. I do not speak of death after acute pain.

After Christmas I went back to life, Langfeld, and the philosophers. Langfeld had been caretaker for the Harvard Laboratory ever since Münsterberg's death six years before. The philosophers had not arranged life too well for Langfeld and me. Here, by their own act, they had on their hands two vigorous, egoistic, youngish psychologists, each with ideas of what should be done in the same laboratory. Langfeld had been director. They asked him to forego that title but did not give it to me, gave him the rank of associate professor because they had given that to me, and then, turning their backs, left the irresistible force and the immovable body to work it out. Only on the principle that philosophers can understand human nature but not cope with it can the enormity of their neglect of the consequences of their action be forgiven.

In 1924, therefore, when Howard C. Warren asked me, on Titchener's advice, to come to Princeton for more rank and less money, I wondered whether I had better give up Harvard and go. My wife said: "Let's not move every two years always!" I wanted to stay, to work at the mission of rescuing psychology from these philosophers. I asked myself this question: Had not Warren and Titchener tossed a coin to decide between Langfeld and me, with tails turning up for me, and would not Langfeld be asked if I refused? I had to trust my intuition, for Titchener and Warren were sphinxes; but I took the chance, refused Warren, stuck to my Harvard mission, and was rewarded. Heads on the other side of the coin, so it seemed to me, must indeed have meant Langfeld, and he was asked to Princeton and accepted. It is pleasant to think back now upon this difficulty, because it makes so clear my feeling of warm affection for Langfeld that persisted until his death thirty-four years later. He shared so much thought and endeavor with me in a never-stagnant correspondence, but we never would have managed it sitting in the same chair, as the philosophers thought we might.

In the summer of 1923 my wife and I went abroad, my first trip and my last until 1959, to see quickly something of western Europe and then to turn up at the VIIth International Congress of Psychology at Oxford. That was fun, to get to know the persons with the great names, to experience C. S. Meyers' friendly courtesy, to find how charming Henry Head could be, to meet the Claparèdes and the Piérons, to discover that this young-looking Zwaardemaker was really the great authority on smell (he was then aged sixty-six). The most exciting persons were, however, Köhler and Koffka, for Gestalt psychology was just getting to be known in America. The *Psychologische Forschung*, the organ of that new school, had not yet reached its fourth volume and we Americans—like William James in the 1870's and J. McK. Cattell in the 1880's—were all eager to know just what magic German psychologists had contrived.

I have never been in Germany. That lack in my education was a matter of some shame and also some bitterness before Hitler destroyed German science, but I could never afford travel with our children needing support and education. Nor could I ever afford to take a full sabbatical year by sacrificing a half-year's salary. What I did about this deficiency of mine was to compensate. I wrote my *History of Experimental Psychology* largely about German psychology, with a map of German universities as a cover-lining, and when, after G. E. Müller's death, German psychologists wrote me to ask questions about their own compatriot, I felt I had triumphed over space and budget.

In 1925 came the crisis of the *American Journal of Psychology*. Stanley Hall, who founded the journal in 1887, had taken Titchener in as one of the cooperating editors in 1895 and Titchener had made the *Journal* the organ for himself and the Cornell Laboratory. He chafed, however, over not having control, and, when Hall wanted to sell it in 1919 and I had the thought that Titchener, Langfeld, and I might buy (little I knew what Hall would ask for it!), Titchener resisted and then wrote me that a patron of Cornell wanted to purchase the *Journal* for Titchener and Cornell. Dallenbach came on to Clark to negotiate, ostensibly as Titchener's agent.

None of us on the outside knew then that Dallenbach himself was the patron and had borrowed money on his note to his father in order to get the *Journal* for Titchener, who, always self-confident, regarded himself as ruler through natural right even though one of his subjects had provided the cash to ransom the *Journal* from Hall. This arrangement worked for the first few years, for Dallenbach was even more loyal to Titchener than I. Then the inevitable happened. Dallenbach had to assume all the financial risks and he needed to pay off his debt while making the *Journal* a scientific success. When fiscal wisdom came into conflict with editorial policy, financial realism won (it had to), and Titchener awoke to find he was working for Dallenbach.

Titchener, his honor sullied, resigned in anger at the end of the 1925 volume, and Dallenbach turned to Margaret Washburn at Vassar, Madison Bentley at Illinois, and me to save the *Journal*. We agreed to form a joint Board of Editors, each with sovereignty

over what papers he accepted, and that plan, essentially dangerous, worked because of Dallenbach's skill in avoiding crucial
frustration for any of us. Titchener opposed us to the extent of
founding the *Journal of General Psychology* with Carl Murchison,
who had gone to Clark when I left, but Titchener died before
the first number of this rival journal could appear. In principle
I disapproved of privately owned scientific journals, but Dallenbach always worked for the common weal and I cemented my
friendship with him and stuck with the *Journal* for twenty-
three years. I resigned at the end of 1946 because I was tired of
spending my time in making apt the inept writing of inexperi-
enced authors and because I thought such work should pass to
younger men.

Titchener's death brought me the offer to succeed him at
Cornell. Had difficulties been the only assets that go with a job,
I should have accepted, for Cornell actually presented more
problems than Harvard. But Cornell was poor, there seemed to be
little prospect of advancement there (whereas at Harvard the
limit seemed to be the sky), and my mission at Harvard to rescue
psychology from the philosophers was still unfulfilled. So I stayed
in Cambridge, and Madison Bentley, who was older and much
better suited to solve Cornell's problem at that time, went to
Ithaca.

This call was my last important offer elsewhere. I was now
forty-one and getting too old to move. I had come through the
period of grueling decisions. Never for a moment have I regretted
any one of these many decisions to stay put or to move. Does that
mean I am pliant and adjustable? Certainly, after gaining at
Clark the reputation of being a trouble-maker, I was trying hard
to make my energy—and I had a lot of it—work for the common
good and not for obviously selfish ends.

In 1926 Morton Prince, a Boston Brahmin, an M.D. known
internationally for his research on dissociated personalities, appeared, bearing $75,000 from an anonymous donor (the sum was
later increased to $125,000) to use for establishing a department

of abnormal psychology under a faculty of arts and sciences in order to bring abnormal psychology and normal psychology closer together. He offered the endowment to Harvard, hinting that he might try Yale if we did not fall in with his wishes. Even in the 1920's conventional psychiatry had little relation to academic psychology and the tradition of Charcot and Janet in Paris and Freud in Vienna was even farther away from the German tradition of Wundt and the American functional tradition. Prince wanted to marry these separate interests and vocabularies, so he specified that his new "department" must not be in a medical school, where it might turn into conventional psychiatry.

Should Harvard accept this gift? The philosophers, McDougall, and I debated it. In the 1920's it was hard to find a clear distinction between abnormal psychology and the normal psychology of personality. Alfred N. Whitehead recalled how London University had had a foundation for an annual prize for the best essay on the conduct and character of King William II, and how, in the course of a century or so, new thought on this topic became more and more difficult to create. Parliament had had to change the use of the benefaction; similarly Harvard might in a couple of centuries find that abnormal psychology had become the psychology of personality. I suggested that we add the phrase *dynamic psychology* because, being vague, it was flexible in interpretation, and because it did indeed connote the field of personality and multiple personality in which Prince's primary interest lay. My suggestion was adopted, and the Fund for Abnormal and Dynamic Psychology brought into being what was called the Harvard Psychological Clinic. It was hardly a clinic, for therapy was not its immediate purpose. The aging Prince was made an associate professor for two years, and Henry A. Murray was brought in first as understudy. Presently he became the able and successful commander of this enterprise.

It is interesting to see the deliberate forces of History working here through the wills of Prince and me. Dynamic psychology was getting itself born near the turn of the century, when Freud in Vienna was discovering the role of the unconscious and Külpe in Würzburg the imagelessness of thought. Prince's act was designed to help bring the two trends of psychology together, just as Janet had tried to do in Paris back in 1895. Prince helped History along, but he was also a consequence of History's inevitability. By the 1920's many psychologists were beginning to think along similar lines, especially those who wanted psychology to do more about motivation or "human nature" or what was called *personality*. Similarly I thought that I was making a novel suggestion about the addition of the word *dynamic* to the deed of gift, whereas I too was being little more than History's agent. You can always get other people to go your way if you have the wit to follow them.

A little later Edgar Pierce, an 1895 Ph.D. of Münsterberg's, died, leaving his estate to Harvard for "additional instruction in philosophy and psychology and the development of the Psychological Laboratory." The estate amounted, after Mrs. Pierce's death, to $872,802. The word *additional* created much discussion in the councils of the University, for we argued that our budget in 1928, when the gift was accepted, must be guaranteed forever so that the Pierce increment would be truly an addition. The Harvard Corporation finally granted that view in modified substance, but it made no real difference because the funds of the University were expanding and our budget continued to expand after the Pierce Fund had been added to it.

How often I have blessed Pierce for his phrase "and the development of the Psychological Laboratory." At this time McDougall had left Harvard and the determination of the policy for the Psychological Laboratory depended on the six permanent professors, who were five philosophers and I. I was the youngest. The Laboratory then had an annual budget of $2500 and had to rent out the time of the mechanician to get money to buy materials and tools. I still paid out of my own pocket the salary of my secretary, the only secretary in the whole department. The five philosophers asked me what sum, out of an expected $30,000 income, the Laboratory ought to have. I spent an evening, with advice from no one, figuring out a budget which came to $6100. I could have made it $610 or $61,000, but $6100 was one-fifth of the total income and seemed fair. The philosophers had no desire to spend so much on their laboratory-child, which they regarded with enthusiastic ambivalence, but I stood firm and they were honorable men. I was the expert in experimental psychology; they were not. Thus I became an all-powerful minority, a case where one wisdom controls five ignorances. We could not vote on this matter, for here voting and majority rule would have been undemocratic. So the Laboratory got its $6100 because these five philosophers were honorable and just and ignorant of experimental psychology, and that exact sum still sometimes turns up in the budget as a contribution of the Pierce Fund to the Laboratory.

The 1920's I spent in teaching, administration, writing, and the direction of research. I was Director of the Laboratory *de jure* and chairman of a nonexistent department *de facto*—for we were linked with philosophy in departmental organization and a philosopher was always chairman. The constant stream of demands for letters and conferences took most of my time and I did no important research of my own. That might have been because I was not an experimentalist by temperament, but it is also true that my book-writing, at which I have been successfully productive, has been done almost entirely in the summers because there was no free time for my own work between September and June.

In those days most of the graduate students carried on their experimental work under my direction, but I never learned how to persuade them to work on the problems I wanted to see attacked. Later I found that I could get my crucial problems worked out at other universities if I would discuss the problems in publication. Wever and Bray did their first work on acoustic frequencies in the auditory nerve because I had suggested in 1927 that the frequency theory of pitch was more probable than a place theory—a suggestion that proved at least partly wrong but one which stimulated research and so got an answer. The younger instructors wished that the graduate students would not all turn to me, but prestige counted. Later it was the other way around. The students wanted to work with the younger staff, not with me.

The systematic course—the "two-hundred-lecture course"—I kept up for ten years (until 1932). By that time I felt that no one man could any longer cover the whole field of psychology. Besides, there were by then good texts and handbooks at the graduate level, so that the task of the instructor had become more than to read and assess the literature for graduate students. As I was obsessed by the conviction that we must somehow or other weld our psychologists, all of them Harvard individualists, together into an understanding unity, I conceived the idea of our having the different members of the staff take on different parts of the systematic course, all of us attending each others' lectures. The staff agreed, but I was the only one to attend all of the lectures (taking notes!) throughout the first two years.

In 1939 we gave up this attempt and started the Proseminar for first-year graduate students, a course which has been successful and in which J. G. Beebe-Center and I were for years the chief teachers. The Proseminar was a heavy course, with several examinations. The students did their own reading in the available books, about one hundred fifty pages a week, all in English. With the increase of handbooks and translations, the need of the American graduate student of psychology for German to use in his work had diminished greatly.

The Wednesday afternoon Colloquium for graduate students and staff was begun in 1924, another attempt to get an intellectual understanding among the staff. I wanted communication, not full community, and the Colloquium worked to that end in the 1920's. The staff all came and argued with each other; the students participated in a lesser degree. Those Colloquia stand out in my memory because of two important insights which the discussion brought out:

1. The Gestalt psychologists had baffled us because they seemed to insist that analysis is impossible, whereas we all knew that description has to be analytical and that they themselves believed in description. We taxed Köhler with this difficulty in a Colloquium, only to discover that he did believe in descriptive analysis and was objecting merely to splitting mind, especially consciousness, into fixed elements. That resolved a puzzle of five years' standing.

2. McDougall argued for freedom in psychology, always noting that determinism is not complete. In Colloquium we demanded that he show instances, only to discover that the difference between us lay in basic values. McDougall's freedom was simply my probable error, and McDougall hoped that there would always be left some freedom (probable error) no matter how far science advanced, whereas I hoped that probable error (freedom) would be diminished by scientific progress.

Those early Colloquia were worth while. Later, when the Department became large and forty persons came to a session, I never got intellectual stimulation from them, nor was there good discussion. A good Colloquium ought not to include over twenty persons.

Both the Colloquium and the cooperative scheme for giving the systematic course had failed to bring unity to the Department, but there was another device which succeeded—the staff luncheons. These began in the early 1930's when I brought my lunch to the Laboratory and offered free coffee to anyone who would lunch with me. Later they became an institution in the seminar room, organized under the principle that no one on an academic salary could afford to pay more than twenty cents for his lunch—since enough food for a lunch can be bought for twenty cents in a grocery. Coffee was made for us, but we put together our own sandwiches and used paper napkins for plates. That tended to bring the staff together, though later the Psychological Clinic formed its own in-group and lunch and ate with us only on occasion, and Lashley was but a rare attendant. The conversation at lunch was good, however, and I was never ashamed to invite a distinguished guest to join our frugal meal where talk was so stimulating. These luncheons continued for many years to provide understanding and communication among persons who had been added to the staff, added largely because they represented different basic values in psychology, but nowadays attendance is less general. To some of the key men the in-group is intellectually confining. Quite reasonably they want more varied stimulus.

It was in the 1920's that I wrote *A History of Experimental Psychology*. In the summer of 1924 I had offered a course on the history of experimental psychology at the University of California at Berkeley with the intention of carrying on to a book. I worked hard at the job in successive summers. It seemed preposterous for me to assume my competence in so large a field, and I confess that I was troubled by what I supposed would be Titchener's disapproval of my presumption. Then Titchener died in 1927, and I was as released as was John Stuart Mill by his father's death ninety years before. I took a sabbatical half-year off to finish the writing job in early 1929, and the proof sheets were bound into a gigantic fat volume for display by my publisher at the IXth International Congress of Psychology at New Haven in September 1929. The book appeared in the fall. It was successful, selling 1316 copies in 1930, never dropping below 200 copies per annum, and booming in 1947 after the Second World War to 2843 copies. It is a stiff book, one of which Titchener need not have been ashamed to have me write had he lived. How could so many persons want to read it? They did, however, most of the buyers, and when the first edition had become of age, I revised it radically and enlarged it, believing that many of my immaturities of 1929 I could eliminate in 1950, as I saw more clearly how great men are not the initiators of progress but its agents and how History is an ever-flowing stream through the centuries, a stream of events that occur in the nervous systems of persons situated so that their thoughts and acts become links in the course of progress.

There were many other events in the 1920's which represent

my participation in the professional scene. In 1919–1922 I had been secretary of the American Psychological Association and thus made many contacts with colleagues. In 1924 I became Director of the Harvard Psychological Laboratory and I held the post for twenty-five years. In 1925 Margery, the Boston medium, introduced to Harvard by McDougall, took our attention for a while. My hair was pulled in the dark in the Laboratory one night. Did Margery do it with her toes, or was it done by Walter, her deceased brother? I never knew about the first hypothesis for sure, but the second seemed to me a pseudo-problem with ill-defined terms.

McDougall resigned from Harvard in 1927 to go to Duke. He was unalterably British and thought of himself as in the provinces. The American South was to him another British province which presented an interesting racial problem. For a long time we filled up McDougall's deficit with visiting profes-sors: Wolfgang Köhler, Karl Bühler, Leonard Carmichael, and E. S. Robinson.

In accepting a demotion in rank from Clark's professorship to Harvard's associate professorship, I told myself that good work was important, not rank; still, I chafed at seeing all the men whom I regarded as my peers promoted to be full pro-fessors, while I kept on at the lower rank. If I was to advance, Harvard's philosophers had to arrange it, for there was no psy-chologist at Harvard senior to youthful me. The promotion finally came through after I had refused the Cornell offer. I have always believed that it was due to R. B. Perry's initiative and sense of justice.

In 1928 I was president of the American Psychological Asso-ciation and gave my presidential address in New York at the banquet—the last meeting at which the presidential address for this rapidly expanding society could be given at a banquet. The subject was the paradox between psychologists' insight into personal motives and the aggression of their egoistic productive drives. I have kept at that theme all my life and have got it into the 1950 edition of my *History*. I used to be intolerant of intolerance and to chafe at arrogance, but now I see, just as I was saying in 1928, that the truth must transcend the individual and that the blindness of egoism may be all that the productive scientist is vouchsafed. He contributes thus unwittingly to the stream of History which carries the burden of progress—a progress that becomes apparent to posterity. These interests of mine have continued up to the present and are explicated in two papers reprinted in the present volume (pp. 314–337).

At the end of the 1920's there was at last an American International Congress of Psychology—at New Haven in 1929. Cattell was president. I was secretary. Cattell and I used to clash in committee and I once remarked to him: "We ought not, Dr. Cattell, to be on the same committee; we differ too much." "That," he replied, "is not the trouble; we are too much alike." He meant we were alike in aggressive insistence.

The 1920's were a decade of hard work for me. Having a compulsive temperament, I drove ahead on the eighty-hour week with the firm conviction that I was not so bright as most of my colleagues but that I could make up for the deficiency by working harder. Unfortunately eighty hours is near the physiological limit; I could not have worked a hundred; so I found myself thwarted and baffled for lack of time or brains, since more of either would have sufficed to make me discontent at some higher level of production. I contributed no important research. Although I never saw how to free myself enough from interruption to do research and did not seem to stimulate students into working on my problems, I was mixed in with the stream of American psychology, becoming its agent in the various ways which I have just described, a psychologist at large, as it were. I believed thoroughly in *tout comprendre c'est tout pardonner,* and my personal paradox was that I could promote that doctrine of valueless phenomenology without weakening my own compulsive drives. I accepted compulsions as given and let them work. Of course, I liked having them, though they made me sweat, but I never argued that they were best. I mistrusted them, even in myself, as possible grounds for prejudice and blindness. It may be that the truth has usually to transcend the individual, but I hoped always that it might not transcend me.

Harvard 1930–1942

The 1930's started off with my writing *The Physical Dimensions of Consciousness*. Why I became a physicalist, reacting against Titchener's dualism, is not entirely clear. Dualism, the belief that mind and matter are different kinds of stuff, that the events of consciousness as introspection reveals them are essentially immaterial and impalpable, this faith has dominated psychological thinking ever since Descartes made it orthodox in the middle of the seventeenth century. Physicalism, in its most modern phase which is often called *operationism,* is the view that consciousness, as an object of observation by science, reduces to the operations by which consciousness becomes known to scientists. A sensation, for instance, is not an immaterial something such as redness or pain or bitterness, but the observed data, a man reporting in words the difference between two hues, the rat reporting in action that he knows dark from light. Since the man's words are discriminative behavior, and the rat's behavior is similarly discriminative, and behavior is a physical phenomenon, we can manage in this way to avoid dualism and bring all science, psychology and physics, into relation.

Actually this movement toward the dissolution of dualism was going forward in Vienna at the instance of the logical positivists when I was writing my *History*. P. W. Bridgman, the Harvard physicist, had expounded "operationism" in 1927 in order to make relativity theory clearer. Later he had great influence on American psychologists, but neither they nor I knew about his book then. In an unclear way my book was using this new "operationistic" logic, and I think I may properly be said to have been unconsciously plagiarizing the trend of scientific opinion as it moved on from the past toward the future. In short, I was being the unwitting agent of History, a little too soon to be clear, or perhaps not bright enough to be clear so soon. Later, on the occasion of the 1942 centenary of William James's birth, I undertook to contrast the operational or positivistic point of view with its Jamesian antithesis. That paper is reprinted elsewhere in this volume (pp. 194–209).

Certainly *The Physical Dimensions of Consciousness* was an item in the trend of American psychology away from dualism toward physicalism, a trend which has now ended in an almost complete acceptance of the physicalistic view by American psychologists. My book was a move away from Titchener, but it also served to make his dimensionalism clear. I have long called it "my immature book," but it had some admirers and 105 copies of it were sold in the seventeenth year of its life. It is now out of print and every now and then someone writes to ask where he can get a copy.

When I had finished with the *Physical Dimensions* I went into psychoanalysis with Hanns Sachs, Freud's loyal adjutant, one of the six who with Freud formed "The Committee" that took on responsibility for the psychoanalytic movement after World War I, the six who had rings fashioned like Freud's. Sachs had been Director of the Psychoanalytic Institute in Berlin, but, being Jewish, had come to Boston in order to leave Hitler behind.

Why did I undertake analysis? To know why you wish to be analyzed is almost equivalent to not needing to be analyzed, for the motives are bound to lie beneath the surface. I told Sachs that I was insecure, unhappy, frustrated, and afraid. I told him that I could no longer work, that I had to be rescued to productivity, that my honor was involved since I owed achievement to Harvard. Some of the younger men in the Laboratory let me see that my lack of productivity in research cost me some of their respect, yet my character was not changed by that realization. I could perceive vaguely that a difficulty arose from my thwarted compulsions. To be compulsive is to be perpetually dissatisfied with yourself, or so it seemed to be with me; and at that time my level of achievement was surely further below my level of aspiration than usual. So Sachs, kindly *gemütlich* soul, took me on in 1934–1935 for 168 sessions. Although I felt that he became somewhat of a Titchener-substitute for me, I never managed the degree of transference, either positive or negative, that I think now might have made the analysis more successful.

Four years later, Sachs and I, at my suggestion, discussed the question of whether my analysis had indeed been successful or not, and how you can tell when any analysis has been successful, discussed it in print for the benefit of our colleagues. What I believed then that I got out of the analysis was a knowledge of the technique, the reassurance of knowing that I had not left a reputed remedy for my trouble untried, the realization that even what is called successful analysis does not create maturity, and an appreciation of the fact that we have here a procedure which claims validity but which lacks scientific control and the means of validation. The analyzed analysts themselves taught me that analysis does not guarantee maturity or integration, for they turned out to be as vain, competitive, boastful, jealous, and ego-involved as most of my other friends—not Sachs, who was indeed mature and wise, but the young men. Had I then had Sachs's book about Freud to read and to show me the nature of the relations among Freud, Jung, Adler, and Rank, I should hardly have undertaken analysis with the hope of gaining maturity. For Sachs's and my printed discussion of the problem of my psychoanalysis, see pp. 127–142 of this book.

The analysis did not, however, injure me, except that the $1680 which it cost me at the special reduced rate added to my money complex, which had grown with the advent of my two daughters in 1925 and 1931. (The younger at the age of twelve figured out that she should get her A.B. one year after I had retired, and exclaimed with alarm, "Who is going to pay for me while I get my Ph.D.?") What really brings at last the measure of maturity that any man obtains must be living and experience, and in that way the analysis did mature me. I was wiser about human nature for having been analyzed, wiser for finding the analysts human and without a magic to dispense.

At least that is the way it looked then. I went into analysis at forty-eight. At forty-nine I was done with it and disturbed because I had not gained the maturity I sought. At fifty-two I wrote this paper about it, finding progress in myself but unable to attribute it to the analysis. At fifty-six I remarked to my daughter, so she says, that I thought I had at last attained a degree of maturity. At sixty-four when I wrote the first draft of this biographical account of myself, I was sure that I had finally captured maturity, but I must have been uncertain of its permanence or I should not have been so vehement in my expressed determination to hold on to it. Now at seventy-four I can afford some amusement at the whole tumultuous fifty years (or was it sixty?), a half-century of *Sturm und Drang*, as the Germans refer to adolescence. Could this be gerontic endocrine change? No, that did not come until after age seventy. But it is a wonderful period, these seventies—at least so far! Now let me get back to my story which is still halted in my late forties.

In 1933 President Conant succeeded President Lowell at Harvard. Lowell had not cared much about psychology, but Conant did. He said to me during his first year that he thought that the day of the physical sciences had passed and that the day of psychology was dawning, a prediction wholly borne out for psychology and utterly wrong for physics. One of his first acts was to appoint what must have been his first *ad hoc* committee, a committee to find "the best psychologist in the world" to elect to a chair at Harvard. I was on that committee, which was chosen to favor "biotropic" psychology (the kind that faces toward biological science), not the philosophical kind. Conant was shocked to find how generally psychologists contradicted each other about who was the best psychologist in the world. Evidently the psychologists did not know, but eventually the committee decided that the best was K. S. Lashley, and I have always been proud of the fact that he was appointed by Harvard's Governing Boards before he knew he was being considered. He was informed that he had been elected Professor of Psychology at Harvard and asked whether he would accept. He did and was given space in the new Biological Laboratories. Thus psychology grew and became geographically scattered. The Clinic under Harry Murray was down by the river, Karl Lashley was over in Biology, the conservative core of the social and experimental psychology (Gordon Allport and I) remained in Emerson Hall, and we had an annex over in Boylston Hall. The daily staff luncheons helped to keep us from falling apart.

We were, however, still tied up with philosophy. After twelve years my mission at Harvard was still unfulfilled. We were then a *de jure* Psychological Laboratory in a *de facto* Department of Psychology in a *de jure* Department of Philosophy and Psychology in a Division of Philosophy in a Faculty of Arts and Sciences. Lowell would have kept it thus, but under Conant my constant pressure at last created change. In 1934 I had the pleasure of moving to the Faculty that the Department of Philosophy and Psychology be divided into a Department of Philosophy and a Department of Psychology. The motion passed readily and Conant made me the first chairman for psychology. I had been acting as a chairman without authority for a dozen years. We were, however, still part of a Division of Philosophy and Psychology. Two years later I had a second pleasure: I moved that the Faculty abolish all divisions in order to leave the departments autonomous, except those departments that asked for divisional amalgamation, and that motion passed. Now at long last we had access to the Dean without a philosopher as intermediary. My mission was accomplished. How simple it seemed, and how silly!

The change was a *de jure* recognition of *de facto* independence already nearly acquired, and it would have come about if I had never come to Harvard. History had this event up its sleeve all along. In innovation Harvard prefers to be either first or last. In this case it was gloriously among the last of the big universities to make this change, and I was on the spot to witness the formalities and to contribute to it about as much as a minister contributes to the success of a marriage. Thus I had another lesson as to how the free action of a personal will in a naturalistic world is a delusion, of how little History's agent determines History's course.

The next thing after my analysis that took my time and attention was the first of the Boring, Langfeld, and Weld textbooks. I had thought that I would never write a textbook, since there were too many and their writing drained research. Most authors of texts hope, however, to achieve the perfect text that will end all other texts, and H. P. Weld of Cornell came forward with the suggestion that Langfeld and I cooperate with him in getting out an authoritative text, in which the various chapters would be written each by an expert, and in which psychology would assert its coming of age by showing that it could give facts to students without feeding the facts through a cloud of controversy. The book was to be science but to have no special point of view. Facts were to be stressed. Controversy was to be left out. Dubious truths were to be omitted. The names of researchers were not to be included unless they were such that the students ought to learn them as the names of great men. Since facts belong in the common domain, the undergraduate ought not to be taught as if facts were a function of the latest man to work on a given problem. Thus the first "BLW" was called *Psychology: a Factual Textbook*, and it came out in 1935. It was full of fact and not easy reading, but it was a success in that it preempted the field as an elementary text for universities which wanted a stiff introductory course and as an advanced text for colleges which wanted a second course in general psychology.

One of the most stimulating experiences of my life occurred when Langfeld invited Weld and me for a week to the hospitality of his house in Princeton while we worked over chapters received from various authors. We expected to disagree vigorously and I went to the conference with misgivings. Mrs. Langfeld escaped to Baltimore to leave us free to fight our differences out. We did disagree, but in this intimate contact with no jealousies we came gradually into agreement.

Since then I have seen this phenomenon happen to other committees. Put a group of men, who want the same result but who disagree on means, together for a week or two without interruptions and they will find (1) agreement, (2) a firm conviction that they are right, for each has conceded so much that he cannot believe that he did it except to gain the truth, and (3) a euphoria that makes them want to tell everyone else about their great success. (That is why Harvard's Committee on General Education in a Free Society was so sure it was right, although it had no means to propose for testing the truth of its conclusions.) Changing your opinion once shows that you have an open mind. Changing it twice suggests, however, that your mind may be weak.

The chief complaint about the first "BLW" was that it gave too much priority and space to the topics of sensation and perception, so we did another volume in 1939 which diminished the importance of these topics and placed them last in the book. In general users preferred this change, but certain staunch conservatives at Cornell, Brown, and other places continued to use the first book and regretted that we had yielded to pressure from the majority. After the Second World War in 1948 we published a much larger, more thorough, better written BLW. It too was a success, but it had lots of competition.

Along about 1939 I got into problems of the apparent visual size of objects at different distances and the moon illusion. At last I was doing experimental research, and, as observations had to be made late at night, I was free of interruptions. I still did not have time for detail and had to leave that to A. H. Holway, my able assistant. We published jointly, but eventually I got most of the credit because I was better known and because I published interpretative summary articles under my own name.

On the size-distance function we showed that objects do not appear to get smaller when they are removed from a distance of twenty feet to a distance of two hundred feet provided the clues to the perception of distance remain intact. Interfere with the clues and the objects shrink rapidly as they recede.

The moon illusion is a size-elevation problem. The moon higher up in the sky usually looks smaller, although the size of the image on the retina is unchanged. We showed that the illusion depends on the position of the eyes in the head and is reversed with respect to the earth when the observer is reversed, *i.e.*, when he looks at the moon lying on his back. We never found out why elevating the eyes in the skull shrinks the moon's size. Astronomers hailed our discovery as settling the moon problem because it took it out of astronomy into psychology, but some physicists felt that we had failed because we could not explain the shrinkage. It is a popular problem and the publication of our results led to a great deal of correspondence with persons who had thitherto been strangers. For a summary of this research on the apparent size of the moon, see pp. 115–126 of this book.

Ever since my analysis I had realized that I must save myself from sterility by hard work and not by psychoanalytic magic. For that reason, I had been working on a second volume of history, the book that finally appeared in 1942 under the title, *Sensation and Perception in the History of Experimental Psychology*. When I began the first history book in 1924, I meant to cover the entire field of experimental psychology as I then conceived its limits. What I published in 1929—699 pages—was but the introduction to the whole account and not so very experimental at that. (I might have changed the title to "Men and

Systems in Modern Scientific Psychology," but I forgot all about the title until after I had published.)

Now the question arose as to whether I could handle the history of research on sensation and perception in a second volume. I feared I could not, for I was no expert in the field of vision and I knew that, as long ago as 1896, König had a bibliography in this field of over ten thousand titles. I resolved, therefore, to try my skill with vision first, and, if its chapters seemed passable, to go on to finish the book. Since these chapters, when done, seemed not too bad, I finished the book, dating the preface 6 December 1941, as the day before the Japanese attack on Pearl Harbor and thus the last day when pure scholarship could be undertaken with a clear conscience, as it seemed then.

This book too had success, although it was more specialized than the first history and thus sold fewer copies. There were some complaints about the treatment of special topics, but not many. Certainly the book got by, perhaps less because of its accuracy than because there were few persons competent to criticize it. I have never felt free of the sense of solemn responsibility in knowing that my quick decisions of an afternoon may make history in the sense that hundreds of graduate students then learn what I have said and have no way of knowing if I was wrong. (In 1911 Titchener reproved me for buying an encyclopedia. "No one," he said, "has the right to use an encyclopedia, unless he knows enough to tell when it is wrong!")

Harvard 1942–1950

Emotionally the Second World War was harder on me than the First. In the First I was in the Army, with a job prescribed and no inner doubt about doing the most that I could. The Nation kept reassuring me of the importance of my effort, for at camp I had all the sugar I wanted while my family at home scraped along on a meager allowance. Hitler was, moreover, a greater threat to my basic values than had been the Kaiser, so I hated him more and worried more about victory. It would have been a relief to have had the Army to circumscribe my role, instead of being left to feel that, if I were but powerful enough, I might determine the issue of the war alone and that any effort of mine which fell short of victory was inadequate.

Actually I was too old to be in uniform and I had to begin war service by taking on more teaching at Harvard as the younger staff and the secretaries moved out nearer the front. One of my first war sacrifices was to support heartily the migration of my efficient secretary, the only one who ever worked the eighty-hour week, to the firing line in the National Research Council. The Emergency Committee in Psychology was formed in 1940 to promote the contribution of American psychology to the war effort. I was not on that committee, but I knew seven of its nine members well and followed its work closely.

Ever since the First World War there had been talk about military psychology and the need for a textbook in that field. Now the Emergency Committee brought that project back into its crowded agenda, but it seemed to be getting nowhere with it. With the BLW experience behind me, I was sure that the chapters could be written by various experts and edited into a unity, and I made this proposal in 1942, was invited to present it to the Emergency Committee in May, and left that meeting as chairman of a subcommittee authorized to get the book written and published. This was wonderful therapy for my frustration. I now had a war job into which I could pour effort. We got a good committee, which included Colonel Joseph I. Greene of the *Infantry Journal*, the wise academic in the Army who presently, because of his wisdom and humanity, became my close friend.

Colonel Greene thought that a popular book on military psychology, one addressed to the common GI soldier, helping him better to understand the psychological weapons with which he fought, would be a more valuable achievement than a text at a West Point level. We then got Marjorie Van de Water of Science

Service into the committee and went ahead. Fifty-two authors contributed material for the book, but Miss Van de Water and I rewrote and rewrote their material and shuffled their parts around to get the whole. She knew how to write the popular style, and I learned from her, eventually enough to do it on my own. We batted chapters back and forth between Washington and Cambridge until one of us was satisfied with the other's latest revision. It was great fun. Never before had I tried consciously to manipulate my English style, but now I was learning to do just that. Eventually I thought that I could come nearly up to the Van de Water standard, and I think I also kept out some of her more feminine phrases and illustrations. When copy for the book turned up in academic circles, it met with shocked astonishment, for academics do not write to the man in the street or in the front line. The Chairman of the National Research Council, Dr. Ross G. Harrison, was startled, but he accepted our judgment of what was good for the services. One of my idealistic graduate students, when he picked up a copy in my office, contented himself with laying the book down again vigorously and remarking, "It stinks!" But the GIs and the public liked the book.

The little volume appeared in the summer of 1943 under the title *Psychology for the Fighting Man,* a twenty-five-cent paper book under the imprint of the Penguin Series and the *Infantry Journal.* It eventually sold about 380,000 copies—perhaps the widest sale for any book sponsored by academic psychologists. The royalties brought the National Research Council about $10,000 which could be put against the $4000 expenses of my committee, but the services of the fifty-two contributors had been free. Certainly this was a successful undertaking, one which helped to place the importance of psychology more than ever in the consciousness of the American public.

Later this same committee got Dr. Irving L. Child to collect materials and publish a similar book, *Psychology for the Returning Serviceman,* for people at home were worrying about the adjustment of the returning GI to the reality of civilian life. I had little to do with this book except for one hectic period in the fall of 1944 when we were trying to accomplish the impossible in the way of rewriting before a deadline. That strain brought on an ulcer attack, for the ulcer, my badge of productivity, was still with me.

At that same time I was supposed to be rewriting the materials of *Psychology for the Fighting Man* into a true textbook of military psychology, stepping the style up to the West Point level and adding new content from what I knew about psychology in general or what the authors of the BLW texts knew. The ulcer attack held that up, but the book came out as *Psychology for the Armed Services* in the summer of 1945, two years after the other. As far as I know, it was all right, but it had no phenomenal success. West Point later used it a little, but they wanted tougher chewing for their cadets. My style regulator should have been set higher; there should have been more tables, more quantitative graphs, more of the odor of science, less of the tang of human nature. It was also true that West Point wanted to stress leadership, and that requirement was an impossibility since there were not enough data available for constructing detailed chapters on leadership at a rigorous scientific level.

In May 1942, when I was forming the subcommittee on a psychological military text, R. M. Yerkes was organizing, under the Emergency Committee, his Survey and Planning Committee. The purpose of this committee was to bring psychologists together with more time for deliberation and discussion than was available in the meetings of the Emergency Committee. Yerkes asked five others and me to make up his first committee and we met for a week at the Training School in Vineland, New Jersey, in June. During the three years that the war continued, this committee met nine times at Vineland, always for at least four days, sometimes for a week. We worked morning, afternoon, and evening. The suggestion that we take off one afternoon to migrate to the Atlantic Ocean to swim never prevailed. We accomplished a great deal in the way of recommendations to the Emergency

Committee and I think that much collective wisdom can be said to have issued from us. The psychology of collective effort in conference, which I have mentioned above as applying to Langfeld, Weld, and me when planning the first BLW text, held sway here. The committee members represented divergent points of view and conflicting value systems, and we were a little afraid of each other at first. Everyone of us, however, wanted success in the war effort, and that common goal brought us together. As we got to know one another better and to achieve unanimous recommendations by compromise, our belief in the importance and correctness of what we were doing grew. Our egos throve, jealousies evaporated, and we worked efficiently.

One of the greatest achievements of the Survey and Planning Committee was the reorganization of the American Psychological Association, the "APA." The committee was convinced that American psychology needed to speak with one voice and also to think, if not with one brain, at least with a set of brains connected by commissural fibers. We wanted to bring the APA and its scion, the American Association for Applied Psychology, as well as some of the other smaller societies, together into a single unitary group.

The Survey and Planning Committee prepared the way, got a first draft of a constitution together, and organized an Intersociety Constitutional Convention in May 1943, a convention of which I was chairman, ably assisted by E. R. Hilgard. The philosophy that I kept emphasizing was that of the American states in 1787. Every society which joined the supersociety would keep its sovereignty. There would be a central office to accomplish all communal functions, and societies could delegate their sovereign functions to the central office when they wished administrative relief. On that basis the AAAP joined with the APA, the Society for the Psychological Study of Social Issues came in, but the Psychometric Society stayed out. After the Convention younger men took over the planning and the rewriting of many drafts of the Constitution, but I was elected as the first chairman of the

Policy and Planning Board of the new APA, a board which was to carry on the function of the old Survey and Planning Committee.

The war had one great effect upon psychology at Harvard. It taught the social psychologists that they had a common mission with the cultural anthropologists and the modern empirical sociologists (the field sociologists, the polling sociologists, not the arm-chair and library kind). They were all studying human nature in its social setting. Now at Harvard they proposed the great fusion: social psychology, cultural anthropology, and sociology were to form a new department and to bring clinical psychology along in with them. Let the peace not dissipate the advantages of the recent war.

Fusion, however, means fission. It takes an out-group to make an in-group. The new arrangement would split psychology down the middle and leave the experimental and physiological psychology of the laboratory outside. I was doubtful, but these human naturalists were sure. I gave in when one of them, like the Prince of Wales before Stanley Baldwin, pleaded with me for the right to marry for love. Whatever the others may have hoped, it was I who suggested publicly that the Psychological Laboratory ought, after forty years, to get out of Emerson Hall into more suitable environs. For two decades I had longed for a laboratory where the milkman could deliver milk and collect yesterday's bottles without offending academic dignity. Our new Dean, Paul H. Buck, the latest and best of a long series of deans who had all been sympathetic and helpful to psychology, showed his statesmanship by lending vigorous support to both sides of this fission. In 1945 a new Department of Social Relations and Laboratory of Social Relations were installed in the top of Emerson Hall with decent outside funds for development, and residual psychology was freed for expansion in a wonderful new Laboratory in the basement of old Memorial Hall.

There was really no good name for our horn of this dilemma. We were "biotropic" and the others were "sociotropic." The sociotropes would have had us called *physiological psychology*, but, while we included physiological psychology, we also claimed all the psychology and behavior of the individual organism and asserted that, as residuary legatees, general psychology and instruction in the history, systems, and general theories of psychology came within our competence. We also maintained that biotropic abnormal and clinical psychology fell with us whenever we might find means for providing for them. So we kept for ourselves the word *Psychology*. We might have been called *Experimental Psychology*, but the sociotropes insisted that they experiment too, as indeed they do.

Meanwhile we were getting our grand new 108-room Psychological Laboratory set up in the basement of Memorial Hall. The space had been partly a dirty, messy cellar and partly the old commons kitchen of the 1870's. S. S. Stevens discovered its possibilities, and developed the government-supported Psycho-Acoustic Laboratory in one end, starting in 1940. That laboratory grew, and then Stevens was given the job of planning the whole space for the combined laboratories of psychology. As usual he threw himself into the job, devoting a year of his life to the undertaking, and it is remarkable what cinder-block walls, asphalt tiles, paint, glass bricks, furred-down ceilings covering pipes, and twice as much fluorescent light as necessary will do to make the inside of the Pyramid of Cheops look like the Waldorf-Astoria.

We were very happy, and the immediate accessibility of the books and journals in general and experimental psychology gave me a sense of expanded power. I, now the patriarch, was given a huge office supplied with Münsterberg's refinished desk with a glass top put on it, for at first we thought we had plenty of space. Soon, however, President Lowell's bon mot, "These professors followed the gas law" (will fill all of any space in which confined), became clear again. We were jammed full and regretted earlier expansiveness. The Navy had spent about $100,000 on making the Psycho-Acoustic Laboratory. Now Harvard had spent $150,000 more. It cost more in 1940–1945 to fix over the cellar of

Memorial Hall than it cost in 1906 to build all of Emerson Hall.

In September 1946 the University of Pennsylvania, in connection with the celebration of its Bicentennial, held a special convocation to commemorate the fiftieth anniversary of the founding of its Psychological Clinic, the first in the world, and to confer the honorary degree of Doctor of Science upon six psychologists of whom I was one. The others were John Dewey, famous philosopher and once entrepreneur of functional psychology; R. S. Woodworth, often called the Dean of American psychology, still writing books up to the age ninety; H. H. Goddard, pioneer in the study of feeble-mindedness; L. M. Terman, of Stanford-Binet fame; Wolfgang Köhler, the effective exponent of the distinguished school of Gestalt psychology. I was proud to find myself in such honorable company, to sit next to John Dewey on the platform, and indeed to have my first honorary degree. Köhler and I were the babies of this group, just under sixty. Dewey was eighty-seven years old. Now Dewey, Goddard, and Terman are gone. Woodworth, Köhler, and I remain.

When the fission with Social Relations occurred in 1945, I found myself suddenly chairman of the department again, without even having been asked whether I would serve. In 1921 I had picked up from E. P. Cubberley at Stanford the dictum that a departmental chairman ought to resign at age forty-five, leaving power to younger men. If his prestige does not then give him influence enough, he does not deserve power. I liked that thought, but I had only belated opportunities to put it into effect. I was Director of the Psychological Laboratory from 1924 to 1949, having been persuaded by the Dean, when I tried to resign a year earlier, to stay on to round out a complete twenty-five years as director. I was *de facto* chairman of a nonexistent department for ten years (1924–1934) until I was forty-eight (three years beyond Cubberley's limit). Then, when the *de jure* department was created, I became its chairman for two years, but resigned in 1936. After that I was landed in the chairmanship again for three years when the new Department of Social Relations was created. It had not been easy to follow Cubberley's dictum, but in 1949 I was at long last free of the administrative responsibilities I had had for the Department and the Laboratory, and also, as it seemed then, for the American Psychological Association. I was nearly sixty-three years old, much older than I felt.

It seems proper here for me to say a word about Stevens. Of all the graduate students who have worked especially with me, he was the one in whose ultimate success I had the most certain belief, in whose future I made the largest investment of identification. Outsiders used to think of him as my favorite, and indeed he was, but with good reason, as the outsiders kept finding out when they learned what he could do. In the early days I taught Stevens some of his knowledge and even how to write well. Now he instructs me. I watched with a paternal pride his early research in psychoacoustics and his publication with Hallowell Davis of the book on *Hearing*. I stood by when he designed the laboratory in the cellar of Memorial Hall. I inveigled him (what a job!) into organizing and editing the Stevens *Handbook of Experimental Psychology*. I rejoiced when he succeeded me as Director of the main Psychological Laboratory—he was already the successful Director of the Psycho-Acoustic Laboratory. I was the astonished and delighted witness of his return about 1953 to personal research, first in psychoacoustics, and then in general psychophysics with his steady cumulation of experimental evidence for a substitute for Fechner's law for measuring sensation, a century after its first formulation. My relationship with Stevens has been very rewarding for it has been genuinely paternal. Always I count Stevens' many successes as my own, not publicly, of course, but in my secret thought. He and I for thirty years have thought alike about departmental and laboratory policies and have perhaps provided for Harvard's psychology, as I waned and he waxed, the most durable continuity it has had since Münsterberg died or perhaps ever. At any rate I note how it is in these relations that the older man through the younger obtains one of the most satisfying reimbursements that the academic profession has to offer and also, by identification, manages a little grasp on immortality.

When finally I found myself released from the administrative responsibilities of both the chairmanship of the Department and the directorship of the Laboratory, I turned to the revision of my 1929 *History of Experimental Psychology*, getting out in 1950 a real revision, expanded by 25 per cent, with half of the enlarged book new writing and many alterations in the old parts that were taken over. What pleased me most about the revision was that I felt that it was more mature, that the discussion was structured about a wiser conception of what is going on when science advances. I had also solved to my own satisfaction the question why American psychology, while attempting to copy German introspective psychology in the late nineteenth century, nevertheless went functional. That matter had troubled me in 1929. Also I got into the new account the paradox of how History controls the achievements of Great Men and yet consists of what they do. I said, when the book came out, "If it does not last another twenty years, it should at least last ten." It did. In 1959 more than 2200 copies of it were sold. During the thirty years of the two editions, 36,000 people bought it of the original publisher, besides a few thousand more who purchased a reprint from another publisher. Some of these matters of the dynamics of the history of psychology are discussed elsewhere in this book (pp. 314–337).

Harvard 1950–1960

The 1950's became the best decade of my life. At last I had got my level of aspiration down within reach of my abilities. Other people had ceased to be jealous of me and some honors came to me. It was an honor to be chosen to edit and form the policy of the new journal, *Contemporary Psychology*—much hard work, but an honor too, a recognition of present, not past, ability.

It was the best decade, but it began with a tragedy, the death of my younger daughter, the one who at the age of twelve was worried about the money that would be needed for her Ph.D. I thought of her as the brightest of the six of us, but perhaps it is more correct to say that it was her intense compulsions that pushed her toward the top in her academic activities and in her music. In compulsiveness she was an exaggeration even of me. She could not stand second-rateness, and failure was unthinkable. So she pushed herself to the top in a progressive preparatory school, completed her freshman year at Swarthmore where competition was fiercer, and then, in her sophomore year, died. One can say that compulsions are not enough, that had she equaled Francis Bacon by sheer force of her will she still would have been inferior to Goethe, that after Goethe there was still Aristotle to keep the perfectionist in place. But I—I had lost part of myself, for she was made in my image, was better than I, and had come to nothing. Ten years later I write these words with moist eyes.

Still, the 1950's were the best decade.

As I have already remarked, it was in 1950 that I wrote the first draft of the present autobiography, which was intended to become a chapter in the last of the four volumes of *History of Psychology in Autobiography,* the collection of the intellectual histories and the self-analyses of fifty-eight important European and American psychologists. Only nine of those fifty-eight are living now—only two, R. S. Woodworth and Sir Frederic Bartlett, from the first three volumes that ran up to 1936. The present account is the original long draft of 1950 as it stood before it was halved for publication. It has, of course, been updated and revised as of 1960.

In 1951 my wife and I bought an old farm at Harborside, Maine, on Penobscot Bay—shore land, abandoned fields, good fields, a brook, woodland, and a high hill that is sometimes called a mountain, 137 acres in all, a comfortable farmhouse with seven or ten rooms, depending on what a room is, a deep, never-failing well, and a huge barn built in 1820, the year Maine separated from Massachusetts. I was sixty-five, the age at which some professors retire, and I decided that at last I could quit the four-thousand-hour year and relax in summer.

In Maine I now had a study with an old dining-room table for desk, shelves and drawers constructed by me, a typewriter, a dictating machine, and a calculating machine, along with duplicates of the important reference books. Thus I could work half the day on letters, editing, writing, and other professional work, and be out of doors the other half, improving trails, carpentering, splitting birch logs for the fireplace with a ten-pound sledge. Our grown children and our grandchildren could join us here and did, and they liked the freedom of the great open spaces. My younger son is always on the water, but I am not water-minded. Thus I "relaxed," but the compulsions kept on. I always have a long list of things waiting impatiently to be done —a biography of a deceased colleague to write, a big birch to be cut first down and then up. Not only does this rural institution bring the three generations of our family together; my wife and I drive the 260 miles to the farm about once every other month the year around, and, though firmly typed as "summer people," we now have very good friends among the "natives," feeling proud that they have been willing to accept us even though we were not born in Maine.

Harvard's age for retirement is sixty-six, and I was well past sixty-six in June 1953. Nevertheless one may be asked to stay on. In December 1951 President Conant's office had called and said the President wished to see me. I had said, "Of course; when shall I come?" The voice replied, "No, *he* would like to call on *you.*" At once I knew that this must be Harvard's courtesy operating in this delicate business of retirement. We fixed an hour six weeks off at 5 P.M., and at 5:00:15 P.M. Mr. Conant knocked on my door. He invited me to stay on teaching two years more, and to that I said yes. He then added that, when the two years were nearly up, I should call on him and we would decide about a third year, and then, if I stayed, a year later we would discuss a fourth, "but after that," he continued, "you'd be seventy and hardly anyone stays after seventy." Hardly anyone does, although a Nobel Laureate colleague stayed until seventy-two. I, with my tenure renewed by President Pusey, did indeed stay until nearly seventy-one, and that was just about the right time to quit from my point of view. I was grateful for the extra four years; I needed the activity and responsibility. I am grateful for the many, many things Harvard has done for me, far beyond the call of necessity, and I rather think I was asked to stay more because of my thirty-one years of loyalty enthusiastically given than because my diamond mind had scratched the surface of civilization deeply—for that, I take it, is Harvard's usual criterion for promotion.

Various things happened in the early 1950's. I wrote some papers that I like. I gave one of the two addresses at the dedication of the new psychological laboratory at the University of Texas in April 1953. Alice Bryan of Columbia and I had published a set of studies of the status of women in American psychology. I initiated that because she was a feminist who saw women as denied their professional rights, and I was on the other side thinking that women themselves for both biological and cultural reasons determined most of the conditions about which she complained. I thought that joint study by the two of us was the way to cancel out prejudices and leave truth revealed. The truth, however, was still left masked by compromises, until, some time after the collaboration was over, I published my own paper on the woman problem and felt that I had now said my own last word, even if not the very last one. This paper appears elsewhere in this book (pp. 185–193).

In 1954 the United States was passing through a stage of hysterical fear of Communism and subversion, spearheaded by Senator Joseph McCarthy. The American Psychological Association wished to satisfy its many socially minded members that it was ready to do something, if possible, to protect academic and scientific freedom from these violent attacks by the anti-intellectuals. It appointed a Committee on Freedom of Enquiry to see what could be done, by way of psychological research into people's attitudes or by way of crystallizing opinion—and action perhaps—in other learned societies. The Committee had five members, sociotropes, all emotionally stirred about these problems and the attacks on science and the universities, and it had also me, as its chairman, who was also stirred but not so deeply as to fail to be amused when I realized that what was wanted of me was my reputation as a nonsocial experimental psychologist. Actually, I was chosen for political conservatism. Entirely unknown to this generation was the Clark episode of 1922 and President Atwood's quite genuine fear that I was an active member of a subversive Bolshevik cell.

The Committee held five meetings from June 1954 to January 1956, including a convocation of representatives of learned societies in October 1954, but Senator McCarthy had already been discredited and condemned by the U.S. Senate in December 1954. Did we do any good? We tried and failed to get funds for a research on attitudes among Government employees. Our sessions were certainly good therapy for the committee members who, frustrated, could not bear inaction. Our very existence must also have comforted a great many of the then twelve thousand members of the American Psychological Association who believed that their profession was under attack and should not remain complacent. I myself, being neither a sociotrope nor a clinical psychologist, felt somewhat uncomfortable in my involuntary role as social therapist. It was natural that the Committee fade in 1955 because the hysteria had faded, but there was another reason. I had been elected editor of the new journal, *Contemporary Psychology*, and had no time for extracurricular activities.

In 1955 the American Psychological Association was publishing ten journals, of which four carried book reviews. In general, book reviewing was not popular with the editors, for it was something foreign added on to a different principal activity. The Association decided, therefore, to start an entirely new journal devoted solely to the reviewing of psychological books and, after much discussion, the name *Contemporary Psychology* was chosen for it, with the vague thought that such a magazine might someday expand to include timely articles about the contemporary scene. It was plain that the new journal was to be addressed to all psychologists, or at least to all members of the Association, and that it could not on that account be highly technical. I was elected editor for a term of six years. We started work in March 1955. Volume 1 was to appear in January 1956. Presumably I would send in my last copy—for Volume 6—just after my 75th birthday in the fall of 1961.

Within this vague framework I made policy. With an eye on the *New Yorker* and the *Saturday Review,* I tried to set the magazine on its way toward an informal, interesting English style. We called the journal *CP,* fully aware that those initials had always meant Communist Party but determined to break down the old association and establish the new. We won. Nowadays no psychologist thinks of anything but us when he hears *CP. CP* put in an editorial page and gave itself a mind. Always it has been *CP* who thinks, plans, decides, not the editor. That page, *CP Speaks,* seems to have been successful. At least there are some readers who turn to it first when a new issue arrives. For two examples of the editorials in *CP Speaks*—the more sober ones—see pp. 338–346 of this volume.

This biography is not the place to discuss all the facets of *CP's* policy nor all the ways in which *CP* has adjusted to the variety of human responses that impinge upon every editor. On the other hand, there are three matters of policy so deeply founded in the value-system of *CP's* editor that they seem to enter properly into this autobiography. Here they are.

The psychologists feared autocracy—the putting of all the value-judgments of all their books into the hands of a single editor. Illogically but effectively, *CP* met that risk by distributing autocracy among thirty socialized Consultants. That was also a bit of necessary wisdom, for no one man could deal wisely with all the books or find proper reviewers for them in so broad a field as psychology, but the device was also an imposition, for thirty separate idiosyncratic autocrats, who would never in the world agree with each other on all value judgments, nevertheless look democratic.

Unfavorable reviews brought out the cry, "Monopoly!" If *CP* is unfair, who is left to do justice? Well, reviewing has to be idiosyncratic. The authors would ask for multiple reviews, but two independent reviews tend to be redundant, and anyhow *CP* was in no position to double its size. Instead it put in a department of dissents, called "On the Other Hand," printing there critical letters and "counterreviews" and dissents to dissents, aiming always at an ultimate average justice by a cybernetic process of successive diminishing, antagonistic dissents. This scheme works pretty well.

In the reviews and the letters *CP*—who is, of course, I—was resolved that personal attack should be eliminated. Wound the ego and objectivity takes flight. *CP* set itself to keep all criticism *ad verbum*. No *ad hominems*. Of course the effort fails of perfection. There is always a *homo* who uttered the *verba*, but a writer can come nearer detaching himself from his words than from his integrity or intelligence. Scholarship advances best if dissent is confined to ideas and kept as impersonal as an idea can be. The more caustic letters, the more brutal ones, that have come to *CP* have so far all been rewritten by their authors before publication in a more impersonal vein. Perhaps anger has an ethical function, but brutality has not—and much of the brutality offered for publication is autistic.

CP was fully a half-time job for me (half of forty hours a week, not half of eighty), and for Edith Annin, my able assistant editor, it was full time and over. Thus I was able to carry it along during my last two years of teaching, and how I liked it! Somehow or other the writing skill of him whom Titchener had called "the uncultured engineer" had improved enormously during forty-five years of trying, and the editorial skill for making the texts of other people smoother and brighter has gone along with the writing. I felt I was giving American psychology something that it needed and also wanted.

In the spring of 1960, alas, came the time to think of retirement, for my successor needed to be chosen eighteen months in advance of his first issue, so that presently he might go to work assigning reviews. For the first time I found myself in a position of importance that I did not wish to surrender. I had fantasies about being a Churchill, and keeping on a second six years, but the wisdom that age is supposed to have told me that no older man has the competence to assess his own competence. *CP* has, indeed, been good geriatrics for me, and I shall quit shortly after my seventy-fifth birthday, content with having had a new adventure in communications.

It was in my final active year before retirement that a new activity turned up. I was asked to put Harvard's Psychology 1 on television.

No one ever undertook an important new activity with such inadequate advance information. Harvard, stimulated by the Ford Foundation which paid half my Harvard salary, asked me to produce Psychology 1, which I had given in the classroom with almost no interruption for thirty-three years, on Boston's educational TV channel. In all innocence I figured that Psychology 1 at Harvard included about twenty-eight fifty-minute lectures, and that I would thus need fifty-six half-hour programs. There was, however, not so much time available; thus I settled for thirty-eight half-hours from 6 October to 28 June, with no holidays.

I have always liked mastering new media of communication. Writing *Psychology for the Fighting Man* in GI language was one; *CP* was another; and this would be still another. But how I worked, changing the Harvard lectures over into TV demonstrations. I had able assistance but the week went thus. Saturday and Sunday: get up new lectures. Monday: conference. Tuesday: free, except for phone calls. Wednesday: "walk through" and planning of movements in morning; rehearsal with camera crew in afternoon; program in evening, followed by inspection of kinescopes of past programs. Thursday and Friday: free except for telephoning.

I had no prompter. I had notes in my pocket but never had to use them. Except when demonstrations made me move around, I sat on the corner of a table and talked in a friendly, enthusiastic, paternal manner to the red lights on whatever camera was on the air, calling the lights in my imagination "Papa, Mamma, and Johnny." So my TV audience was three. Perhaps ten thousand outside, but I always doubted that. The talks were gay— not without wit, some said. I got to like the enterprise. There was some fan mail—from colleagues, from old students who had rediscovered me, from high-school children with papers in science to do. All during the year following I received letters from over the United States where the kinescopes were being shown and they were still coming after three years. It was a great experience. I would not consider doing it again.

The next year I had retired. Psychology at Harvard had had, since 1928, some money from Edgar Pierce's bequest. At last the Corporation decided to create an Edgar Pierce Professor of Psychology. I held that chair my last year. It was probably my impending retirement that hurried authority into the decision. Now, of course, I am Edgar Pierce Professor of Psychology Emeritus, and I like the title.

My first year of retirement, 1957–1958, was a biographical year. First there was the memoir of Robert Yerkes for the American Philosophical Society. Yerkes, Terman, and I had been quite close, but now Yerkes had gone. After Yerkes, Terman died too, and his son asked me to write his memoir for the National Academy of Sciences. He said his father would have especially wanted me to do it. I worked hard at it to produce what I thought was a good account of the dynamics of a life. Meanwhile, the editors of the *American Journal of Psychology* had planned a commemorative number of that journal when its chief editor, Karl M. Dallenbach, was retiring as professor at the University of Texas. I was to do that, also as a complete analysis of a man, and, tutored by *CP*, I added pictures of Dallenbach at different ages and in different situations. My fourth undertaking of this sort was to write an intellectual history of Karl S. Lashley's research from 1917 to 1950. There was to be a commemorative volume in which would be reprinted twenty-nine of his more important papers. I wrote a preface as a kind of preview of what was coming in the volume. Lashley died before the volume could be published, so this undertaking turned out unexpectedly to be a kind of obituary. It was, however, becoming plain that I did this sort of thing well and that I was likely to become the unofficial biographer of psychology's great unless I resisted. So I decided against any more obituaries immediately and have since declined two. Now here I am busy at my own. These biographies of Titchener and Terman are to be found elsewhere in this book (pp. 246–294).

The next year, 1958–1959, I went on Phi Beta Kappa's circuit from October to March. At their planning I visited eleven colleges for two or three days each, gave at each from five to thirteen lectures or talks (but the thirteen was a mistake by an overeager college), and in informal sessions got as close to the students as possible. There was always one big formal lecture, but soon I found I had a repertoire of ten talks, and they all ran so easily ad lib from notes on cards before me that I could ask casually on being led to the talk whether it would be to thirty or six hundred persons. I think these talks went well from the point of view of the colleges. The students were stimulated and I slipped into a vein of ready humor. On the other hand, I was too informal to please all. Many would have preferred orations or a polished lecture in traditional Phi Beta Kappa style. I talked mostly about the psychology of discovery, the psychology of the history of science, and the history of psychology, and also about man as a machine.

Next I was asked to lecture at the University of London, with a fee and expense money that made acceptance possible. I had not been across the Atlantic since the Oxford International Congress of Psychology in 1923. There had never in this long interval seemed to be enough money, but I was also held back by the fact that I do not speak French or German and the only reason for going to the Continent would be to talk psychology to psychologists. Now I accepted with pride and alacrity, though I knew I could not leave *CP* for long—*CP*, which had never been without me for more than ten days. I arranged for seven lectures in three weeks, at London, Cambridge, Manchester, and Edinburgh. My wife went along and we had a wonderful time. The British were all cordiality. At the second London lecture at Birkbeck College they anticipated my birthday by a day with a huge cake with seventy-three candles on it. Cambridge was stimulating in one way, Manchester in another, and Edinburgh perfectly delightful. They all said: Come back and stay longer, but I probably shall not.

I returned to America, strangely enough, with the impression that anti-intellectualism, which American psychologists deplore, actually infects these same American psychologists themselves. That thought arose because I found so much respect for the history of psychology among the psychologists of the United Kingdom, whereas I think history is looked at askance by psychologists in the States.

I have said that the 1950's not only moved me out beyond the constant jealousies that younger men face in our competitive society but also brought me honors. *CP* was one. The Sc.D. from Clark University in 1956, the remedial degree as it were, I have already noted. The cordiality with which I was received after more than thirty years of dubious status pleased me enormously. And then there were two other honors.

In April 1957, when the Society of Experimental Psychologists met at Harvard, just before my retirement, the annual dinner of that select society, of which I am a charter member, was turned into an occasion for recognizing the significance of my impending metempsychosis. President Pusey of Harvard was there, made a little speech, and received from more than 150 donors a check for nearly $5000, starting the "Edwin G. Boring Library Fund." That not only engraves my name forever in the Harvard Treasurer's Report but also puts a beautifully designed bookplate bearing my name in countless books. Besides all this, thirty-four former pupils sent me specially inscribed reprints of their publications dating from 1925 to 1956, all recognizing the various ways in which their authors had sensed my influence. It was a red-letter evening.

Then, in the fall of 1959, just before my wife and I went abroad, I was summoned to the convocation of the American Psychological Association meeting in Cincinnati. There the American Psychological Foundation bestowed their Gold Medal on me as a "psychologist whose lifetime career has made a truly distinguished contribution to the content and status of the science of psychology." The citation itself was long but the scroll that went with the medal claimed for me a sevenfold usefulness as (1) an experimentalist, (2) a teacher, (3) a critic, (4) a theorist, (5) an administrator and statesman, (6) a popular expositor, and (7) an editor. Needless to say, this ovation wiped out much of the loneliness of the Philadelphia boy who had no playmates. The huge audience rose when I went to the platform and again when I left it, just as they used to do in my fantasies sixty-eight years ago when I was six.

Thus I come right up to the present instant. I keep wondering what will come next and whether my seventies will still remain the best decade.

Perspective

Is there anything clear and simple that can be said to give unity to such a hodgepodge of a life? It is a hodgepodge. Even if one were to list one example of each of the seven kinds of achievement for which I was given the Gold Medal, it would still require a feat of analysis to reveal what is invariant in all of them. Of course the chief invariant is the single personality. It remains the same old I that does all these things, and the I has continuity, for the marks of its insecure childhood still show. Attitudes show a continuous development. And Psychology, that social institution that is known for a science, encompasses them all, a life-long devotion to an arbitrary division of knowledge that did not have to be bedded down between biological science and social science, yet is. Is this enough? A man is not a congeries of phenomena that needs to be telescoped into a theory. We could let the matter rest there.

There are, however, three things that occur to me in connection with this kaleidoscopic life, three out of many, and I should like to set them down here because my story seems to need a summary.

It is clear that every scientific career must rest upon a personality whose attributes affect or even determine the important choices. The little boy with no playmates in the Philadelphia home wanted love and power and often got neither, or else found that the one precluded the other. No wonder he grew into an adult who disliked controversy and anger, who urged tolerance and the understanding that precludes blame. His insecurity, both real and felt, threw him into a restless, compulsive search for what he called *maturity,* a capacity to accept reality without loss of avidity. The psychoanalysis did not seem to help the deficiency much. At most it acted so slowly that it could not be distinguished from the maturation that grows out of varied experience and advances one toward the goal of *tout comprendre, c'est tout pardonner.* Eventually that goal seems to have been nearly achieved—in my sixties and early seventies. How? I do not know. There was some material success. Living shows that many causes of human contention are impermanent and trivial. Some of the diminution of ambition and the need for power may indeed have a physiological base. I count this personal phase of my life a success because I ceased to be tormented by unsuccess, and also because there is some evidence for a consensus that I have in some degree been successful. (Never mind, kid, if you are a sissy. Drive ahead into life, scared as you are. It can come out all right and sometime you may feel that you got to wherever you wanted. A mere fifty years may do it.)

Then there is the fact of the hodgepodge itself. Titchener once said to me: "Choose a field in which you can be the most expert person alive." Just then I chose psychology's history and, although I never reached the prescribed goal, I came near enough to be among the top few, at least in America. The historian would not have applied the name *history* to this business of finding where the present came from; this success was only within psychology. As I look through my other "successes" I think I see that they were planned to be successful, that I undertook new ventures because I believed that I could succeed in each with sufficient pains. I trusted myself to take the pains. Easy success and clear failure had to be avoided; the target lies between. Thus the hodgepodge comes out of this need for success, for a well-managed success could often generate both love and power.

Finally, there is the attitudinal invariant that is founded on this personality and runs through most of my scientific and historical work. It is the love of tolerance and the paradoxical intolerance of intolerance. This attitudinal constant moved along from youth into adulthood. It emerged to scientific view in my attack in 1928 on the blinding egoism of scientific controversy. I have stuck with this faith all along. *Tout comprendre, c'est tout pardonner.* "Enthusiasm is the friend of action and the enemy of wisdom." Presently, however, I came to see that enthusiasm is necessary to drive research forward even when it blinds the researcher to truth. Egoism must have its due. It is motive power. And criticism is the fly-wheel. Let the pendulum of cult and theory swing as wide as it will; posterity is the safe assessor. It will see more clearly the distinction between today's fact and foible, and posterity's posterity will do still better. To be keenly aware of this motivational predicament is useful in science for it provides the critics who keep wasted motion minimal. Yet not everyone in healthy science can do without egoism and prejudice. Science needs temporary blindness in order to get ahead. I took my stand with posterity whose tolerance is assured, but I also learned to be somewhat tolerant of the motivating power of intolerance. *Tout comprendre* . . . Here then is basic attitudinal invariance based on the pattern of a man's personality, influencing his thought and action throughout his life.

No wonder then that I think that current psychology requires for its understanding a knowledge of its genesis in the minds of the men who went before, and that this genesis cannot be divorced from the personalities and attitudes of those who contributed to it. Current thought is best assessed if one knows the psychodynamics of its history.

Selected Letters

Letters

A great part of my need for social stimulus has been met through the mails, often in a correspondence with interesting acquaintances whom I have never seen. My files for 1919–1960 contain about forty thousand letters by me and an equal number to me, most of them quite unimportant, for I have been too lazy to cull them. (My daughter started to sift them in her spare time, but *A* took her all winter, and she never got to *B*, for she found she wanted to read the letters she retained.)

I thought it impossible to search these files for interesting samples, but my indomitable editor was resolved not to leave this potential mine of personality untouched. She turned prospector and produced nine nuggets, which seemed to me astonishingly well suited for their purpose. What else remains in the mine we do not know.

Gestalt Psychology and Positivism

1936

To Kurt Koffka at Smith College
Koffa's crucial *Principles of Gestalt Psychology* (1935) had been reviewed by me at length in the *Psychological Bulletin* (January 1936, vol. 33, pp. 59–69). According to Koffka, the book was intended to be a definitive text of Gestalt psychology, perhaps the only one. I was at that time an enthusiast for the modern positivist position in psychology—which we tended to call *operationism*—the view that all scientific concepts are defined in terms of the operations by which they are observed. Since the operations of observation are physical, this view tends to destroy the

dualism of mind and matter and to reduce everything to physical processes. Koffka was holding to the reality of direct or immediate experience, and I was complaining about the lack of rigor of the resulting immediately intuitive mental processes. E. C. Tolman was also in correspondence with Koffka on this general issue.

Dear Koffka:

I am very grateful to you for your discussion of your relation to operationism, and I shall not attempt to extend this correspondence into a complete reply, but just make a comment or two that may serve for the time being.

As our discussion develops, it becomes clearer to me that the antithesis is more between immediate experience and mediate constructs than anything else, although it is by way of operational procedures that some of the terms get themselves changed.

I really have no quarrel with reification; we obviously must work in terms of things. But I cannot convince myself that scientific things are ever immediately given. Perhaps the question here really arises between Tolman and me, as to whether the implications of observation are for a discrete class of things (Tolman) or for neural things (E.G.B.).

All this is to say that I am fully aware of the problem of regress if operations be substituted for the things that they reveal. In fact, I tried to explain in a paragraph of my review of you that operationism was used to compel agreement and pursued along the regress only until agreement had been achieved.

As to the main issue and my challenge that you could not write your psychology for a congenitally blind man, there you seem to me to avoid the issue by the trick of appealing to the similarity between touch and vision. My thesis here was that the intellectual appreciation of the world is not immediately sensory. Perhaps I was thinking of [Douglas] McGregor in our Laboratory who got working on color sensitivity because he is color-blind, and who seems to me to know more about color vision than most normal-eyed psychologists. However, what I really have in mind are things like the fourth dimension and Riemannn space. My thesis was that hyper-spaces and special spaces are just as intelligible and understandable to the geometricians as simple Euclidian space—I should have said as scientifically intelligible if I had been sure whether to call geometry a science. Now then, it seems to me that the real scientific world is just as real as some hyper-space and just as understandable—and also no more so. This is what a world of constructs is like, and it is a safe, secure world, where definition is rigid and the vagaries of immediate intuition do not apply.

I am still taking things quietly, but I do want to go to Worcester and I am planning to do so. If the thing proves too strenuous, I can go to bed early Thursday night while the rest of you argue. So I shall hope to see you there.

April 1, 1936

Sincerely,
Boring

Psychic Energy and the Psychoanalysts

1937

To Hanns Sachs in Boston

Hanns Sachs, Freud's close associate, Director of the Psychoanalytical Institute in Berlin before Hitler's day, had analyzed me (more or less; see pp. 53-55) in Boston and two years later loaned me the monograph on energy and drive by S. Bernfeld and S. Feitelberg. He remarked that Bernfeld was familiar with experimental psychology and that he (Sachs) wanted to see what I, an experimentalist, would think of the discussion. Sachs was hoping, I doubt not, to enhance in my thinking the scientific status of psychoanalysis by this analogy of motivational intensity to physical energy, of psychic force to physical force. I remained unimpressed but sought to be tactful and to instruct my quondam analyst as to what the rigorous experimentalist thinks about this kind of intellection.

Dear Dr. Sachs:

I promised you a report on the Bernfeld-Feitelberg *Energie und Trieb,* and it is easier for me to write it and send it to you now than it would be for me to try to revive present impressions next fall. Your mail is probably forwarded to you somewhere, but it does not matter whether you read this now or next fall, and I shall not expect a reply until we meet.

A judgment of this sort is a very much more difficult matter than I had supposed it would be, for the reason that it raises questions of fundamental scientific values. I see now that the problem of the value of the B-F contribution is a phase of this much more general topic of discussion that you and I have up, the thing that arose out of [Harvey C.] Lehman's article and the problem of the statistical vs. the insightful method of studying the dependence of productivity upon age.

I want to suggest to you a fundamental dichotomy in approaching these matters.

1. There is the intuitional or insightful method of seeing and understanding scientific facts and relationships. This is the method that is typified by Goethe's outlook upon the world, especially in his excursions into science. It is therefore the tradition of the phenomenological approach to scientific problems, and in fact I think Goethe belongs in that tradition. The line of development is through visual sensation and perception: Goethe—Purkinje—Johannes Müller—Hering—Wertheimer and the Gestaltists. Maybe people like Husserl and Stumpf belong in the line somewhere. In general, it is the tradition of German psychology, although there are, of course, plenty of specific exceptions to this generalization. It is fundamentally the method of philosopher-psychologists. I think the psychoanalysts belong in this tradition too, and thus I am ready to find you on this horn [of the dilemma] and myself on the other. I rely on your knowledge of Goethe to make the thing clear to you, his impatience of Newton's experimentalism when experiment went directly against the obvious in observation. It is the method of the expert

who brings his wisdom and personality into a situation in order that his reaction to it may solve the problem. This kind of expert does not know how he works; there can be no book of rules, and he cannot easily transmit his skill to others except by long personal association with them. Those who hold with this view magnify the importance of the human mind in scientific work. They speak of observation as if it were a special skill acquired in high degree only by a few with special aptitude. Goethe's being able to see the sheep's skull on the beach at the Lido as two extra vertebrae is an example of the insightful nature of such intelligent observation.

2. Opposed to the intuitional method is the experimental method. This is the attitude which mistrusts the human mind instead of magnifying its capacities. The experimentalist—I use the word very broadly—is conscious chiefly of the inadequacy of intuition, partly because it can seldom reveal most of the hidden truth, partly because it gives free rein to wish projection and thus prejudices the results. Of the Germans in psychology I think of Helmholtz as most representative, but I also think of Helmholtz as not so typically German as the other psychologists in Germany and Austria. (Mach too seems to me less German than the others.) Newton, partly because he contrasts with Goethe, is an example of the attitude par excellence, and I am wondering whether experimentalism may not be more at home in England and America. Of course, I can only come to such a conclusion by the intuitional method, so I do not trust my own judgment. If we were to make a decision of this sort, it ought to be by some such procedure as [Harvey C.] Lehman used to get at age and productivity. The genius of the experimentalist's attitude is that in making an observation he does not want to know what bearing it will have upon his conclusion. The observations must be prior to an experimental massing of many of them or to statistical treatment. If it is obvious what bearing the observation will have upon conclusions, then he has the observations made by someone else who does not know what the problem is. I once disturbed Pro-

fessor Whitehead by saying that the psychologist was much more modest than the philosopher in his study of the mind, because he knew enough about the mind to mistrust it as an instrument of observation, and perhaps I even went further and said that no one ought to trust his conclusions unless he mistrusted the objectivity of the human mind.

I think you can see what I am driving at. You and Freud and Goethe and philosophers and most medical men belong on the intuitional side of this dichotomy. Newton and Helmholtz and most American psychologists and I belong on the experimental side. Harry Murray is trying to get on the experimental side, but thus far most of the constructive work of his Clinic has actually been on the intuitional side. Operationalism is clearly a tool of the experimentalist, but my colleague, Gordon Allport, is enough of an intuitionist to oppose it. The Gestalt psychologists are all intuitionists, and I think that is one of the reasons why they are having difficulty in adapting to the psychological situation as it is constituted in America.

Now what about B-F [Bernfeld-Feitelberg]? This monograph seems to me to represent excellently the intuitional tradition. I do not like it very much, but then I am definitely on the other side. If you ask me as an intelligent person to predict the future of the two sides, I have no answer, for I see advantages and defects in both.

Take the main points of the monograph. The relation between Chatelier's principle and the conservation of drive: a very interesting analogy, a very illuminating picture of how drive works, provided you really know how drive works so that you can tell about it, and provided your audience really knows about physics. It does not tell anything more; the analogy between A and B does not increase the probability of A's being true just because B is true, because you have to know first that A is true to know whether the analogy is valid or just a happy literary form. So it is with the Weber-Fechner law that this section makes me a little angry. The section is an illuminating discussion, but of course the

Weber-Fechner law is not true in the sense that it can be expressed by a mathematical formula. It was German intuitionism from Fechner almost to the present that preserved this formula in the face of other German observation that could have shown that the formula is essentially not true. The curve has a different shape from what the formula would give, although fact and formula coincide throughout one region of the stimulus. But why should B-F then talk about the Weber-Fechner law as if it were clearly established? Because they come to it from the outside, like every layman, see in it an analogy for their purpose, and thus create the illusion of dealing with the matter scientifically by writing mathematical formulae, when there are no data in existence that will really justify the use of the formula. They have plenty of distinguished company, but yet I feel that the really distinguished thing would have been to transcend the trite formula which has been accepted uncritically for so many years.

So you see it is also with the death instinct and the law of entropy. A very clever analogy indeed, and, if it is right, then a knowledge of either illuminates the other; but there lies not here, nor anywhere else, valid definition of what psychic energy might be.

The study of the temperature difference between the brain and the body is very interesting for its own sake, but it does not seem to me to bear particularly on the general thesis of this monograph. To say merely that the brain is able, under certain circumstances, to maintain a temperature differential, is not really to give a suggestion as to how psychic energy can exist or operate. It is not that differential that makes the muscles move or that is resolved when the goal is reached, so that the muscles stop moving. Of course the organism has got energy, the energy of the food it eats and the oxygen that it breathes, and it is this energy eventually that accounts for nervous induction and muscular contraction and the work that is done, but no conception of the organism that does not take into account the fact that it works essentially as a release mechanism is going to work out—so I think. All these things about psychic energy have to do with the persistence of the organism in redirecting itself in the face of frustration toward the original goal and the obliteration of this persistence when the goal is achieved. That does not seem to me to be literally an energetic problem. It is the problem of the train dispatcher controlling the course of the trains in a railroad system, where most of the actual energy comes from the coal in the locomotives' tenders.

But when I have said all this, I come back to my original difficulty. I am criticizing Dr. Bernfeld and his colleague less than I am criticizing the intuitional method of work, and in that criticism I am saying little more than that I mistrust the intuitional method because it does not mistrust the prejudice and bias of the observer.

June 28, 1937

Sincerely yours,
Edwin G. Boring

British and German Contributions to Psychology

1947

To Sir Frederic Bartlett in Cambridge, England

F. C. Bartlett, not yet Sir Frederic, visited America in 1947 and later wrote to me from England about the relationship of American to British psychology, thus eliciting from me this frank appraisal of what I thought was the proper perspective on British, German, and American psychology. These views, which seem to me to have strong and broad support, were essentially also the views of E. B. Titchener, all his life a loyal British subject in all respects except British psychology. During the First World War Titchener remarked of England and Germany, "I could wish the psychology of the Allies was as good as the psychology of the enemy." These were, therefore, very old opinions of mine, first given me by Titchener. Sir Frederic now not only gives me his benison in the reprinting of this letter, but also reminds me of how much experimental psychology has advanced in England since 1947. He is, of course, right.

Dear Bartlett:

Here is your delightful letter of 12 August and the reprint of the Oliver-Sharpey Lectures. Both are interesting. We did indeed enjoy seeing you in America and everyone seems to remember your visit with pleasure—not only here at Harvard, but elsewhere when the matter is mentioned. It was a pleasant thing to have had happen, and also a good thing.

You speak now of relations between Britain and America in psychology, and that moves me to write you somewhat at length on the matter, even though the secretarial help is missing and I am going to have to ask you to put up with my inevitably bad typing.

I presume to think that you and I may speak frankly to each other on so important a mattter. I have the impression that you are not quite realistic about it, but then at once I hasten to say that you may think my comment, when it has been explicated, is a sign of my egoism. Let us leave, then, such personal problems aside, and let me tell you directly how I see the relationship as an American and its background from our side.

America began its psychological career with that mixture of boasting and basic inferiority that is characteristic of all insecure ambitious people—and nations. We knew—James knew in the 1870's, the rest later—that there was this new movement in Germany, and to Germany America turned.

It is my belief that from 1890 to 1920 most Americans would have said that the only important country to contribute to the new psychology was Germany, with America coming along second. Certainly I thought that and reflected it in my *History of Experimental Psychology* (in which some have thought the insertion of the word *Experimental* was an error, though it gave me excuse for offending Spearman by leaving him out). My body has never been in Germany, but I find now that often I know more about the history of German experimental psychology than do Germans as they write to me. If 1920 is too late a date to set for America's recognition of Germany's preeminence, then make it 1910. The important American Ph.D.'s in the 1890's were German, but not so much so later. My point is merely that Americans can recognize superiority elsewhere, for all their tendency to boast, which I hope may be less now than it used to be.

In this same period Britain was almost nowhere. Bain, Ward, Stout were not in the right tradition. Spearman did not win respect. Myers did, but he was isolated. England did not get laboratories and chairs. Oxford's psychology was a joke—to the American experimentalists. There were some [British] books that we used over here. Parsons on *Colour Vision* might easily have been the most used, though not Parsons on *Perception*. We thought Parsons a bit insular, citing British sources when the basic things were German and occasionally American. But we used him. Still there was not much. England was the backward country. France [was] the one that had advanced in abnormal psychology but not in scientific psychology. Italy was twenty years behind the times. The little countries were good, but only in proportion to size. Up to Hitler our graduate students felt that they had not quite managed to get educated if they had not been to Germany. They never thought that about England.

But this situation kept gradually changing. America became steadily more independent and self-assured, and Germany less important. You can see the change—I mean I can, an American can if he is old enough or knows enough—from 1890 to 1900, to 1910, to the War, to 1930, to Hitler, to the next War. The First World War gave American psychology a tremendous boost. We tend to forget that it was relative to what it worked on when we think about the even greater boost that American psychology got from the Second World War.

There is no doubt in my mind that American psychology had passed adolescence in the 1920's, was feeling quite independent of and superior to the German psychology of 1930–1934, was not let down at all when Hitler let Germany down.

In the 1890's and for some time thereafter the relationship was asymmetrical. We turned to Germany. Germany did not turn to us. The Germans liked to have American students in their laboratories, but they never found support for them. The Americans exported themselves; the Germans did not import them.

Great Britain, however, has never counted very strongly. We felt simply that the British were backward. There was at least the Cambridge Lab, but that was only one. A few Americans got contact with it and came back with an alumnus loyalty to it. Occasionally one found in America some soul loyal to London, like R. B. Cattell, but rarely. There seemed to be nothing more to scientific psychology than Cambridge and what one found in the *British Journal*. It was all right, but it was utterly out of proportion to the stature of the nation. So I think the Americans did not take Great Britain very seriously in psychology. A particular research got the same attention wherever it was done and published, but institutionally Britain seemed weak.

Well, now you see a little of what is going on in America after the Second World War. Last June the American Psychological Association had 5090 members. [By 1960 it was 18,215.] I do not know how these are to be broken down, but, even admitting the large number of semi-incompetents, we have a huge institution on our hands. You know the list of journals. American psychology is confused with its problems. It wonders how it is going to get unity out of its chaos. But it does not feel dependent. It may want to know about the psychology of Cambridge, England, but it also wonders how to find out about the psychology of Berkeley, California, and Cambridge, Massachusetts, and all the other places. The meeting of the American Psychological Association in Detroit 9–13 September will be a bedlam. My hurried count just now shows 48 sessions of about 4 papers each, 23 symposia, and innumerable lectures and business meetings. And so on. Since I think size works against quality, I can not boast about this; but I think you can see how America might be so wholly occupied with self-integration as to be unlikely to pay much attention to Great Britain and Europe.

And that is all I meant to say. Great Britain in the next years is likely to be much more aware of America than America of Great Britain, and that is all right. We had that relation for decades to Germany. Ideally you ought to send your people over here and you ought to come over yourselves. Just now we are so overwhelmed with students and problems it is hard to be hospitable, but that will not always be true. At present, with dollars and pounds the way they are, [migration west] is impossible, but it may not always be. The principle is there, and I think that the laws of the distribution of attention declare that the closeness of this international relation depends more on you than on us.

It would be pleasant to see you in Edinburgh, but I shall not be there. There is, as I told you, the problem of expense, but also there are too many more important other things to do. It was, let me repeat, magnificent to have you here this winter, and I hope you will come again, and that your colleagues may also come over.

August 28, 1947

Sincerely yours,
Edwin G. Boring

Who Designs the Designer?

1948

To B. F. Skinner at Monhegan Island

Skinner gave the William James Lectures at Harvard in the fall of 1947, published *Walden Two* in 1948, giving me a copy inscribed "Garry Boring: Toward a better world?" and was appointed Professor of Psychology at Harvard beginning in 1948. *Walden Two* described an imaginary Utopia in which the lives of the members of the community were designed and shaped under the mechanics of operant conditioning so that motivational conflict and therefore unhappiness were abolished. Here and elsewhere, as in his *Science and Human Behavior* (1953), Skinner argued for determinism and against freedom in respect of human action, and I kept objecting to the atmosphere of missionary zeal that permeated his argument, because the zeal always sounded as if it were intended to promote action whereas it ought to have been presented as the inevitable consequence of past events. Frazier, the entrepreneur in *Walden Two*, and Skinner in *Science and Human Behavior* both talked as if they themselves were free. Once I rewrote a paragraph of the latter book in deterministic language just to show how dull it became if you gave up the concept of freedom.

Dear Fred:

Lucia and I have finished *Walden Two*, I reading aloud to her. We got a great deal of fun and discussion out of it and I want to say that I think you have done a remarkably good job. I wish I were reviewing it for someone now, but, of course, that would not do.

It takes a while to decide what the intent of the book is. I was misled by Mike's [R. M. Elliott's] having said it was a novel. When I found out it was a conversation between Socrates, Glaucon, and the other stooge, I understood much better what was going on.

Of course, what I kept thinking was: These people acted rationally, and people do not act rationally or we should not have war or most of our social phenomena. Frazier's answer to that would seem to be: Only the free act rationally, *i.e.*, Frazier and maybe some of the Planners. The rest of the community is behaviorally engineered and not free, which is O.K. since freedom is a delusion anyhow; a synonym for Frazier's being abnormal is being rational. Even there your deftness eventually covers up an objection, for Frazier is acting God and not free of ambition and the power need.

That leads to my chief criticism of the job. With the best effort in the world, I can not make real to myself the motivational life of any of the community members. What is it like to live without a sense of social competition? Could you do as good a job for

members of this community as Margaret Mead did for uncom-
petitive islanders (was it the Arapesh?), as Ruth Benedict did for
the Japanese in *The Chrysanthemum and the Sword?* What about
ambition? When, where, and how is it a driving force in *Walden
Two?* A vivid picture of what happens to the psychology of sex
when pride, vanity, competition, possessiveness, acquisitiveness,
and economic security are out of the picture would be a valuable
lesson to humanity. But I could not write the chapter. Could you?
You make Frazier, Burris, and Castle [all Planners in *Walden
II*] real as conscious beings, but the community people are not,
and Steve and Mary seem to me to go blank, once they have
made their decision [to join the engineered community]. Having
joined up, they drop out of the book, when what you want to
know is what it would be like to have made that decision. It's
the difference between John Galsworthy and James Fenimore
Cooper. The community people are as much pawns as another
Redskin biting the dust. Frazier, Burris, and Castle are done in
an approach to the Galsworthy manner, the inner stream of
thought.

I do not suppose you could do that sort of thing, but, until it is
done, this book seems to be an exegesis of behaviorial facts and
relationships, not a practical move toward "a better world." It's
hard for me to tell whether you share this view or not. But that
is not to belittle the job; simply to pick out a bigger one. What
I am trying to say is that the basic freedom-determinism antinomy
is involved even in talking about these things. Most people face
this issue where reason is found not to compel action by saying:
It ought to be done! What do they mean by *ought?* It is one of
the most used concepts in the discussion of social relations; yet I
doubt if it can be given clear meaning except as warning that
there is an antinomy just around the corner.

Our summer goes fairly well. I am still prevented from many
of the normal activities by a bad foot, but we get around by car
and boat. Tuesday we went down the bay with an outboard
motor and landed at three islands we'd never been on before.

One is the second largest cormorant rookery on the Atlantic sea-board, and it was full of large but helpless fledglings. The home life of the young cormorant would shock any child psychologist. . . . See you anon. We shall not go back until the 18th or perhaps the 25th. Our best to Eve.

July 24, 1948

> Yours,
> Garry

Effort without Means

1947

To Lewis M. Terman at Stanford University

My correspondence with Lewis Terman was long and voluminous. Terman was no mere mental tester, as some ignorant people thought, but a liberal who read widely and thought deeply. On the occasion of this letter he was soliciting my participation in the support of peace, and I was saying how many valuable things I had to do that promised greater success and that I thought wise men ought not to let the intensity of a need affect their judgments of what to do about the need. In later years I would have said, "Enthusiasm is the friend of action and the enemy of wisdom," but I had not invented that aphorism in 1947.

Dear Lewis:

Yours of August 8 waited around here until I got back from Maine and did something about piled-up obligations.

Now I shall tell you my general frame of mind about the international situation. The great pressure for people to do something is a pressure that arises from the need for doing something, not from any rational judgment that there is something which can be done. People are stirred up and they have to do something about their emotions. One thing to do is to blame other people. The physicists have been blaming the social scientists for not being able to control opinions the way the physicists can control atoms. Beyond that you form an organization and try to put

your power back of it. That seems to me about as foolish as undertaking a problem in science without a method. It is true that
those things are undertaken. Cancer research is an instance. It
is thought that if enough money and brains are poured into
cancer research something must come out of it, and I am certainly not against it, but merely pointing out that it is a very
inefficient kind of research because it is determined by need instead of by there being a feasible method. Well, the scientists
who were in the war say that need there produced a great many
things including the atomic bomb. Yes, but the whole development of subatomic physics since the 1890's prepared for it, and
there is nothing comparable in social science to make us think
that we shall get ahead to controlling human action in the next
fifty or one hundred years.

In the first place it is clear that man is not rationally controlled.
By that I mean that he is not well integrated. He will hold certain premises and still not find that he has to be consistent with
them. If someone points out clearly that he is not consistent with
them, he meets the situation with a rationalization. The difference between reason and rationalization is that rationalizations
are special pleadings gotten up to make your emotional determination seem rational. So let's not have too much energy spent
on reasonable analyses of situations in order to get peace. It
does not work. Everybody knows that war is undesirable, but
that has no effect at all in putting war off.

If the scientists think that they are exceptions to this rule, then
let them think so, but they are not. The irrationality of scientists
in their scientific work and in their personal controversies has
been a theme with which I have dealt for a long time—in my
presidential address of 1928—in the last chapter of my *Sensation
and Perception* (1942). I should not want to find myself working
in a matter of this sort with a man who believes that he himself
is motivated by conclusions drawn from basic premises. This
belief puts me off of almost any cooperation with other scientists
that is basically psychological because they do not understand

the factors of human motivation. It also puts me off of working with such psychologists as the members of the SPSSI [Society for the Psychological Study of Social Issues], since they are more in the hands of their emotions and needs than in the employ of clearly formulated ideals and techniques.

It seems to me that one can apply individual psychology very roughly to nations. The Russians seem to me to be in an adolescent stage. I have one daughter just passing out of it, another getting into it, both of them very somatotonic persons. It is an intolerant, egoistic stage. The concepts of nationalism and sovereignty are strong. The adolescent wants freedom. Freedom is a negative concept, really a rather crazy thing to want, because it does not say what it is that you want, merely what it is that you do not want (control). But the Russians are acting like a strongly activated egoistic half-baked adolescent. They don't want war, but they'll fight rather than take the long-range view of cooperation and compromise. There is not a thing that can be done with that except to keep to the primitive conditions. In the States and Great Britain we have a much more mature psychology. Our police power works pretty well. We know that fighting is a disadvantage in the long run and we don't want it— not now, although Britain has only recently come to that view. They are nowhere near it in South America.

So the thing to do is to wait until Russia has grown up and gotten mature, even though a big hunk of civilization gets sacrificed on the way. There seems to be no alternative. And when that happens, then we have the same problem over and over again. The Yellow Peril will come true some day, and the Chinese will be just as adolescent then as the Russians are now. That's the only safe guess. So with Russia incorporated into the family of western nations, there will then be the West-vs.-the-East fight. The process of civilizing the globe is a very, very slow one and a very long way off.

I said that the scientists themselves did not seem to realize the silliness of egoism in important matters. Neither do our representatives in government. The very thing that we are fussing about with the Russians is what all the lesser statesmen in Washington are doing, representing local interests and failing to compromise on the larger issues.

I am not so pessimistic as I sound. It seems to me that history has a way of working itself out. It is hard to think of oneself as that part of the present which may get obliterated under nature's wasteful method, but that is just a form of egoism. If every salmon egg insisted on being a fish, we would have too many salmon. Civilization stays because it is useful and has a functional value. The Russians and the Asiatics are not going to upset that, but that does not mean that it is written in nature that Rome should not fall, or Great Britain, or the United States.

You can show this letter to Dr. Blackwelder although I do not think he will be interested in it. He will probably think that I am immoral and irresponsible, whereas I think that I am more mature than the person who interprets history in a narrow egoistic manner. Allport has just hopped on me in the last *Psychological Review*, because I do not support morality enough. My feeling is that his support of morality—he would not approve of this letter at all—is soft and not clearly thought out. You ought to be clear and tough first and moral afterward.

August 15, 1947

Yours,
Garry

Determinism in the History of Originality

1952

To Lewis M. Terman

This letter, from my rewarding correspondence with Terman, is about the naturalistic interpretation of the history of thought and discovery, the debunking of genius and originality, the insistence that the scientist must regard the belief in freedom of choice as a delusion. If this letter seems inconsistent with my

1948 letter to Skinner about his *Walden Two,* it is not that I resist his contention that the belief in freedom is a delusion, but that I feel that Skinner impresses his reader as not being a good robot. It takes very careful writing to prevent a zealous robot, eager with a mission, from seeming self-contradictory.

Dear Lewis:

Your letters always provoke me into reply because they have so many interesting things in them.

Now this question of a naturalistic explanation of the progress of thought. I think of it as very much the same through the centuries in any socially integrated culture and through the weeks or hours in the mind of a single person who will have turned up with something original in thought at the end of the process. You can take the naturalistic point of view toward it all, even if you can not fill in all the cause-effect items. Thought in society or in a person is very much like a rat in the maze trying to find a goal, not always clear at the start as to what goal there is or that there is any solution to the problem of hunger. You try this, you try that; you try a blind alley, perhaps repeatedly before you abandon it; you learn the long way around and then discover the short way there; presently you are substituting "vicarious trial and error" (Tolman) for straight trial and error; your first success does not mean perfection but the beginning of learning. Insight helps tremendously in getting there, be it the insight of the chimpanzee without frontal lobes or the insight of Isaac Newton.

Imagine an explorer trying to make his way west across the United States from ocean to ocean before there were roads or maps. He has lost his compass but he does have the sun to guide him. The general effort is to go westward, but he knows full well that he must sometimes turn eastward in order to get around some obstruction so as to get on westward. It is a matter of trials and errors and corrections, and, if the goal is the Pacific, he is never sure of a success until he gets there, because he might have landed himself off in a great huge 1000-mile blind alley where he would eventually be blocked. That seems to me the way progress in history goes, as well as on the part of the individual.

Now suppose you have had an exact record of the course of this explorer, and it's 200 years later when all the country was mapped and the topographic sections even were drawn up. Then you would know the best route and you would see his routes as he explored. There are portions of the route that would seem unimportant because, having started along one valley, the only thing to do is to go to the end or to the place where there was a pass on one side or the other. You would find choice points in the record. You would say this decision was vital; here he made the right choice. You could regard all his subsequent progress as dependent on that choice. And you would also see where he made the wrong choice, either because he had to retrace his steps, or because it took him on an elaborate roundabout way. Thus you would say that one of the more important crucial right choices, since the other alternative would have been very bad for progress, was a great step forward, like a lemming's choice which seems to us to determine everything afterward.

My point here is that Lashley's principles of cerebral physiology apply to the progress of history. There is equal potentiality for the course of progress, and there is also mass action. If progress got ahead by one route; then it does not have to get ahead by another route; if it is blocked in that one route because some man who could have taken the right choice made the wrong choice, then there are still the other routes. That is the *Zeitgeist* naturalistic theory of history, which I am busy promoting. Mass action comes into history because the larger the possible number of routes, the greater the chance of rapid progress.

Now all this means that some of the choices in getting across the Continent or getting along through history or doing some good thinking in your study, as viewed a posteriori, were crucial, and that is simply to say that they were sufficient causes but not necessary ones. There could have been other routes to the goal, but some sufficient cause was necessary, although not necessarily this particular one. The important thing is to realize that sufficient causes, viewed a posteriori, look like necessary causes because history does not repeat itself and these things only happen once. (I avoid going into the question as to how you establish dynamical relations in history where you cannot experiment, where you do not have controls. You see the problem about history.)

The other important point concerns the antecedent of a crucial, sufficient (though possibly unnecessary) choice. If you know the antecedents, then you simply extend the naturalistic theory backwards. If you do not know them, then you reify your ignorance into some concept for ignorance, like free will or genius. I am holding that unpredictable genius is always evidence of scientific ignorance.

It seems to me that this is the naturalistic view that scientists must take and that freedom is out of place in science. The philosophers tell us that freedom is just as good a concept for interpreting reality as is determinism, and I have there simply to admit my inability to transcend my own scientific prejudices. My whole temperament makes me feel that they are probably right, that most wise people are caught in certain presuppositions which curtain them off effectively from some more nearly absolute level of understanding of the truth, but I can not argue this because I do not know enough. For myself I am content to believe that naturalism holds in the world and is capable of a complete explanation of it, and that the complete explanation includes the explanation as to why scientists and others often want to believe in freedom. I do not mind freedom as a concept in value at all, if you believe that it is a useful delusion that ought to be cultivated and that cannot be escaped. The only argument that delusions are undesirable and ought not to be cultivated is, it seems to me, an esthetic one. Certainly delusion often helps survival. (I could write a long dissertation on that sentence.)
April 21, 1952

Yours,
Garry

The Rigorous Use of Words

1934

To Robert M. Yerkes at Yale University

My correspondence with Yerkes was as large as my correspondence with Terman, and the two wrote constantly to each other, but each pair of us talked about different things. I dealt more with ideas in talking to Terman, whereas Yerkes wrote to me about practical matters, administrative affairs, and the activities of the entrepreneur. This letter concerns the use of words. Yerkes wanted them to have exact meanings, whereas I was more sympathetic with Humpty Dumpty, who said of authors and their words, "The question is, which is to be master—that's all." I felt that the scholar with the English language at his command—and it is at his command if he is a scholar—can, writing somewhat dangerously, express more delicate meanings than the rigors of mathematics or logic would ever allow. Yerkes, though neither mathematician nor logician, nevertheless felt safer with verbal rigor.

Dear Robert:

Of course, as you say, we cannot discuss these fundamental issues by correspondence, and we do not meet easily. However, you have done me such a big compliment by taking my little book [*The Physical Dimensions of Consciousness,* 1933] so seriously, that I wish at least to make some comment on these issues and perhaps relieve your mind in some quarters, even though I add to its worry in others.

Do you know, I can't get interested in the use of words. Or perhaps I should say that I am tremendously interested in ideas and realize that they have to be expressed by words, but that I do not particularly care what the words are if the meaning can be got. Thus in that little book I did what I could to get *dimension* accepted, but that was because I thought there was a special idea in it. (I conclude now that there were two ideas in it:

Titchener's and mine, which seem to be different as I go over part of my large scientific correspondence with him—212 letters.) If anybody has another word now, all right, especially since I am being bothered by a still later discovery that the physicist has a third use of the word. So it is with *consciousness*, a very nice useless word for an equivocal concept, which can be now—so I would stake a good deal—absorbed into a physical system with or without change of name. (If consciousness is a Lucy Stoner, it would still keep its maiden name after marrying physics, but it might be old-fashioned and give it up.) And I cannot get very much excited about *psychobiology*, a very good idea which seems not to be misrepresented in the word at the present time. The same goes for the *self*; and so on. (Am I hurting sacred things?)

I think my thought is that words should be the coy maids of science, who sit back and hope they will be wanted, who put their best features forward, but whose fate is decided from outside historically when the dance is done by the statistical fact of how many asked them and how many left them alone. This may be an unpleasant thought, but I am content to leave it thus. A good idea and a good word for it will certainly be such if they get accepted and used, and what other people do about accepting them is something that I do not have to worry my head about.

I am beginning to think that I may have overdone Lashley a little in the PDC [*Physical Dimensions of Consciousness*], and your admonishment of me I take in the part of a good friend. The pendulum has to swing over before it comes back, and we have needed something to emphasize the lack of rigid constraint on the nervous system. It is a little embarrassing to have been sitting on the pendulum while it swung instead of waiting omnisciently at the golden mean for its return, but sincerity and a little intelligence are about all that one can hope for—certainly not infallibility.

I do not know quite what to say to you about the *self*. The PDC was admittedly a little book which attempted to apply a point of view to bare sensory phenomena. After [the principal chapters] I wrote a chapter on attention, learning, and intelligence simply to indicate the way in which I thought that point of view could be extended to more complex or "higher" problems. I think the systematic point of view from which all of the logical part of the PDC follows is Bridgman's operationism, and with that as a can-opener I am beginning to find meat in many of the old uninteresting tins upon psychology's shelves. All I can say of that is that it seems to me to work and to give decent interment to some futile problems and to bring others out into a useful life in the community.

It was awfully good of you to write so fully, and I hope this letter will in some inadequate way indicate the good will which you inspire in me.

November 8, 1934

Sincerely yours,

Garry

Titchener's Letters

1945

To Robert M. Yerkes

This letter covered ten different items, each of which had arisen from a question in a letter from Yerkes, but I quote here only the most interesting topic, the one about Titchener's correspondence. My comment to Yerkes here explains why no letters to Titchener are included among these samples: the assured Titchener did not invite correspondence about ideas with a satellite like me. The moon may noticeably affect the earth's tides but not its majestic course about the sun.

Dear Robert:

Titchener's letters! You know I had a treasured folder of 212 of Titchener's letters and felt that something important must be done about them. I let it go for years and years, partly because it was a question whether Weld as literary executor would do something, and then I sat down to them and went through them, went through them with a great sense of depression and disappointment. What seemed so great and important and marvelous at the time turned out to be small and petty and personal. So much of it was important because it was ego-involved, because it was advice to me, because it was critical of others in a context that included me among the elect, because it was politics of putting the Cornell point of view ahead of the enemy. And it picked up that basic need for dependence which I notice Franz Alexander says all peptic ulcer cases have. Finally I worked out of the whole batch of letters what little psychology there seemed to be left in them and published that. [*American Journal of Psychology*, 1937, vol. 50, 470–483; *Psychological Review:* 1938, vol. 44, 92–95.] I send you along a reprint in case I may not have sent you one when I published it. It was a very disappointing experience but also a maturing experience. It showed of what stuff hero worship is made.

· · · · · · · · · · · · · · · · · ·

September 10, 1945

Garry

The Nature of Freud's Research

1954

To Robert M. Yerkes
From another long letter to Yerkes I quote a brief comment about Ernest Jones and the nature of psychoanalytic discovery.

Dear Robert:

· · · · · · · · · · · · · · · ·

I have finished reading Ernest Jones' *Freud*, the biography of the immature part of his life up to 1900, and must now write the review for the *Psychological Bulletin*. Freud is not too mature or enthusiasm-producing a character in this 1880–1900 period, even when he is presented by such an admirer as Jones, but unfortunately the thing stops blank there, because this is only Volume I, with Jones' assertion that the early nervous, irritable, capricious, now conceited and now self-punitive Freud was very different from the calm, mature, wise man that "all of us knew." This handicaps me in my review. I am also interested in what in the world Jones means by "discovery," for he says he is describing Freud's discoveries. Well, they are somewhat like the discoveries of a naturalist, I suppose, observing animal behavior without experimental controls or any controls of either kind. He gets a hypothesis and a patient seems to fit into it and then another patient, and his own self-analysis puts him into the pattern, and presently he draws a generality in the way that all science gets generalities out of the induction of particular cases. But it is not convincing to me. It needs more rigorous control.

.   .   .   .

January 26, 1954

Garry

Selected Papers

The Moon Illusion
1943

Some of my experimental research, even though its volume is not large, ought to be represented in these pages, but research reports, especially the papers of thirty and fifty years ago, are too extended for inclusion. I regret that for this reason nothing of my "Cutaneous sensation after nerve-division" (1916) can be included, for this paper played an important role forty-five years ago. Instead I have turned to the experiments with A. H. Holway and D. W. Taylor on the moon illusion, but even here the original reports are too long and discursive. Instead I give my summary of the work as printed in 1943, a paper which is, I think, clear as to the findings, the method, and the remaining problems, but which tends, being a summary, to be somewhat more categorical than a report of research should be.

The fact that the horizon moon is much larger in perceived size than the moon in the heavens is so obvious that it must have been recognized by primitive man, even though there are still many persons, some of them with Ph.D.'s as well as many city dwellers without Ph.D.'s, who have never heard of this phenomenon. (On the history of the illusion, see Reimann, 1902.) The great Ptolemy described the phenomenon, noting correctly that it holds not only for the moon, but also for the sun as seen through fog and for the constellations. The phenomenon would thus seem to be celestial. Ptolemy suggested that the great perceived

Reprinted with permission from the *American Journal of Physics*, 1943, vol. 11, 55–60.

size of the horizon moon may be due to its comparison with terrestrial objects, and this is the most common explanation today.

Stated so simply the explanation makes no sense, however. Why should contrast make the moon seem large rather than small? The horizon moon subtends the same angle as an horizon object 230 ft. wide 5 mi. away, or as an object 46 ft. wide 1 mi. away. So the moon is, in this sense, "bigger" than a house, although smaller than a field or a hill. If it looks large by contrast, it must be because a smaller size is expected. Undoubtedly there is a contrast effect, one that makes the horizon moon seem large as compared with the memory of the more familiar moon in elevation, but this contrast is a consequence of the illusion, not its cause.

This common explanation does, however, insufficient justice to Ptolemy. He was not so naïve. When he spoke of the comparison of the horizon moon with terrestrial objects he was thinking, not of the objects at the horizon, but of the objects between the horizon and the observer. An extent of filled space is nearly always perceived as greater than the same extent of empty space. The horizon, Ptolemy thought, ought to look farther away than the zenith, and that might make the horizon moon look larger than the zenith moon (cf. Helmholtz, 1866, pp. 290–292, 360–362).

Ptolemy's theory, elaborated by many philosophers, is illustrated in Fig. 1, in a diagram similar to one drawn by Robert Smith (1738, pp. 49–70, esp. pp. 62–67). If the zenith is perceived as nearer the observer than is the horizon, then the arch of the heavens would appear to be ellipsoidal, as if extending along the curve *HzH* for an observer at *O*. Actually the moon more nearly describes an arc of a circle *HZH* and always (practically) subtends the same angle at *O*, as shown in Fig. 1. Thus the moon, actually at the zenith Z, appears to be at a nearer, false zenith *z*, and looks smaller than it would if perceived farther away. If a near object subtends the same angle as a far object, the near object must be smaller than the far—that is the argument. The

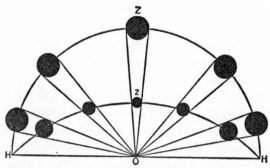

Fig. 1. Ptolemy's theory of the moon illusion: O = observer; H, H = horizon; Z = true zenith; z = perceived zenith. Adapted from Robert Smith (1738).

argument was plausible enough, because comparison with terrestrial objects between the observer and the horizon ought to make the distance to the horizon seem greater than the empty undifferentiated distance to the zenith.

Yet the argument is wrong for the simple reason that the moon in elevation looks farther away than the moon on the horizon—to all who have observed the moon much and thought about the matter. If asked why, they say, "The moon is so much smaller in elevation; of course, because it looks farther away"—thus inverting Ptolemy's logic.

If the moon appeared to be nearer at the zenith than at the horizon, then certainly it ought to seem smaller at the zenith. Perceived size is known to be thus dependent upon perceived distance. The brain habitually corrects the size of the retinal image for the distance of the object. A man 40 ft. away puts on the retina an image half as tall as a man 20 ft. away, but he looks just about the same size because his distance away is perceived and a correction is made in the perception (Boring, 1940; Holway and Boring, 1941). But in the case of the moon it is not the perceived distance that determines the perceived size. On the contrary, the perceived size would seem to determine the perceived distance.

There has been no end of discussion of the moon illusion. Both Gauss and Helmholtz proposed studying the phenomenon with mirrors, but never undertook the experiment. They would have had trouble. The horizon moon is apt not to look large when seen in a small imperfect mirror.

The amount of the change in perceived size of the moon was measured by Pozděna (1909). He equated the size of an artificial moon close at hand to the size of the real moon at different elevations, and he found the ratio of the perceived diameter of the elevated moon to the perceived diameter of the horizon moon to be about 1/2.5.

Schur (1925) showed that this phenomenon is not necessarily celestial. It appears for terrestrial artificial moons if the distances are but great enough. She found a ratio of the diameter of the zenith moon to the diameter of the horizon moon of 1/1.2, when the moons were 4 m. away, and of $\frac{1}{2}$ when the moons were 33 m. away. Since the change in this ratio was asymptotic to the ratio $\frac{1}{2}$, she concluded that the illusion would hold in maximum amount for distances beyond 33 m. She worked indoors and did not find it practicable to get an artificial zenith more than 33 m. above the floor. Her finding means that the illusion holds for the moon in elevation at those greater distances where the clues to the perception of the distance are not fully adequate. Since one can easily perceive 33 m. along the ground, this result also suggests that the illusion is really the smallness of the moon in elevation when seen through empty space, not in bigness on the horizon. That is about how the problem stood until recently.

IS THE PHENOMENON PHYSICAL?

The evidence is overwhelming that this phenomenon depends upon the physiological properties of the observer and not upon physical factors external to him—not upon refraction, nor upon atmospheric haze which might make the horizon look more distant than the zenith. Here are some of the reasons.

The difference in size does not appear in photographs. The camera is fairly faithful to the subtended angle. I have seen one photograph, made by the late W. R. Warner who constructed the Lick telescope. It shows the moon successively at different elevations on the same negative. The diameter of the image *increases* about 20 per cent as the moon rises, due undoubtedly in part to creeping on the plate, for the moon in elevation shines through less atmosphere and is brighter. This enlargement is too great for the 2 per cent increase that would be caused by the fact that the zenith moon is nearer to the observer by the radius of the earth.

If the large horizon moon is viewed through any physical instrument that is perceived by the observer as near to him, then the perceived moon loses its great size. That is why it usually looks small in a poor mirror where the glass or the frame is visible. The horizon moon looks small when viewed through a tube or when pinched between the thumb and forefinger. Bring your fingers tangent to the limbs of the horizon moon and it shrinks at once. Take your fingers away, and it snaps back to its inflated size.

When the moon is big on the horizon, lie down on your back with your head toward the moon, hanging the head over a log or stone or the edge of a table. The moon, huge but a moment before, is now quite small, small enough to make you exclaim. Or stoop over and view the horizon moon between your legs. Again it shrinks. So the perceived size of the moon must depend on the properties of the biological viewing mechanism and is thus truly an illusion.

CONDITIONS OF THE ILLUSION

Recently a series of experiments on the illusion has been in progress, experiments carried out from 1936 to 1941 by Dr. Holway, Mr. Taylor and myself (Holway and Boring, 1940a; 1940b; Taylor and Boring, 1942). We arranged to project an artificial moon on a white cloth screen, 3.5 m. away from the observer and placed always a little to one side of the real moon's azimuth. The observer controlled a series of apertures in the projection lantern, adjusting them until the artificial moon matched in perceived size the real moon at its different elevations.

This judgment of equality is not so easy to make as one might think. Abstracted equivalences are always troublesome. Heterochromatic photometry, for instance, is difficult because the observer has to abstract from the hues to equate the brightnesses. These equations of judgments between the real and artificial moons were "heterotelic," that is to say, the observer had to match in size two objects which were at different distances. He cannot, of course, see the size of his own retinal image, and, when he is aware of the distance, then his brain automatically tends to correct for distance—at least approximately when the distances are not too great and there are sufficient clues to tell him what the distance is (Holway and Boring, 1941). The retinal image remains, nevertheless, the primary determinant, so that there is some conflict and uncertainty. A man 40 ft. away looks about as large as he did 20 ft. away, when he is seen with two eyes in good light with perspective obvious. But a man 1000 ft. away looks smaller than one 20 ft. away even under the same good conditions for knowing about distance—just as parallel railroad tracks seem to get closer together in the distance. This difficulty of the judgment accounts for some of its variability.

We also used mirrors in the apparatus shown in Fig. 2. There is no reason why mirrors should not be used, provided they are invisible. These mirrors were front-aluminized optical surfaces without frames. They were placed at the ends of long 5-m. arms, which could be rotated to place a moon at any desired elevation. We had two arms and two mirrors so that two moons at different elevations could be compared directly.

The black arms and the black clips that hold the mirrors are quite invisible when a bright moon is shining at one from the mirrors, but there is a difficulty. The mirror cannot be placed near the real moon, but opposite against a dark part of the

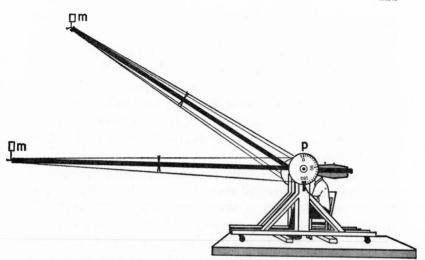

Fig. 2. Mirrors for the moon illusion. The positions of the mirrors *m, m* are controlled by strings. Each mirror is at the end of an arm that can be elevated, and the angle of elevation is read on the protractor *p*. The observer has his head (behind the protractor) immobilized by his biting firmly on a rigid biting board. The projection screen for an artificial moon is not shown.

sky. Then on a hazy night the mirror is no longer invisible, because it becomes a rectangular patch of bright haze seen against the black sky behind it. So the illusion then fails to appear, as is almost always the case with visible mirrors. It is often better, therefore, to use the real moon, if only one has the patience to wait month after month for cloudless nights when the moon is full and to stay up late enough for nature to provide the desired elevations. Still, without the mirrors we should never have known the size the moon would appear to have if it could be seen below the horizon.

In the early experiments we were able to measure the changing perceived size of the moon as it ascended, but we did not get smooth functions. The observed points fell to one side or the other of what seemed to be the average curve. Then we found the difficulty. We had left the observer free to move his head—

just as everyone before us had done. When you look at the moon in nature you move your head, or your eyes, or more often both.

If the head is fixed in a vertical position, the eyes can be raised about 40° above the horizontal or a little more. The neck can easily be bent backward another 40°. If you stand erect and look at the zenith, you almost inevitably have to bend the body backward to get the remaining 10°. It is important, therefore, to know whether the eyes are responsible for the illusion or whether it is the neck.

We arranged to immobilize the head by having the observer bite firmly on a horizontal strip of metal, a biting board, fixed in the apparatus of Fig. 2. We could then study the illusion up to 35°. Vision begins to get blurred when the eyes are raised as much as 40°. We could also make the plane of the biting board vertical, so as to work with a supine observer who was looking straight ahead at the zenith. Finally, we pivoted the biting board in such a way that the head could move and leave the eyes always looking straight in front at a mirrored moon.

Here is what happens. For the erect observer the perceived moon gets smaller as it ascends from 0° (straight ahead) to 35°, and the full amount of shrinkage is reached in that span. Fig. 3 is the average of results for two observers who always agreed pretty well with each other during the six years of experimentation. The ratio of perceived diameters in these data is 1/1.9— about what Schur got with an artificial moon at 33 m., a little less than what Pozděna got for the real moon.

If the observer is supine looking straight ahead at the zenith, the same kind of function is found—only then does one have to use mirrored moons, because the real moon in Massachusetts does not often get to the zenith. If the supine observer hangs his head over the edge of a table to see the moon ascend, then the moon starts small at the horizon and gets larger as it ascends. If the angle of the biting board is controlled so that the observer always looks straight ahead from his skull at the moon, then there is no illusion. If the moon is placed by mirrors

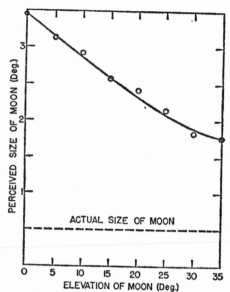

Fig. 3. Perceived size of the moon as a function of its elevation. The curve is the average of data for two observers, erect with heads immobilized. The perceived size is measured by the angle subtended by an artificial moon, equated in size to the real moon but only 3.5 m. away.

below the horizon, then, for an erect observer, it shrinks as it descends below the horizontal. So the maximum size is straight ahead.

If the supine observer sees the moon rise from 25° below "straight ahead" to 35° above—a total range of 60°, which is all he can get out of his eyes—then the perceived moon first expands up to the straight-ahead position and thereafter contracts.

Strange things happen if the observer is allowed to use only one eye (Taylor and Boring, 1942). Immediate memory then affects the perception. If he makes binocular and monocular observations alternately on the same evening, then the illusion holds for monocular observation, although the data are a little less reliable. The binocular judgments have affected the monocular. But, if the observer is made monocular with a patch over one eye for an entire evening, then the illusion fails.

Persons who have lost an eye appear not to have the illusion. Some of them give smooth functions with no change in the perceived size. Others, who are sophisticated about the fact of the illusion, believe that they see it, but do not report consistently. Presumably the illusion depends on binocular vision.

There remain two special points for consideration. Why do the perceived angular diameters of Fig. 3 vary between 1.7° and 3.5°, when it is well known that the real moon subtends an angle of only about half a degree? There is no satisfactory answer to this question, but the difference is consistent with what is called the *size-constancy phenomenon*—the fact that a distant object does not look nearly so much smaller than a near object as its retinal image is smaller. These perceived sizes of the real moon are measured by the diameter of an artificial moon only 3.5 m. away. If the small image of a distant object matches in perceived size the larger image of a near object, then the image of the near artificial moon must be made larger than the image of the distant real moon if the two are to match. But the precise answer to the question will not be forthcoming until the quantitative relationships that express perceived size as a function of distance have been worked out. Just now we know these functions only up to 200 ft.

The other point concerns the emotional accompaniments of the illusion. When the erect observer sees the large horizon moon he exclaims "Oh!" with a rising inflection—generally. He is surprised and pleased. With a supine observer with head hanging over the table edge, or anyone doubled over and looking between his legs, sees the tiny horizon moon, he exclaims "Oh!" with a falling inflection—generally. He is surprised and disappointed. Why?

The supine observer sees the zenith moon large, but he never exclaims about it. He says it does not appear large to him, yet he equates it to an artificial moon just as large as the artificial moon to which, when erect, he had already equated the horizon moon. Nor does the erect observer ever exclaim about the small size of the moon in elevation. He just takes it for granted, as if that were the size the moon really is.

The answer must lie in memory and expectation. The moon is usually seen in elevation—in cities almost always. That is the size it is. One carries these absolute impressions around with him. Thus the large horizon moon comes as a great surprise. The observer, supine or doubled over, has just been seeing the horizon moon large. He is surprised when his change of position makes it small.

So comparison does come in, but it is not as Ptolemy thought, a comparison with terrestrial objects. It is comparison of the moon with itself seen previously. This fact makes it unsafe to try to demonstrate the nature of the illusion by asking anyone to lie down and observe a zenith moon or one high in elevation. Apparatus for the measurement of the perceived size is needed. But it is always safe to ask him to try shrinking a large horizon moon by doubling over to view it from between his legs.

THEORY

There is no satisfactory further theory for explaining this phenomenon. It is not due to physical causes outside the visual mechanism. It is not due to the greater brightness of the moon in elevation, when atmospheric haze is diminished. It depends on raising or lowering the eyes. Movements of the head, neck and body do not cause it.

The theory most generally held by psychologists cannot be true. It is that the eyes when raised tend, because of the balance of their muscles, to diverge or at least to converge less. Thus an effort for convergence is necessary to keep the binocular image from doubling up, and the clue from innervated convergence is the clue to perceived nearer distance. If the theory of Fig. 1 were correct, this clue might explain the illusion; but we have seen that the moon in elevation does not look nearer. It appears to be farther away, because it is seen as smaller. This theory, moreover, would require that the moon below the horizon look still larger than at the horizon, whereas it looks smaller.

When the eyes are raised they also rotate slightly, the one relative to the other, and in such a way as to produce a stereoscopic effect in which high objects would look nearer than low. This theory would work out satisfactorily for the smaller moon below the horizon, but it too is inconsistent with the fact that it is the horizon moon that looks nearest.

There remains only the suggestion that the effort of raising or lowering the eyes shrinks the perceived size of the moon—a theory of inhibition or drainage. Since we do not know why muscular effort in the visual mechanism should affect visually perceived size, in these cases where the clues to perceived distances are missing, we are forced to leave the problem there without ultimate solution.

References

Boring, E. G. Size constancy and Emmert's law. *American Journal of Psychology*, 1940, vol. 53, 292–295.

Helmholtz, H. v. (1866). *Physiological Optics*. Vol. III. (Trans. by J. P. C. Southall.) Optical Society of America, 1925.

Holway, A. H., and Boring, E. G. The moon illusion and the angle of regard. *American Journal of Psychology*, 1940, vol. 53, 109–116. (a)

Holway, A. H., and Boring, E. G. The apparent size of the moon as a function of the angle of regard: further experiments. *American Journal of Psychology*, 1940, vol. 53, 537–553. (b)

Holway, A. H., and Boring, E. G. Determinants of apparent visual size with distance variant. *American Journal of Psychology*, 1941, vol. 54, 21–37.

Pozděna, R. F. Eine Methode zur experimentellen und konstruktiven Bestimmung der Form des Firmamentes. *Zeitschrift für Psychologie*, 1909, vol. 51, 200–246.

Reimann, Eugen. Die scheinbare Vergrösserung der Sonne und des Mondes am Horizont. *Zeitschrift für Psychologie*, 1902, vol. 30, 1–38, 161–195.

Schur, Erna. Mondtäuschung und Sehgrosskonstanz. *Psychologische Forschung*, 1925, vol. 7, 44–80.

Smith, Robert. *A Compleat System of Opticks*. Vol. I. Cambridge, England: Author, 1738.

Taylor, D. W., and Boring, E. G. The moon illusion as a function of binocular regard. *American Journal of Psychology*, 1942, vol. 55, 189–201.

Was This Analysis a Success?
1940

When I undertook analysis with Hanns Sachs in 1934–1935
most of the "orthodox" psychologists, and thus most of my friends,
regarded psychoanalysis with disapproval. At best it was to them
a mistrusted mystery, and my own scientific integrity seemed to
them to be open to some doubt. The skeptics wondered: "Does
psychoanalysis really work?" and I found myself wondering too,
right after the analysis in 1935 and again five years later when
I thought that the personality change that I had so anxiously
hoped for ought to have become clear if indeed it had occurred.
Accordingly I proposed to the *Journal of Abnormal and Social
Psychology* that it solicit from well-known psychologists accounts
of their analyses in order that we might thus have a poll of scientifically competent ex-analysands. The scheme worked, at least
far enough to excite considerable interest, for the entire set of
these reports was later reprinted together and sold by the American Psychological Association until the edition was exhausted.
My report came first, and I alone among the analysands got my
analyst, Sachs, to comment in print upon my discussion of his
analysis of me. That report too is printed here.

This paper has provided a very interesting perspective on that
quest of mine for the kind of maturity that I wanted so desperately when I first sought analysis, for it shows what I thought of
myself in 1935 and also five years later in 1940 when I wrote the
paper. The five years had provided considerable progress toward
my goal. The first draft of the Autobiography printed in this book
was written in 1950, and thus is able to note further progress

Reprinted with permission from the *Journal of Abnormal and Social
Psychology*, 1940, vol. 35, 4–10.

during the next ten years. Now the current draft of the biography, revised in 1960, shows much more advance toward being the kind of person I wanted to be. I had in 1960 not read this report on my analysis during the twenty years since it was written, and reading it now shocked me. Was I really so disturbed, so fearful and insecure, only twenty-five years ago? Yes. The description is clear. A great deal can happen in twenty-five years, and some of it was my progress toward my self-determined goal. The rest was the goal's regress toward me, a simple lowering of my level of aspiration as age quiets ambition.

It seems strange that a psychologist after his psychoanalysis should not have a message for his colleagues, when there has been so much questioning of psychoanalysis by the orthodox psychologists; and yet it is true that four years after my analysis I still cannot assess with assurance the significance of the experience in my life. Since, nevertheless, my hesitation is a datum in itself, I welcome this opportunity to make it in specific detail a matter of record. Apparently psychology is not yet in a position to validate or invalidate psychoanalysis experimentally—with selected groups and carefully chosen controls. Hence we are reduced to the collection of case histories; and critical autobiographical histories by sophisticated, scientifically minded persons ought to be worth more than the enthusiasm of naïve persons about an event which has helped them. With this conviction I join the present symposium, realizing that no considerable part of the total picture of psychoanalysis can ever reside in the private experience of a single person.

The reason for my undertaking psychoanalysis was primarily therapeutic, a need arising out of the basic tenets of my professional creed. My ambition has always been strong, my entire life formed about a drive for scientific productivity. Such success as has been my lot seems to me to have depended more upon persistence than genius, for my ethic has been that a successful psychologist works at his job eighty hours a week and fifty weeks a year. Though I think now that this drive has grown out of my need for approbation ("affiliation," "love," Murray, 1938), I did not before my analysis recognize that origin. Viewed from the distance of the present, the 1920's seem to have been for me a fairly effective decade, and my *A History of Experimental Psychology*, a successful book as psychologists' books go, appeared in 1929. After that I got into another job of writing, *The Physical Dimensions of Consciousness* (not nearly so good a book as the other), which I finished in the spring of 1932. Later in that year I found myself in an emotional crisis, a crisis so accurately timed that I wonder sometimes if in some vague way I did not sense its coming, if I may not even have driven the second book through to completion that it might be done before the crisis should occur.

When it came, the crisis seemed to leave me sterile, troubled with autistic thinking and all the interferences with attention that arise from emotional disturbance. About the sterility or its cause one cannot, of course, be sure. Presumably every ambitious academic person passes periodically—perhaps even annually—through depression, periods during which he is beset by the conviction that he is making no headway. *Ex post facto* I see that the 1930's have been less effective for me than the 1920's (and this in spite of the analysis!); yet the cause is not certain. The decade of ages 33–43 is likely to be more productive than the decade 43–53, so Lehman's (1936; 1937; cf. Miles, 1939), curves seem to prove. It is perhaps enough to say that in 1932–33 I was depressed, that I seemed to achieve little, that the thought of my professional accomplishment's diminishing rather than increasing in the future seemed utterly intolerable to me. So evident was my emotional disturbance that many of my associates urged analysis upon me, and into psychoanalysis I went, therefore, as a last resource. My difficulty was psychological, and I was a psychologist. It seemed that there must be some way whereby I could regain full control of my attention, and, since I knew of nothing else, psychoanalysis was worth a try. In public I saved my face by the rationalization that the psychoanalysis of an experimental psychologist might result in some important insight into the relation between the two fields.

The first analyst I saw repelled me. He seemed too mercenary. We had not talked half an hour before he explained that, were I to miss any conferences, I should have to pay just the same. I know, of course, the reason for that rule; yet he seemed to be thinking less about my health than about his own pocketbook.

Then I met Dr. Hanns Sachs, onetime Director of *Psychoanalytisches Institut* at Berlin, a pupil and friend of Freud's. I liked him at once. He reminded me of Titchener, whose image has always dominated my professional life. I still feel a warm friendship for him, uncertain as I am of the effects of his analysis. He is wise in general knowledge, in history and literature, although the rigors of positivistic science are not for him. Ready as he was to learn about American psychology, he never could have liked it. We arranged for the analysis in December 1933, but Dr. Sachs was too busy to take me on before the next September. So desperate was I then that I did not see how I could wait three-quarters of a year; yet I had to. I mention this point to show that my initial attitude was favorable to a successful analysis.

From September 1934 to June 1935 I had 168 analytic sessions, five every week. I missed none by inadvertence or on short notice, although by planning for professional engagements long in advance we skipped a few. I had what I think was my share of emotion. I wept. I threw things. And once, right after a session, I found myself quite unmoved by a lecture from a traffic policeman, so much calmer was that usually enraging performance than the analysis.

The expense seemed to me to play the role that was expected of it. The analysand is supposed to make a sacrifice in order to obtain the analysis; this sacrifice secures his serious cooperation. I knew how many seconds cost one cent, and often, as I lay on the couch awaiting the next free association, I found the new idea would be an image of the pennies scurrying by as costly seconds were lost without any progress in my therapy.

So I liked my analyst, I suffered, and I felt impoverished—all favorable auspices for a successful analysis.

The analysis was not didactic. Most people, I think, do not realize how little of conventional psychoanalytical theory and terminology there needs to be in an analysis. My analyst had no belief in word magic. He did not care what terms were used so long as we worked ourselves clear as to the meanings. He was, moreover, dealing solely and particularly with ME and not with the human mind in general. It was I, not he, who wanted to make the generalizations.

Now we come to the difficulties.

All through the analysis I felt the inadequacy of the psychoanalytic philosophy, a philosophy which seemed to me to be a loose and indeterminate mixture of voluntarism and determinism. This failure of the discipline to take a firm stand on so basic a matter troubled me greatly—and still does. I recall that toward the close of the analysis the analyst reinterated, "Where there's a will, there's a way," implying that, if you do not do what you can do, then you do not want to do it. That philosophy roused my ire, for it was offered as a motivation, not as a mere tautology. After all, psychoanalytical therapy is founded on a belief in the inadequacy of voluntarism and in the meaninglessness of the concept of will.

I do not believe that I can be said to have got the intimacy and efficiency of personal relation with my analyst that is called *transfer*. I liked him, and sometimes I was angry with him. He was a very important person in my life that year, but I doubt that he was much more important than a few others, like the president of my university, who can determine, I should suppose, depression or elation for every departmental chairman, since it is the president who decides whether the chairman shall prevail or fail, whether he shall be wise or foolish. There are those who will say that this fact proves my analysis to have been unsuccessful. The point is that I did not know then, nor do I know now, whether my analysis was "successful"; and my analyst himself has never pronounced his judgment. I gathered that he thought it would have been successful if I thought it was; but I needed him to tell me what I should think.

It seems certain to me that we fell far short of the recovery of old memories which are made so much of in the literature. I think it is true that we came to no assurance about any event of my childhood that was not already in my normal repertoire of reminiscence. Though we tried to work on only a few dreams, none of them came to that self-consistent closure which is supposed, I understand, to indicate a correct dream analysis. It would seem that I have no important hidden past, or that it is irrelevant to this psychosis, or that the analysis failed. (Perhaps I was too old at forty-eight for psychoanalysis; Hamilton, 1939, p. 465.)

There is one objective fact about my analysis which I must add to complete the record. It may have been crucial, though I think it was not. The situation of 1932 that threw me into analysis was suddenly altered in the spring of 1935 toward the close of my sessions. Thus the analysis, which started for the purpose of clarifying one situation, ended by needing to clarify another. Since it was I myself more than the particular situation that wanted clarifying, I do not see how this event could have changed the analysis from success to failure. Psychoanalysis is supposed to be something more than the mere practical adjustment of individuals to particular situations, needing to be repeated whenever life presents a new unpleasant surprise.

We come now to the main issue. Did my analysis help me to understand myself better? Did it give me a new insight into my motivation, and was there, with this insight, any new appreciation of reality that should permit me to dismiss my foolish emotions for what they were and return my attention to psychology, where I wanted it to be? Let us consider the question of insight first, and of therapy second.

As to insight. I was certainly confused before the analysis. Believing as I did that the most important thing in my life was my professional ambition, I went to analysis to have it unentangled so that it could proceed. But I also believed then that my need for personal relations ("affiliation") and for approbation was fundamental. It seemed plain to me that the damaging of the latter had injured the former, though I was fairly astonished that there should be anything in my own constitution that could thwart my ambition. Nevertheless, I entered analysis without a clear belief as to the causal relation between personal needs and professional ambition. I entered it, more than that, with some sense of guilt about pressing for the right of those personal needs to exist. What the analysis did was to sanction these needs. If it did not discover them, at least it reassured me in respect of them. For a year or two after the analysis I felt a little suspicious, fearing that analysis had proved only what I should have liked it to prove; but I confess now that I have no misgivings about the result, that I am assured that the analysis is right, and that it is a mild relief not to feel guilty about this sector of my egoism.

Now as to therapy. It is true that I hoped for a personality change. I did not like what I had. There lay, however, a mystery in psychotherapeutics. I could understand how free association could reveal the hidden parts of the mind, but I never could see how their revelation could alter the personality. Over this riddle I puzzled from September to March, being nevertheless fairly patient, for I am an experienced subject in experiments and know better than as subject to take on responsibility for an experiment. By April, however, I was beginning to worry. There ought, I thought, to be some revelation if the analysis were to be complete by June—and I "had" to complete it by June. I had not the money to continue, nor did I have the time. Too many colleagues were being inconvenienced by the necessary adjustments to the schedule of my appointments. In May I began to be alarmed, but there was no help coming from the analyst. Then in June I found that he was going abroad on the 22nd and that my last session would have to be on the 21st.

By the 15th I was asking desperately what to do about my personality, which, for all the emotional upheavals of the past few months, seemed to me still no different from the outmoded bundle of incompatibilities that I had had to get along with for so long. To my question there was only a partial answer. It was on the 20th, I think, that we agreed on the fact that the analysis had reached a point of diminishing returns and that it would be unprofitable to continue in the fall, and then the analyst cautioned me as to the impossibility of knowing whether the analysis had been successful until some time afterward, perhaps a month. I ought, he said, to get clearer about it in time. That to me was an unsettling anticlimax. I had eagerly awaited a light from heaven, at the very least to be changed from Saul to Paul; and all that happened was that the analysis petered out in an uneventful session on June 21 and my analyst went abroad!

The aftereffects were somewhat worse than the analysis. I was distraught. I had tried a last resource, and it had failed. Yet, unwilling to accept so bitter a conclusion, I found myself seizing on the analyst's casual statement that I ought to wait a month. I waited anxiously, hoping for a new personality by July 21. None came. Finally I sought out my psychologist-friends who believe in psychoanalysis, and we sat in conference discussing this sad immutability of my personality—on August 21, as I suddenly realized. Their advice was patience, the less haste the more speed; wait at least until December 21, they urged. So I waited, through all of one sabbatical semester, a semester during which I had planned to write on the other volume of my *History of Experimental Psychology*. That precious sabbatical, filled as it was with the emotional reverberations of the analysis, was an utter loss. Not only was I unable to write; I could not even read effectively. And finally I ceased to expect a miracle. I was sad and distraught, knowing that I had wasted one of the four precious sabbaticals that are due me during my life.

Now, four years after the close of the analysis, I find myself quite uncertain as to whether it has made any important change in me. Too many other things have happened for me to say why I am as I am. I have not yet regained the productivity that I so confidently expected in 1932, but for its loss, of course, I can find an alibi in academic administrative responsibilities. I am somewhat calmer about this thwarting of ambition; but as to whether that calm is the result of the analysis or of my advancing age, with only fourteen years now left before my retirement, who shall say? (Cf. Miles, 1939, pp. 555–562; Hamilton, 1939, pp. 464–479.) True, the analysis had had this advantage: having been analyzed, I can no longer feel that I have left any available stone unturned. But that would be a rather small return for so large an undertaking. Perhaps I am a little more aggressive. Perhaps I speak up more readily with the confidence that what I have to say is important. Perhaps less often do I meet contradiction with the conviction that the other man is presumably right. But I am not at all a calm or well-poised person. My "need for affiliation" is still dominant. Cruelty and arrogance—whether in Germany or at Harvard—have an effect upon me so disturbing that the newspapers can throw me out of work for an evening, and a simple local act of aggression, not even directed at me, can stop creative work for half a day. There is so much about this personality of mine that would be better if different, so much that analysis might have done and did not!

References

Hamilton, G. V. Changes in personality and psychosexual phenomena with age. In E. V. Cowdry (Ed.), *Problems of Ageing*. Baltimore: Williams & Wilkins, 1939. Pp. 459–482.

Lehman, H. C. The creative years in science and literature. *Scientific Monthly*, 1936, vol. 43, 151–162.

Lehman, H. C. The creative years: "best books." *Scientific Monthly*, 1937, vol. 45, 65–75.

Miles, W. R. Psychological aspects of ageing. In E. V. Cowdry (Ed.), *Problems of Ageing*. Baltimore: Williams & Wilkins, 1939. Pp. 535–571.

Murray, H. A., and Associates. *Explorations in Personality*. New York: Oxford University Press, 1938.

Was This Analysis a Success?

Comment by Hanns Sachs

This is my analyst's reply to my comment on his analysis of
me. Sachs was handicapped, of course, because he was bound
by Hippocratic ethics not to discuss in detail what he knew in
confidence from his analysand. Later Franz Alexander undertook
to strengthen the case for psychoanalysis by commenting on this
limitation of Sachs's comment (*Journal of Abnormal and Social
Psychology*, 1940, vol. 35, 305–323). Alexander was undoubtedly
thinking that Sachs had not been free to go into "the one objective fact" that I had thought was not crucial but which he
had thought "amounted to a potential trauma" which might without the analysis have produced a breakdown, perhaps a depression.

Every analyst of sufficient experience has observed the therapeutic effect of psychoanalysis, but it remains still an open
question in how many cases anything approaching a full cure
can be achieved and how the result compares with the necessary
sacrifice of time, exertion, and money. Any attempt to clarify
these problems deserves an analyst's most intense cooperation. I
shall, therefore, try to describe what I consider to be the fundamentals of the problem and point out its difficulties. The discussion of Professor Boring's paper will serve as an excellent
approach to the general viewpoint.

Reprinted with permission from the *Journal of Abnormal and Social
Psychology*, 1940, vol. 35, 11–16.

I see no reason to contradict Professor Boring's statement which terms his analysis, with some minor exceptions, unsuccessful. I cannot raise an objection when he declares it as doubtful that the favorable changes have been the effect of his analysis or rather of extraneous circumstances; but I want to add the warning that these "doubtfuls" will be present with almost every therapy—except of an acute illness—and will be absolutely unavoidable in psychotherapy where the psychical adaptations and the modifications of reality work hand in hand in a most insidious manner.

The causation of this partly absent, partly doubtful success may, of course, lie in the inefficiency of the analyst, who made some mistake or overlooked some important aspect. Of this, I cannot myself be the judge. Anyway, there are some objective factors which might furnish a sufficient explanation. The analysand in this case, although suffering in various ways, had no neurotic symptom. It was clearly a case of character analysis which has to be considered from a different angle than a strictly "therapeutic" analysis of a clearly defined—and diagnosed—neurosis. In such a case it makes all the difference if the character has retained some of the infantile flexibility or if it has been cast a long time ago in a fully developed and strictly preserved form. With a personality like the one before us, where, for example, professional pursuits are not a spurious interest that could be given up easily for the sake of other aims and where the claims of family life have a deep and lasting influence on the character formation, a start for a new way of living, of a totally different emotional life, offers not much chance. This fact does not mean that psychoanalysis or even character analysis has to abdicate unconditionally in face of such reality factors as are evident or could be ascertained before the analysis. Age, for instance, is a highly important factor, but it cannot be justly evaluated on the sole basis of the number of years. I want to emphasize that all these facts, such as age, professional life, family ties, money situation, etc., have to be taken into consideration, not merely in regard to their objective and present importance, but still more in relation to the question of how strong their hold on the personality of the analysand is, how far they form an intrinsic, inseparable part of it, and what role they played in the evolution of his character from early childhood on (sublimation). In technical terms this means the investigation of the superego and of its infantile origin.

When the analyst thinks he has gathered sufficient material to decide these questions, then—but only then—he has to face the two fundamental problems of a character analysis. First, is the power which analysis has at its disposition and which consists (for the sake of brevity I use technical terms again) of the libido that has not been transformed permanently into superego functions—is this power equal to the task of producing a fundamental change of character? Secondly, is it advisable in the best interest of the analysand to attempt such a task, even if one cannot be sufficiently sure of the success? These questions are quite different with a neurosis or with a case where the sublimation cannot be maintained any longer and, showing already the fissures of an impending neurotic breakdown, has therefore to be considered as equal to a manifest neurosis. One does not hesitate to wreck a slum tenement which endangers the life and health of its inhabitants, but one feels differently in dealing with a dignified and respectable house which has given comfort and shelter for a long time, even if it causes to its inhabitants a good deal of inconvenience.

In one point my opinion about the therapeutic value of this special analysis differs from that pronounced by Professor Boring. It is about the "one objective fact" of which he says: "It may have been crucial, but I think it was not." This fact amounted, as I see it, to a potential trauma; that is, I have some good reason to assume that this fact, without the analysis, would have produced the danger of a breakdown in the sense mentioned above, probably tending towards depression. What might have happened cannot, of course, at least for an outsider, constitute a convincing proof as compared with what *has* happened. But this circumstance, as already mentioned, is one of the constant difficulties of psychotherapy. I may add that even in this point I do not want to claim the beneficial influence as a consequence of psychoanalytic technique in its strict sense. A lifelong, very intimate friend, to whom the analysand could have confided in many repeated and unrestrained outpours all his woes and worries, might have done him the same service. But it was not accidental that such a friend did not exist; and I put it down in favor of psychoanalysis—and not as a small thing, either—that it was able to provide on short notice a stopgap for the missing friend when such a stopgap was most urgently needed.

In taking a more general view of our problem it has to be kept in mind that the healing of mental and organic illness has proceeded on different lines. In the beginning they were identical; the primitive mind conceived every pain and sickness as the working of magic, as the influence of evil spirits or of malevolent witchcraft. Consequently all therapy was magical too. With the progress of civilization and reality adaptation the scientific view, regarding organic illness as the result of disturbing processes in the organism, was soon—though far from completely—evolved. Mental healing remained for a much longer time on the magical level; the witch-expelling exorcism was still in universal use at the beginning of the eighteenth century. A scientific attitude, making psychogenic causes responsible, was, even among the most progressive minds, not existent till the middle of the nineteenth century and seems generally even today far less acceptable than in the matter of organic illness. All scientific knowledge in psychotherapy is therefore comparatively new; it has not only to fight against resistances which elsewhere do not exist, but it carries still not a few traces of its origin from a belief in magic. The expurgation of these traces is one of the major claims of psychoanalysis; it means that not only the hope for working miracles, but even the aim at such effects has to be abandoned.

I have mentioned already that from a purely therapeutical—not so much from a psychological—point of view the situation is quite often rendered neither perspicuous nor unequivocal, because of the constant intermingling and interaction of psychic facts and modifications of reality. I will quote a case in illustration; yet, even in selecting as clear-cut a case of therapy as I can find in my experience, I feel a pang caused by the necessary oversimplification. The patient, who had been an addict first to morphia, then to cocaine, had, after a pause which had been the result of an unfinished analysis (conducted by another analyst), taken to drinking. The alcoholism had lasted several years in the most severe form when he entered the analysis with me. In the meantime other methods of psychotherapy together with several stays in nursing homes, closed institutions, etc., had been tried without the least success. During the third year of his analysis he became free from the addiction for several months. Then came a full relapse. The analysis lasted approximately four years and resulted in full abstinence. A few months after the end of the analysis he had a relapse which lasted two weeks. Since then, for nearly seven years he has been absolutely free from drug addiction in any form. I consider this as a signal success of psychoanalytic therapy, and I feel proud and happy when I think of it.

But it is not for this reason that I quote it here. There is a hitch in the story. Just after the end of the analysis a total change in the surroundings and circumstances of the analysand took place. This change, it is true, was by no means on the easy side. On the contrary, he needed all his determination and resourcefulness to see it through. It is also true that I never heard of a severe case of alcoholism, at the verge of delirium tremens, cured by a change in the reality situation. But who can answer the question—except purely theoretically—whether or not just this sort of emergency at just this particular moment was necessary to set his feet on the road to full recovery?

Another obstacle to the correct appraisal of the therapeutic value of psychoanalysis is the absence of any yardstick or general rule concerning the following facts:

1. The seriousness and extent of the neurosis.
2. The strength of the forces opposing the therapy (primary and secondary gain, reality situation, traumatic experiences, etc.).
3. The extent and the duration of the therapeutic result.

It would be much easier if we could find at least a strict interrelation between these three factors, but even this is not the case. As to the first, patients which are in fact near-psychotic may impress not only their acquaintances but even the psychotherapeutist for a long time as fairly normal, whereas others who are called perfectly crazy by themselves or by their friends suffer only from a passing neurotic spell.

This is not the place to discuss the second point adequately; the deeper factors—e.g., the amount of masochistic satisfaction which the patient acquires by his symptoms—would need a detailed exposition. Instead of it I will mention one of a more superficial kind. A patient who wants to be cured of a neurosis becomes aware that he cannot set himself free without giving up an important gratification, such as a pervert phantasy, masturbation, or certain habits to which he is addicted, and he reacts accordingly.

The difficulty of forming a right estimate of the extent of therapeutic success has been referred to in this discussion. I shall add here that the members of the patient's family behave sometimes very much like the father of the dumb girl in Molière's *Médecin malgrè lui;* when his daughter has been cured of her mutism and breaks out in an endless streak of wild talk, he implores the doctor who cured her to make her tongue-tied again. Some patients behave to the therapeutist in a manner like that of a criminal to the lawyer who has got him off: they deny that they ever were seriously involved, and they want to forget all about it.

I cannot end this discussion without giving my personal

opinion of the problem as precisely as I am able to formulate it. Psychoanalysis is—as Freud has emphasized repeatedly—far from being ideal therapy, since it is neither certain, nor quick, nor easy. That admission, however, does not alter the fact that psychoanalysis is getting nearer to the roots of the evil than is any other therapy; instead of taking care of the surface, psychoanalysis works on causation. It is, therefore, not only the most thorough therapy but in a good many cases the only efficient and durable one available at present. Since it has given, moreover, an opportunity for the fullest investigation, progress in other methods would not have been possible and probably for sometime will not be possible without the help, instruction, and instigation which psychoanalysis gives to them. For the psychoanalyst the therapy is the indispensable instrument for any advance in his science and almost the only source of material that furnishes possibilities of gaining new insight. In the matter of the proof and verification of psychoanalytic theories, the psychotherapeutic proceedings gives opportunities to check up on single instances, but I should never consider it possible that psychotherapy in isolation from the rest of psychoanalytic investigation and experience should be used for this purpose. The proof—I repeat that I am voicing my personal views—lies in the combined force of all the experiences, tests, and explorations which can be made over the whole range of psychic life, pathological as well as cultural, and brought together after each of them separately has been demonstrated as fully as its special nature permits.

The Logic of the Normal Law
of Error in Mental Measurement
1920

This paper is one of my dearest, one of my least influential, and, as I still firmly believe, one of my soundest. In 1918, when the First World War reached America, I went from Titchener's introspective Laboratory at Cornell, where consciousness was regarded as the only proper subject matter for psychology and where mental testing and the study of human and animal behavior were taboo, to work under R. M. Yerkes at intelligence testing in the U.S. Army. After the Armistice in November, Yerkes brought me to Washington to be in charge of the section on results in the mammoth report, *Psychological Examining in the United States Army* (Memoirs of the National Academy of Sciences, 1921, vol. 15, 890 pp.).

In Washington I found that some mental testers, not all, thought that they could discover that a "true" scale of intelligence could be obtained by seeing how the arbitrary test scale must be altered to make the distribution of a large homogeneous sample normal. This was Quetelet's old view (1846) that the normal law is given a priori in nature, is the "true" law of any "natural" distribution. This view seemed to me so preposterous that I went to the Library of Congress to read up on the theory of probability and came away with the conviction that the psychologists' statistics of the late 'teens was founded upon unproven and unprovable assumptions.

Reprinted with permission from the *American Journal of Psychology*, 1920, vol. 31, 1–33.

When the Army released me, I went to Clark University and wrote this paper, which I read in Cambridge, Massachusetts, at the meeting of the American Psychological Association in December 1919. Ralph Barton Perry, the Harvard philosopher, heard it and liked it, and I have always supposed that his approval of it had something to do with my being called to Harvard, since the Harvard philosophers were the men to make this choice and the "brass instrument psychologists" who could talk about logical fundamentals were less common then than they are now.

I thought that the paper undermined current statistical procedures. I have no knowledge that anyone else ever thought so (or perhaps S. S. Stevens did); yet this effort clearly belonged to the *Zeitgeist,* for the criticism, as the paper shows, had often been made before—by George Boole (1854), for instance, who noted that to assume random distributions are normal is to believe that ignorance of a fact can determine what the fact shall be. The paper tells of the others who anticipated me, and the history of psychological statistics shows that the statistical sophistication was moving my way but slowly, indeed so slowly that I ventured another protest against the law of insufficient reason twenty-one years later ("Statistical frequencies as dynamic equilibria," *Psychological Review,* 1941, vol. 48, 279–301).

I was and am still impatient at the statisticians' stubborn complacency and have wondered whether by 2050 this whole period of statistical effort in American psychology might have become an enormous historical joke. In my family we talk about my making this protest every twenty-one years. The next time would be 1962 at age 76, and then 1983 when I am 97. But perhaps Lancelot Hogben's *Statistical Theory* (1958), which expounds my "truth" with a sophistication of which I am incapable, will get listened to. *Contemporary Psychology,* under my editorship, has reviewed Hogben (Sept. 1960, vol. 5, 273–276) and I wrote there an editorial on "The QPF Tradition" (p. 290), meaning the Adolph Quetelet, Karl Pearson, and R. A. Fisher tradition.

The paper is reprinted in its entirety except that the comments in the elaborate footnotes, which constitute about 30 per cent of the original paper, have here been deleted to save space. In 1920 I thought footnotes were scholarly. In 1929 and thereafter I have published books that I think are scholarly and that have notes in them, yet no footnote. It is better not to try to bifurcate the reader's thinking.

No amount of practically successful "mental measurement" in laboratories, school systems, factories, or the Army can relieve us, if we do not wish to waste time, of the necessity of stopping, every so often, to take account of first principles.

Psychophysics, with more than half a century of history to its credit, has repeatedly found the need to eliminate its logically unfit and reorganize its forces: it is a long cry from the principle of the just noticeable difference to the principle of the psychometric function. The mental test as a newcomer had first to prove its right to consideration. Now that it has been accepted it must pass under the critical eye and learn to conform. And what needs to be said, in way of admonition, applies especially to the mental test, although for no other reason than that the mental test is the lustiest form of mental measurement that one meets today. It, especially, merits a discriminating encouragement.

1. THE NATURE OF PROBABILITY

We can get nowhere in an understanding of mental measurement unless we appreciate the relation of the unit of measurement to the frequency of occurrence of the different measures. In statistics we deal repeatedly with frequency distributions; and we know, very often, the frequencies before we are assured as to what they are frequencies of. It is not unusual to attempt to calibrate a scale of measurement in terms of frequencies—an attempt that always demonstrates the necessity for a definite understanding of the relation between the two. Frequency distributions, however, have a way of absorbing some of the mystic power that is commonly supposed to inhere in the normal law of error, the "probability curve," which is itself a frequency distribution. Into the mystery of this function, a mystery connected with its supposed a priori nature, we can pry only by studying its origins, logical and historical. On the logical side we must ask what, in scientific usage, is the nature of a probability. In such a beginning we are setting ourselves no mean task, but a necessary one if we are to avoid muddling.

The early history of the theory of probabilities is a history of the solution of problems arising in games of chance (Todhunter, 1865). An applied mathematics of probability preceded the pure. For us the most significant principle that this period brought forth is one that is implicit in the famous theorem of James Bernoulli in 1713.

This theorem holds that events tend to occur with relative frequencies proportional to their probabilities. If *a* is twice as likely as *b* to happen, then in the long run it will happen twice as often. But how, we may well ask, are we to know the probabilities of occurrence for *a* and *b*? We must exclude the inverse use of the Bernoullian theorem. We can not say that *a* is twice as likely to happen as *b* because it happens twice as often, for this is simply to reason from frequency to probability and ultimately to identify the two. Our problem was to predict frequency from given probability. How then do we achieve this given probability?

The case of the coin appears at first glance fairly obvious.

If we may regard an ideal coin as a uniform, homogeneous circular disc, there is nothing which can tend to make it fall more often on the one side than on the other; we may expect, therefore, that in any long run of throws the coin will fall with either face uppermost an approximately equal number of times, or with, say, heads uppermost approximately half the times. (Yule, 1917, p. 256.)

Thus we read in a modern textbook of statistics. The thesis is: the probabilities are equal when there is no good reason for their being unequal. Von Kries (1886, p. 6; cf. Kaufmann, 1913, pp. 43–45; Stumpf, 1892, esp. pp. 41, 61–79) has called this law the principle of insufficient reason (*"das Princip des mangelnden Grundes"*); Boole (1854, p. 370) speaks of it as "the equal distribution of ignorance."

Against an indiscriminate use of the principle of insufficient reason von Kries inveighs. We are asked to consider before the days of spectroscopic analysis the question of whether there is iron in Sirius. We are completely ignorant, but we can conceive of no greater reason for the presence of iron than against it. The probability for the existence of iron in Sirius is therefore ½, on the principle of insufficient reason. Similarly the probability for the existence of gold is ½. It follows algebraically that the probability for the existence of both iron and gold in Sirius is ¼, of iron without gold ¼, of gold without iron ¼, and of neither of these metals ¼. There were, when von Kries wrote, 68 known earthly elements. The probability of the existence of all these elements in Sirius is the 68th power of ½; *i.e.*, the chance of all the elements existing in Sirius, as well as the chance of no one of them existing there, is about three in one hundred billion billions. But if we had raised in the first place the question of the existence of earthly elements in Sirius, we might, being ignorant and applying the principle of insufficient reason, have said that it is just as likely that there are no earthly elements in Sirius as that there are some. The discrepancy between the three one hundred billion billionths and one half leads von Kries (1886, pp. 10 f.) to declare that *"die Aufstellung der gleich möglichen Fälle muss eine in zwingender Weise und ohne jede Willkür sich ergebende sein"* [the establishment of equally possible cases must be determined in a cogent manner and without any free choice].

Plainly it must. Shutting our eyes reduces our faith in what we see to less than one half. If we would know the nature of our surroundings, we must open our eyes; and, if we would acquire a tenable belief of the chemical constitution of Sirius, we must await the spectroscope. There is no alchemy of probabilities that will change ignorance into knowledge. Expectations must be founded upon cogent rather than insufficient reasons. Nevertheless we can not, it would seem, push this antithesis too far. We can never be completely informed of all the conditions. Thus Westergaard (1890, p. 4):

> In every well-arranged game of chance . . . the balls are of the same size, of the same wood, of the same specific gravity, etc. They are mixed with the greatest care and every ball is apparently subject to

the same forces. Yet such is not the case. In spite of all effort the balls are different, and depart, even though quite insignificantly, from spherical form. One approaches this and another that mathematical form. Every one has a weight and size different from all the others. No ball is absolutely like any of the others. Moreover they can not possibly lie in the bag in exactly the same manner. In short there are a multitude of apparently insignificant differences which determine that exactly this ball and none other shall be drawn.

In the face of such complexity it is hopeless to seek cogent reason for the drawing of the particular ball.

Moreover, there is a logical as well as a practical reason for our inability to predict in the individual case. Westergaard seems to see this when he implies—it amounts to this—duplicity on our part when we arrange the game of chance. We attempt to make the balls all equal so as to equalize chance, we assume that we have succeeded for all practical intents and purposes, and yet in the same breath we expect to be able to draw some particular one of the balls. However, there must be inequalities, including of course difference of spatial position within the bag, in order to make the drawing possible.

Did no such inequalities exist, then one of two things would happen: either all the balls would turn up at once or they would all remain in the bag. (Westergaard, 1890, p. 4.)

In more general terms, we may say that the problem of probability exists only in the face of ignorance. Given all the conditions, we deal not in probabilities but with the certainties of cause and effect (cf. Venn, 1888, p. 122).

Here then it would seem we are landed in a dilemma. If we are in total ignorance of the conditions of our problem, all argument is foolishness. If we know all the conditions, we may argue to an effect but not to a probability. Have we to deal then either with a practical impossibility or with a logical absurdity?

The solution lies in the adoption of a definite intermediate position. [Arne] Fisher (1915, p. 9) lays down a first principle in the case:

It thus appears that a rigorous application of the principle of cogent reason seems impossible. However, a compromise between this principle and that of the principle of insufficient reason may be effected by the following definition of equally possible cases, *viz: Equally possible cases are such cases in which we, after an exhaustive analysis of the physical laws underlying the structure of the complex of causes influencing the special event, are led to assume that no particular case will occur in preference to any other.*

But Fisher, in attempting a compromise, neglects to tell us definitely how much ignorance and how much knowledge make the proper conditions from which we may proceed. We are scientists engaged in very practical work and we wish to know what we may and what we may not do in our statistics.

We can get at the nature of probability by taking a simple instance. The event in which we are interested is, let us say, the toss of a penny. We wish to know the probability that it will come heads. The law of insufficient reason says that, since we can not know that the penny is more likely or less likely to come heads than tails, the probability of heads is one half. The extreme demand for cogent reason would urge that, since we can not know the principal determining factors, this case is insoluble. The "compromise" that Fisher proposes is that we shall analyze the underlying physical laws. We shall find that one side of the penny is heads and the other tails, that the penny is homogeneous, that it spins many times in the toss, and so on, until we are "led to assume" that neither heads nor tails will be preferred. Now the crux of the whole matter lies in the mechanism by which we are led to this assumption. In the case of the penny no knowledge of physical constitution and of the complexity of tossing would ever be valid ground, in itself, for believing that the penny would come heads as often as tails. In the initial instance this fact must be observed (Edgeworth, 1884, p. 230; cf. Pearson, 1911, p. 146). Thereafter we may reason that other homogeneous, one-headed, well-tossed pennies will in the long run come heads fifty per cent of the time, and we may even go farther and reason that a homogeneous, six-faced, well-tossed die will in the long run come up equally often on every face. What we do is to assume probability on the grounds of observed frequency and its conditions.

Let us state the case in roughly syllogistic form:

The tossing of a penny gives, when indefinitely repeated, 50 per cent heads.

The event in which we are interested is a tossing of a penny.

The event in which we are interested gives, when indefinitely repeated, 50 per cent heads.

This leads us to predict what will happen to our particular penny if it is tossed repeatedly; and, what is more important, it defines for us the place of cogent reason and the sphere of ignorance. We must know what a penny does when tossed again and again, either directly from observation or indirectly by inference from other observations. The major premise must be based upon cogent reason and there is no limit to the exactitude of the knowledge. Ideally the major premise may be considered to be indubitably established. Moreover we must know that the event in which we are interested is the toss of a penny in the sense of that term in the major premise. Our minor premise, by "an exhaustive analysis of the physical laws underlying the structure of the complex of causes influencing the special event," must also be established and without limit of accuracy by cogent reason. Of what then do we remain ignorant? Of the manner in which the particular, in the middle term, is subsumed under the general. In other words we know that our event is such an event that if repeated it will yield in the long run heads and tails equally, but we do not know whether this particular event, unrepeated, will be heads or tails.

Of an equal distribution of this ignorance, of a law of insufficient reason, we are saying nothing. But have we attained to a statement of probability by saying of a single event that it is such that, if repeated, it would yield a given frequency of particular cases?

We can not within the narrow limits of this paper escape a

certain amount of dogmatism. We must read widely elsewhere on the logic of chance. This much may, however, be said. It is plain that the probability of the event can not inhere in the event. The coming throw is either heads or tails, not half heads and half tails. An event is not even conditioned upon its probability. If, from a box of one thousand tickets, numbered consecutively, one draws any ticket at all, one obtains that particular ticket in the face of odds of 999 to one against it. The rule of such a drawing is that the improbable always happens. If the probability does not lie in the event, it must lie outside it; and we may here assert that it lies in the series to which the event belongs. When we ascribe a probability to a particular event we are simply seeing that event in a series in which the event is repeated as it varies in some particular phase; or, to put it more picturesquely, we see a series of repeated events telescoped within the single instance. This is our habitual mode of dealing with ignorance of this kind. Unable to prophesy the particular event, but able to prophesy its frequency, we content ourselves with the general in view of our impotence to deal with the particular (cf. Venn, 1888, pp. 119–121; Urban, 1911).

(And we may note in passing that ignorance has not bred knowledge in this process. Where reason was insufficient, prediction failed. We never can tell what will turn up next. We may be able to tell what will happen one way often and another way seldom, but that tells us not at all what the next one is.)

We may seem far from the subject of mental measurement, but not without occasion, as we shall see. Let us turn now to the part played by the normal curve of error.

2. THE ROLE OF THE LAW OF ERROR

The normal law of error (Todhunter, 1865, pp. 71 f., 136, 191–193, 485, 552 f.; Laplace, 1812, pp. 275–277; Gauss, 1887, pp. 102 f., 207) has been both an inspiration and a limitation in statistical measurement. Its formulation by Laplace resulted during the last century in a wide extension and application of the law to numerous forms of scientific, social, and biological measurement; but Laplace is not responsible for all that occurred. There is a bit of magic in the formula. The law came to play the part of a first principle of nature, of an ideal, given *a priori*, to which nature seeks to conform. The mathematicians wrought slowly, but they wrought a god. Against such blind faith later statisticians have protested. They call the normal law a "fetish" and its *a priori* use a "superstition." Nevertheless the "superstition" still lingers and is mixed up with mental measurement. For this reason we are going to enquire, concerning the law of error, what real value it has for us today as a scientific tool.

In the days when the application of the theory of probabilities was largely confined to games of chance (Todhunter, 1865), the logical difficulties discussed above had little opportunity to make trouble. The fact is that the cards in a pack, the faces of a die, and the sides of a coin do in the long run and under the conditions of gaming turn up about equally often. At this level common sense takes care of the theorist. It makes no practical difference whether the reason he assigns for the equality of occurrence is his lack of sufficient reason for any other result or the empirical fact that these things do work in such a way. Nor does it matter if unwittingly he applies to the single event the frequency that belongs to the series and calls it the probability of the event, for he knows by common sense that probability is not prophecy and that he can not be assured of a realization of his expectations except in the long run. The fact is that the principle of insufficient reason and an indefinite conception of the nature of probability do, when applied to games and modified by such unconscious reservations, furnish safe ground for practice even though the logical implications are dubious.

Laplace and Gauss extended the theory of chance to the probability of errors (cf. Jevons, 1883, pp. 375–385). Errors are a new material and it is not plain at once that the old assumptions hold. So far as the development of the law of error goes, these mathematicians were content to make their assumptions and reason abstractly to the general conclusion. Laplace worked in the tradition of the old school. He developed the law of error as the limiting case of the binomial expansion when the number of terms is infinite. This process is equivalent to assuming that, in a given case, an error is the resultant of a large number of sources of error, every one of which may affect the result in one way or the opposite (or affect it or not affect it), *i.e.*, every source of error may, in the particular case, come up "heads" or "tails," as it were (Jevons, 1883, pp. 380 f.; Weld, 1916, pp. 41–56; Boring, 1917, pp. 465–467). Either we have, in practice, to assume the principle of insufficient reason which, applied to errors, does not have the sanction of common sense experience; or we have to achieve an analysis of the case into sources of error and determine for every one that its law is the law of the coin, a course which is ordinarily impossible. Gauss hypothesizes explicitly that positive and negative errors are equally likely, and derives the law on this basis. Logically his assumption is the same as Laplace's, but it is usually stated in a form that suggests a test. If positive and negative errors are equally likely, then the arithmetical mean is the most probable value. To test the validity of the assumption in practice, we have then only to select a series (of observations, say, which are subject to error) and see whether the arithmetical mean occurs most frequently.

Laplace's derivation suggests the nature of error, Gauss's its mode of manifestation. Both these famous mathematicians were arguing from premise to conclusion when they derived the law of error, and science remains in their debt. We have no complaint to make until we find the law applied without an effort to establish the premises in the particular case. *The law will not work for errors, unless errors fulfill its conditions.*

Gauss (1887, pp. 4, 92–94, 129, 139–141) was clear about his assumptions, but he did not hesitate to apply the law to astronomical errors of observation. Some of his followers, it seems, who had not witnessed the birth of the law, were less concerned in its application than with its parentage. In theory of measurement the law was often accepted on its face value, in spite of the fact that a constantly increasing list of exceptions to it was being made out. In such cases the argument for the law seems to have been the practical one that it gave but little trouble in actual use. Thus Urban (1910a, p. 242) recently wrote:

> We are confronted by the shocking situation that a proposition is triumphantly borne out by an immense indirect experience and that it can be proved neither by mathematical deduction nor by direct experience.

Urban (1910a, pp. 240–244), however, did attempt to prove it by showing, under the conditions of the psychophysical experiment, that positive and negative errors of observation, measured from the point of subjective equality, are equal. Faith in the principle was established, however, long before psychophysics furnished this justification.

It is upon Quetelet (1835; 1846; cf. Lexis, 1877, p. 11; Kaufmann, 1913, pp. 12, 163), it seems, that we must fix the responsibility for the uncritical extension of the normal law to various human measures other than errors. In making a man, he holds, nature aims at an ideal and the differences between men represent her degrees of error (Quetelet, 1846, pp. 91–96; cf. Kaufmann, 1913, pp. 110–112). Quetelet refers for evidence to the measurement of circumferences of the chests of 5,738 Scotch soldiers and of the heights of 100,000 French conscripts. His position would be all very well were Quetelet content with supporting his hypothesis by this evidence. He seeks, however, to make it work both ways. He suggests that the deviation of the curve for the French conscripts from the normal law is due to fraudulent rejection for military service.

> This . . . law of continuity enables us to recognize a more remarkable fact: we might suspect it, but here we find it proved,—it is that the number of men rejected for deficiency in height is much exaggerated. Not only can we prove this, but we can determine the extent of the fraud. The official documents would make it appear that, of 100,000

men, 28,620 are of less height than 5 feet 2 inches: calculation gives only 26,345. Is it not a fair presumption, that the 2,275 men who constitute the difference of these numbers have been fraudulently rejected? (Quetelet, 1846, pp. 97 f.)

Of course it is not a fair presumption, since the law depends on the official documents for confirmation. Nevertheless, while admitting the dependence of the law on experience, Quetelet proceeds in numerous cases to analyze experience by means of it. Such a double-edged sword is a peculiarly effective weapon, and it is no wonder that subsequent investigators were tempted to use it in spite of the necessary rules of scientific warfare.

Galton (1869, pp. 26–36) in the *Hereditary Genius* applied the normal law to mental differences and, using it *a priori*, worked from frequencies of natural ability to a scale of equal intervals of ability. He frankly accepted "the very curious law of 'deviation from an average' " from Quetelet, showed that certain mental capacities obeyed the law approximately, and then argued from the law to "grades of natural ability, separated by equal intervals."

The English school of biometricians, which derives directly from Galton, has furthered the *a priori* use of the normal law that obtains today in much biometric and mental measurement (cf., *e.g.*, Trabue, 1916, pp. 29–60). There is an early study by Pearson that illustrates the point (Pearson, 1894; Weldon, 1893). Weldon had measured the lengths and breadths of two large samplings of crabs: one set from Naples and one from Plymouth. The Plymouth batch gave symmetrical distributions, but the frequency curve for the breadths of the Naples batch was skewed. Pearson, by an elaborate mathematical treatment, analyzed the skew curve into the sum of two normal curves, the averages of which did not coincide, and Weldon accepted this result as evidence of "dimorphism." Pearson then applied his method to a symmetrical curve for the Plymouth crabs and found that there was no real solution. He assumed, therefore, that these data were "homogeneous." Further he laid down the general rule that some such analysis must be attempted upon every apparently normal curve before a conclusion can be reached as to the homogeneity of the data. If the actual results can be better represented by the sum of two normal curves than by any single normal curve, then there is heterogeneity. Even curves that approximate the normal very closely must be tested, for they may yield to analysis.

Thus Pearson showed that the distribution of shots at a target, given by Merriman (1884, p. 14), is best represented by the sum of two normal curves. The gun must be thought of as aiming, not at the sixth band of the target as Merriman supposed, but at the fifth and seventh bands (explainable perhaps by a change of sighting during mid-firing). Here then, we find no attempt at all to seek empirical support for the normal law. The crabs were obtained in a single selection and the shots were made in a single experiment, and each set appears, even after it is charted in a graph, as if all the measures belonged together. But we apply the criterion of the normal law and we find the crabs dimorphic and the gun double-sighted (but cf. Pearson, 1895, pp. 344 f.).

Now the very remarkable thing about this easy acceptance of the law of error as the rule of nature is that it has been done all along in spite of very much better available information. Let us get some idea of what has been said.

We saw that Laplace's assumptions were implicit in his method and Gauss' explicit in his text. We had no quarrel with them, but we blamed Quetelet. Did Quetelet's thesis pass, then, quite unchallenged? No, for in the notes to the *Letters* he printed three letters from Bravais (Quetelet, 1846, pp. 286–295; cf. Venn, 1887), who presented figures on the skew distribution of barometric pressures, discussed various reasons for departures from the normal law, and said in brief:

> I think that generally every partial and distinct cause of error gives place to a curve of possibility of errors (or, if preferred, of differences about the mean), which may have any form whatever,—a curve which

we may either be able or unable to discover, and which in the first case may be determined by consideration *a priori* on the peculiar nature of this cause, or may be determined *a posteriori* by observations on the isolated condition of other concomitant causes of error. (Quetelet, 1846, p. 290.)

In introducing the letters from Bravais, Quetelet (1846, p. 286) remarked:

In this memoir I only had in view the examination of the case in which accidental causes have had no tendency to act in one direction more than another.

We have already shown that Quetelet actually established the law by the data and then corrected the data by the law.

In 1869 Galton accepted the law of deviation from an average as applicable to mental ability, but in 1879 he was ready to insist on exceptions (Galton, 1879; McAlister, 1879):

My purpose is to show that the assumption which lies at the basis of the well-known law of "Frequency of Error" . . . is incorrect in many groups of vital and social phenomena, although that law has been applied to them by statisticians with partial success and corresponding convenience. . . .

The assumption to which I refer is, that errors in excess or deficiency of the truth are equally probable; or conversely, that if two fallible measurements have been made of the same object, their arithmetical mean is more likely to be the true measurement than any other quantity that can be named. . . .

Suppose we endeavor to match a tint: Fechner's law, in its approximative and simplest form of sensation=log stimulus, tells us that a series of tints, in which the quantities of white scattered on a black ground are as 1, 2, 4, 8, 16, 32, &c., will appear to the eye to be separated by equal intervals of tint. Therefore, in matching a grey that contains 8 portions of white, we are just as likely to err by selecting one that has 16 portions as one that has 4 portions. In the first case there would be an error in excess, of 8; in the second there would be an error in deficiency, of 4. Therefore, an error of the same magnitude in excess or in deficiency is not equally probable.

Thus Galton argues that the geometric mean is the most probable value with sensory material or data that follow a similar law. The distribution curve in such cases would be markedly skew.

We remarked that Pearson in 1894 gave evidence of being influenced by the sanctity of the normal law. His faith was not great for he noted its limitations in 1895 (Pearson, 1895, pp. 344 f.). In 1900 the faith was gone (Pearson, 1900, p. 173).

It appears to me that, if the earlier writers on probability had not proceeded so entirely from the mathematical standpoint, but had endeavored first to classify experience in deviations from the average, and then to obtain some measure of the actual goodness of fit provided by the normal curve, that curve would never have obtained its present position in the theory of errors. Even today there are those who regard it as a sort of fetish; and while admitting it to be at fault as a means of generally describing the distribution of variation of a quantity x from its mean, assert that there must be some unknown quantity z of which x is an unknown function, and that z really obeys the normal law! This might be reasonable if there were but a few exceptions to this normal law of error; but the difficulty is to find even the few variables which obey it, and these few are not usually cited as illustrations by the writers on the subject.

Pearson (1895; 1901; 1905) in developing a system of skew curves whereby he seeks to adjust theory to nature has performed great scientific service in combatting the superstition of the normal law. The paper of 1894 suffered on account of its occasion, *viz.*, the problem of dimorphism in Weldon's crabs. But not all investigators have avoided initial error; and presently we must return again to Pearson.

These quotations from Galton and Pearson suggest a reason why the normal curve should be of exceptional occurrence. If "log stimulus" gives a normal curve, says Galton, then "stimulus" will not. If x does not give a normal curve, some persons, says Pearson, assert that z, of which x is a function, does follow the law. Suppose then that nature does conform to the normal law; we shall not in practice be fortunate enough to obtain normal curves of distribution unless we have chanced to use nature's own unit of measurement, or some unit directly proportional to it. Bertrand (1889, pp. 180 f.) pointed this out long ago.

La règle des moyennes, il importe d'insister sur ce point, n'est ni démontrée ni exacte. S'il était admis que la moyenne entre plusieurs mesures fût toujours la valeur la plus probable, il en résulterait des contradictions. Quand on mesure une grandeur, on mesure, par cela même, toutes les fonctions de cete grandeur, son carré par exemple, ou le logarithme du nombre qui la représente. Pourquoi la valeur la plus probable du carré ne serait-elle pas la moyenne des valeurs obtenues pour le carré, et la valeur probable du logarithme, la moyenne des logarithmes? . . .

Il ne faut pas, pour écarter l'objection, faire une distinction entre les grandeurs directement mesurées et celles qui résultent d'un calcul. Un mécanicien pourrait, bien aisément, annexer à une balance une aiguille marquant le carré ou le logarithme du poids. Ce carré ou ce logarithme deviendrait alors la grandeur mesurée. Le postulatum admis dans un cas devient donc impossible dans les autres.

A better example would be the distribution in size of the cubical crystals of common salt. In a sample of such crystals we might measure size by the height of the cube or by its weight. Since the latter measure should be approximately proportional to the cube of the former, it is plain that the normal law could not hold in both cases. Now, if nature seeks to conform to the normal law, does she prefer to conform in lengths or in volumes or, perhaps, in some other more "natural" unit? At least, if man would seek the law of nature, he must have cogent reason for his choice of measures. He cannot (as the behaviorist would agree!) tell what nature is doing unless he knows what nature is trying to do.

We have been speaking of France and England, but the reaction against the "Gaussian dogma" was more explicit in Germany. In 1877 Lexis published a *Theorie der Massenerscheinungen* in which frequency distributions were dealt with as normal, subnormal, or supernormal (Lexis, 1877, esp. pp. 34–36). The emphasis was thus shifted from the normal distribution to normal deviations from the normal distribution. The "Lexian ratio" measures this deviation (see Fisher, 1915, pp. 124–126). This point of view has met with acceptance among German and Scandinavian actuarial statisticians, and forms, for example, the basis of Czuber's (1910, vol. II, pp. 34–78) *Wahrscheinlichkeitsrechnung*. We have already seen that von Kries in 1886 did not include among valid logical principles the law of insufficient reason. He was inclined to believe, however, that in many cases the "Gaussian law" was realized (von Kries, 1886, pp. 226–228), and he cites in support Bessel's observations, which Urban refers to as an example of asymmetry (von Kries, 1886, p. 241).

Westergaard (1890, pp. 10–83) sums up the empirical case. He brings together the experiments on the drawing of balls and the like, and shows that with increasing number of cases the relative frequencies lie within a decreasing *Spielraum* and thus in a sense approach the expected frequencies. He then goes on to show that the frequencies of social statistics behave in a manner similar to the frequencies of the experiments on "chance." He is not so much interested in the applicability of the normal law as he is in the facts. The appeal to facts is, however, always a protest against theory which is given *a priori*.

After all, the facts are the scientific business. We have traced what seemed to be a growing realization of the logical inadequacies of a theory, but have we perhaps not been witnessing a deepening appreciation of the facts? When anthropometric measurements were first being made, there stood out the fundamental fact of the massing of cases about the average, the rapid falling off of more extreme frequencies, and the extreme rarity of widely divergent cases. To this extent the normal law was the fact. But as interest centered upon the details, the inadequacies of so simple a generalization became apparent. There was effort enough at reconciliation but, in general, science kept to the facts, and a more flexible system of representations came into use.

There is a pretty instance of the inadequacy of the normal law to scientific description in a research of Pearl's (1907, esp. pp. 90 f.). Pearl studied statistically the number of leaves in a whorl in Ceratophyllum. He found that the distributions for number of leaves were skewed one way at the proximal end of the main stem or of a branch, the other way at the distal end, and that the form of the distribution passed through symmetry somewhere between the two ends. Thus he writes:

The phenomenon of skew variation stands forth in this case, free of doubtful interpretation through selection or any similar factor, clearly and definitely as a phenomenon of growth. In the face of facts of this kind it is difficult to understand how anyone can be so firmly convinced of the *Allgemeingültigkeit* of the normal or Gaussian law, as some biologists still are . . . Skewness in variation is a very real biological phenomenon, which may be changed and modified, not only in degree, but in direction, by various biological factors like growth, as, for example, in the present case.

In other words, if nature is aiming to make something follow the normal law, then, as the stem of Ceratophyllum grows, she changes continuously that something which is to fit the law. The real problem of scientific description is an account of nature's changing. To assume the normal law in such a case would be to shut one's eyes to the fact.

Here we may leave the question of the *a priori* nature of the normal law. There is, after all, no magic in it. It gives us back always what we put into it. If we know from experience what nature is up to, as we do with the coin, then we can proceed upon cogent reasons to apply the law and we get results. If we do not know, we must appeal to nature and see. We have then no reason to expect that we are going to find the law before the appeal is made, whereas we have considerable reason to expect not to find it, since the form of distribution depends on the unit of measurement and we have arbitrarily chosen one of a possible infinite number of units. When we do go to nature we find all degrees of resemblance to the law and divergence from it, and we may even find that the degree of divergence from the normal becomes the significant fact of our observation.

3. THE RELATION BETWEEN THE UNIT OF MEASUREMENT AND THE FORM OF DISTRIBUTION

We have seen that if we alter the unit of measurement we alter the form of the frequency distribution, and that if the change is in accordance with any function other than direct proportionality we get alterations of the skewness of the curve.

Bertrand made the point with especial clearness, and it is strange that a relation so obvious should have received so little attention.

Williams (1918; see also Boring, 1918) recently ran upon the difficulty when experimentally he obtained psychometric functions for memory. He expressed the frequencies for recall of a material as a function of the number of repetitions of the material but he felt, for certain cogent reasons that the student of memory will appreciate, that the repetition was not a satisfactory unit in terms of which to work. The psychophysical effect of an early repetition is presumably greater than that of a late one and Williams would have liked a more truly mnemonic unit. If he could have taken the normal curve *a priori* as the necessary function, he could have adjusted his results to it and have discovered a mnemonic unit that was some particular function of the number of repetitions. Such a relationship would have provided a knowledge of the effectiveness of successive repetitions and would have produced a method for use with other mnemonic measures. All measures eventually could have been interrelated, and a great advance made in the psychophysics of memory. Unfortunately, however, there was no justification for assuming the normal law and, with both law and psychophysical unit unknown, Williams, as he realized, was placed in the dilemma of being able to reason from neither to the other. The way out, of course, was to give up the impossible, and to stick to the observed facts, leaving the frequencies to stand as a function of the number of repetitions.

Trabue (1916, pp. 29–60), in attempting to establish a language scale "with equal distances between steps," ran into the same difficulty. His material—sentences to be completed by the Ebbinghaus method—had no quantitative aspect except the number of arbitrarily chosen completion-tasks that could be successfully accomplished. He chose, therefore, to assume the normal law and to calibrate his material by reference to it, taking the probable error as the unit. (Trabue, 1916, pp. 30–32, 54–56; Miner, 1918, pp. 252–254). His hint of a cogent reason back of the normal law stands quite unsupported (Trabue, 1916, p. 31). Now the language scales presumably do "work"; but if they do, it must be for the reason that this form of measurement, pretending to nothing more accurate than Quetelet achieved, counts his degree of rigor successful.

These two papers are but examples of how the problem of the unit arises in very different fields of mental measurement and how their solution is balked by an inability to assume in advance some distributive function like the normal law (cf., *e.g.*, Pearson, 1906; Miner, 1918, pp. 254–276). In such cases the limitation is pretty clear, for we have to make an assumption and it takes but little argument to show that an assumption in itself can not be fact.

There is, however, a more subtle way in which the will to believe in the normal law gets in its work. Suppose we give up assumption and go to experience, in order to study a special group of related phenomena; and suppose we find that very many of these phenomena, as we measure them, are distributed every one in accordance with the normal law? May we not conclude by analogy that the same law applies to other phenomena? If a penny comes heads and tails equally often, will not a silver dollar? If stature follows the normal law, what about length of forearm?

The answer is that it all depends on how much one knows of the nature of the case. One may reason from the penny to the dollar, if one knows—inductively, from experience—that homogeneity and shape in the penny are the attributes that condition the law, whereas size, chemical constitution, color, etc., are irrelevant. (Even so one may make a mistake; a magnetized steel disk in a magnetic field might give unexpected frequencies.) To reason from stature to length of forearm, however, requires that we know that the size of the forearm is conditioned in the same way as is the total length of the body. It is not enough to know that both forearm and stature depend on the same factors; we must know that they depend upon them in the same way, that is to say, we must know that we are dealing with the same scale of growth. If the forearm were to vary as the square of x and stature as the cube of x, then prediction that the distribution of the one would be like the distribution of the other would be doomed to disappointment. With the coins, we know that the scales are comparable; each is expressed in percentage of heads. But in biological and psychological phenomena we can scarcely hope for any such certain analysis of the essential conditions.

Apparently then sometimes we may generalize and sometimes not. Can we make out a list of the classes of phenomena to which it is safe to say that the law applies? At least we may try. And we shall have to consider five classes.

1. In the first place there are the *Glückspiele*—coin tossing, card drawing, dice throwing, roulette, and the persistent urn or bag with the red and white balls inside—that introduces all students to the theory of probabilities. In such cases the presumption for the validity of the law is stronger than anywhere else. It seems that the red and white balls ordinarily do come out of the bag about equally often if they exist in equal quantities inside. Westergaard in 10,000 drawings got 5,011 white balls. Yet Pearson found that Weldon's 26,306 throws of dice exhibited "a bias toward the higher points." He calculated that the chances of 5 or 6 coming up on these dice exactly one third of the time were less than two in 100,000, but that the chances of 5 or 6 coming up .3377 of the time were as great as two in 16. "Oh well," we say, "you could not expect any real dice to be exactly homogeneous. There is not much difference between .3377 and ⅓." No, and in any real experiment ideal conditions are never exactly realized. All experimental observation is only as accurate as the control of the conditions of observation. The tendency with Pearson's method is to conclude from particular cases against a generality by a method more precise than the precision of the observed cases allows. In general the *Glückspiele* seem to follow the law as well as the faulty conditions of their construction and operation permit (see Westergaard, 1890, pp. 21–38; Pearson,

1897, vol. I, pp. 11–25, 44–62; 1900, pp. 167–169; Fisher, 1915, pp. 127–145).

2. It is generally maintained that the occurrence of digits in the expansion of an incommensurable number like *pi, epsilon,* $\sqrt{2}$, log 7, etc., follows the normal law, and that all digits in the long run occur equally often. Here the law of insufficient reason is peculiarly tempting. If there is no relation at all between the intrinsic properties of a circle and the number of fingers on the two human hands which determined the decimal system, then why should not all digits turn up equally often in the expansion of *pi?* There is no reason why they *should* not. The *fact* is that in the first 707 digits of the decimal of *pi* the sevens occur only three fourths as often as they should, although the other digits do better by the law (Shanks, 1873, p. 319). This case, however, is but a single one, and, as Venn (1888, pp. 111–118, 247 f.) points out, the chances of one digit's deviating from equality as much as do the sevens is one in four. Edgeworth (1905, pp. 128–130) found that there was one chance in ten that the first 1,800 digits of the expansion of the fraction 1/1861 were following the law of chance. Both he and Venn are convinced, however, that the rule of the coin is applicable to such series of digits, and indeed such is the presumption though the generality is here less well established than for games of chance (cf. Newcomb, 1881).

3. In 1904, long after the publication of his first papers on skew variation in homogeneous material, Pearson made the following statement:

[Suppose] we assume a certain distribution of frequency for the character in human populations. This distribution of frequency is given by the Gauss-Laplacian normal curve of deviations from the mean. . . . Now the problem before us is the following one:—Is this assumption legitimate? It certainly is not true for organs and characters in *all* types of life. But it really does describe in a most remarkable manner the distribution of most characters in mankind . . . I should be the last to assert that no human characters can be found that do not diverge sensibly from this Gaussian distribution. But I believe they are few, and that for practical purposes we may with nearly absolute safety assume it as a first approximation to the actual state of affairs. (Pearson, 1904, pp. 142 f.)

Everything hinges here on the word "approximation." The case is very different from that of the coin or of the incommensurable number. We do not know anything about the units with which we are working except that they are the units with which we are working. When we change from the penny to the dollar we keep the same scale, one of proportions of heads in a twofold universe; when we change from pi to $\sqrt{2}$ we also keep the same scale, one of proportions of digits in a tenfold universe, but when we change from stature to the forearm we have no guarantee that the inch means the same thing biologically. And we must use a biological unit, if we are to bind our class together by a biological concept, if we are to predicate the normal law of all *human* characters. That the form of distribution is a function of the unit is unescapable. What we need to know, and what we do not know, is whether the differences that would occur with biologically reasonable variation of the biological unit from the physical unit are small enough to be included within the "approximation." A certain amount of alteration of the scale of measurement still leaves a sensibly normal curve. Have we any cogent grounds for assuming "with nearly absolute safety" that "the actual state of affairs" is not enough differently conditioned from those that we know about as to render it widely divergent from the normal law? This is a reasonable question, and within approximate limits it may be answerable. Certainly we may not generalize with Pearson on any other basis, and certainly Pearson neglects to provide this basis.

4. On such an insecure structure does Pearson attempt to build further. If the physical is normal, why not the mental?

I put the problem to myself as follows:—Assume the fundamental laws of distribution which we know to hold for the physical characters in man, and see whither they lead us when applied to the psychical characteristics. They must: (a) Give us totally discordant results. If so, we shall conclude that these laws have no application to the mental and moral attributes. Or, (b) Give us accordant results. If so, we may go a stage further and ask how these results compare with those for the inheritance of physical characters. (Pearson, 1904, p. 147; 1906, pp. 105–107.)

(The paper is on inheritance.) The assumption of the normal law gives results for the mental characteristics that look like the results for physical characters. Hence we may go ahead with our correlations in each case to indicate the degree of inheritance. The assumption accomplishes little beyond providing the scale for the printed graphs of intelligence; but that was in 1904.

In 1914 we find Pearson still arguing for a normal distribution of intelligence, and the occasions for his argument are certain empirical results which did not show a good agreement with the "Gaussian" law (Pearson and Jaederholm, 1914, pp. 28–36, 46 f.; Pearson, 1914). He is presenting the results of the application of the Jaederholm form of the Binet scale to school children of Stockholm. The samples are very small (261 normal and 301 defective children). There is one chance in 60 that the normal children give but a random deviation from a properly "Gaussian" distribution; there is one chance in 20 that the normal children plus an ideal fraction of the defective children are properly distributed in the "Gaussian" manner. Eight-year-old children taken alone, however, do show an even chance for the applicability of the "Gaussian" law. This is slim evidence, but it appears that it is not yet time to declare the Gaussian image a false god:

There is absolutely no reason why the Gaussian curve should be dogmatically asserted to apply to frequency-distributions of intelligence . . . Still there are *a priori* suggestions that it should be tried. In the first place it does describe with a great degree of accuracy most physical measurements in man, and secondly, the Biometric school has found that it gives good results for many measures of intelligence. It is the view of the psychological joint-author of this paper that its comparative failure as applied to the present data lies rather in faults of the tests applied or in the method of applying them than in the non-Gaussian character of intelligence when adequately measured. (Pearson and Jaederholm, 1914, p. 46.)

This quotation is as near a confession of what the Biometric School is trying to do as we are likely to get. It is frankly seeking always to see Gauss in nature. Its excuse in the case of mental phenomena for a prejudice in favor of this one of an infinity of possible distributions is that the Gaussian curve "does describe most physical measurements in man," and that "it gives good results for many measures of intelligence. The physical agreements, however, are approximate, as we have seen, and the facts with respect to intelligence are questioned (Miner, 1918, pp. 267–279). The real difficulty comes, however, in the grounds for analogy. The implication is that we may reason from the physical to the mental because, in this case, both are "human," and that we may reason from one test to another because both are tests "of intelligence." Now we have no distributions of "humanness," but only of measurements of human characters; and we have no distributions of intelligence, but only of particular measurements of intelligence (Miner, 1918, p. 255). Moreover, in every case the measure is arbitrarily chosen; and it is not even strictly a measure, in the sense of being the sum of equal units, unless we make it so on *a priori* grounds. In an intelligence test, for example, we have no notion whether the difference between 99 and 100 points is the same difference in intelligence as the difference between 9 and 10 points, unless we are ready to define intelligence arbitrarily as the ability to achieve points in that particular test (Pearson and Jaederholm, 1914, pp. 36–38; Miner, 1918, pp. 260–262). Now if we define intelligence with respect to one test, we can not assert *a priori* that any other test is a measure of intelligence, and should therefore show the same distribution. *A posteriori* we may show by correlation that a second test measures an ability similar to intelligence as defined by the first test, but in such a process we demonstrate empirically the similarity of distribution. There is no valid reason for expecting normality in one intelligence test because it has been found in another; and the same reasoning applies to the argument from the physical to the mental (Pearson, 1914, pp. 3 f.).

We are very far, then, from a general conclusion that intelligence, a mental capacity comprehensible apart from the particular instrument by which it is tested, is normally distributed. Still farther are we from stating that mental abilities, whatever their nature, follow the normal law.

5. We have to investigate one more class of phenomena, the psychophysical judgments. In this case no claim for generality has been presented, but the trend of the facts bespeaks attention. Urban (1910a, pp. 257–259; 1909b, esp. pp. 224 f.; 1910b; Keller, 1907) found that the phi-function of gamma is a good hypothesis for the psychometric function in lifted weights and in certain acoumetric experiments. Now the phi-function of gamma is simply the integral form of the normal curve. To say that the phi-function of gamma is the psychometric function is equivalent to saying that the dispositional variations of the psychophysical organism, when measured in a scale of units proportional to the scale in which the stimulus is measured, follow the normal law. If the lifted weights are measured in grams and the psychometric function approximates the phi-function of gamma, then the organism varies in the amount of its disposition for judging "heavier" or "lighter" according to normal law, provided always that the amount of this disposition is measured in grams. This relationship is scarcely obvious and the reader may need to read elsewhere (Boring, 1917, pp. 465–467), before he can accept it. The essential thing to understand is that the applicability of the phi-function of gamma means that the organism is varying somehow in accordance with the normal law, but that the normality of its variation is as much a function of the unit in which the variation is measured as it is in any of the other cases which we have considered.

Now can we generalize? Can we ever say that all psychophysical judgments tend to obey the normal law? Urban makes no such attempt; rather is he against theorizing and for description. "The nature of the dependence," he writes, "is not known and cannot possibly be deduced by any considerations *a priori*" (Urban,

1910a, p. 247); and he refers us for the function to "the results of observation." This, to the scientist, is a refreshing return to facts from the realm of logic and mathematics; but is not final. Something can be said for generalization.

Unfortunately for ease of exposition, there are two kinds of psychophysics. In the one kind stimuli are presented and the observer reports upon the sense impressions. In the case of the stimulus limen, he simply reports sensation or its absence. He is making a brief introspection. In the case of the differential limen he makes a judgment upon the relative degrees of the two sensations, but the judgment is actually little more than a comparative description; the observer may be said to be introspecting here too (cf. George, 1917). In the other kind of psychophysics the observer's attention is directed upon the stimulus and not upon his own mental processes. In no sense does he introspect. Always he is making judgments of the stimulus. In introspective psychology this attitude is called the "stimulus error," but in psychophysics it may be in place. Urban's (1913a; 1913b, p. 274; 1908, pp. 5, 14; 1909a, pp. 264 f.; 1910a, p. 229) experiments are of this kind, as has been much other psychophysical work. There is reason to believe, however, that psychology will profit more in the long run by work performed under the first attitude described.

In the case of the "introspective" psychophysics we are not to expect a generalization because everything depends on the unit. Were the psychometric function to approximate the phi-function of gamma ten times, there would be no reason to expect it at the eleventh. Suppose the eleventh case were the differential limen for auditory intensity with the Fechner sound pendulum as the instrument. Will the normal law hold? Perhaps when we use as the unit $\sin^2 (theta/2)$. If so, it will not hold if we use *theta* as the unit. If it holds for neither, it may hold for some other function of *theta*. The reports upon sensations depend upon *theta* and the momentary disposition of the organism, but in no way upon the scale of units chosen. It is mere luck if the normal law applies. But whatever luck we get is good luck, for the psychometric function gives us the law of the dependence of dispositional variation upon the scale of measurement which we have chosen. A little knowledge of sensory mechanisms is worth the loss of a generality.

When the psychophysical judgments are directed upon the stimulus it may be that we can generalize, for now the scale and the judgment are related. With the sound pendulum we might be asked to judge the height of the fall, which is measured by $\sin^2 (theta/2)$, or we might be asked to judge the angle. In the two cases we would be judging entirely different things, and it is quite possible that the normal law might apply in each. If we found that it applied in a large number of cases, then we might generalize by saying that errors in the judgment of a stimulus, that is to say, errors of observation, are distributed normally. This conclusion, indeed, is Urban's (1910a, p. 243): "We thus obtain the remarkable result that the foundations of the theory of the errors of observation are found in the theory of psychophysical measurement." In other words we would demonstrate psychophysically Gauss' original assumption that positive and negative errors are equally likely.

If there is any general answer to the question: When can we generalize? it is this. We may expect the normal law to hold within an entire class of phenomena, when it holds for a number of cases within the class, provided always that all variations of members of the class are capable of being expressed as variations of some common denominator. In other words, we must be able to see the same thing varying in different situations. With the penny and the dollar, the law holds for the turning up of heads. The things that make the penny different from the dollar, we know to be irrelevant. In lifted weights and acoumetry we may know, by a control of attitude, that we are studying, not kinaesthesis and auditory sensation, but errors of observation. If Urban did know this, then he was supplied with the only possible ground for expecting the one result on the basis of the other.

4. THE LOGICAL POSSIBILITIES
(CONCLUSION)

At last we are ready to take account of stock! There are four logical possibilities, but the circumstances of the case are such that it appears unlikely that the actual mental measurement can make much use of more than one. Let us see.

1. In the first place, there is the possibility of determining *a priori* the form of distribution. This course, applied to the normal law, is popular, but it is usually without sanction. In quantitative psychology we should resist it. We may not assume the normal law in an interpretative study except upon valid grounds. We have seen that the law of insufficient reason furnishes no such grounds. Knowledge simply does not come out of ignorance. The only scientific grounds that are presumptive of the normal law are an intimate knowledge of the constitution of the particular case and of the function that frequencies of occurrence are of that constitution. Such a function comes in science from experience, and, whenever it is thoroughly understood, from experiment. On such cogent grounds we may conclude *a priori* to the normal law or some other form of distribution, and we are following such a logical process in the few cases where we find it legitimate to generalize about the form of distribution for a given class of phenomena.

Two corollaries follow.

(a) If we knew that the normal law had to hold in a particular case, then we could experiment with an arbitrarily chosen unit and determine, by working from the law, the function that the "true" psychological unit, which is following the law, is of the arbitrary unit of the experiment. Any such hope, however, is bound to be illusory, for a knowledge of the constitution of the case involves *a priori* the knowledge of this unit. We may say that, if the dollar is like the penny, we shall get 50 per cent heads; but we can not reverse the argument and say that, because we get 50 per cent heads, the dollar is like the penny.

(b) There is at present very little prospect in the field of mental measurement that our knowledge of the psychological constitution of a mental function or process will be sufficient to enable us to begin work upon a problem with the assurance that the resulting distributions must be normal. There is a bare hint of an exception that awaits verification in the psychometric functions of errors of observation. But the evidence indicates that instances, where there are cogent reasons for assuming the normal law in advance of empirical determination, will be extremely rare for a long time to come.

2. We may begin in mental measurement with the psychological unit, for if we can not determine the unit from the distribution, we may, nevertheless, determine the distribution from the unit. Such, in fact, is the necessary scientific order. The great difficulty is, as we have just pointed out, to find anything that we may properly call a psychological unit. The sense-distance is such a unit. It is a unit of measurement that is mental *per se* (cf. Titchener, 1905, pp. xix–xxxvii). Most of the sensory work in psychology, however, has had to do with the determination of limens and has not made use of the mental unit at hand. The extensive psychophysics of memory has not achieved a psychological unit, nor have the other departments of the psychology of process. In the psychology of capacity or function the case is worse. For example, with intelligence, which is the mental capacity most often measured, we have seen that, not only is there no attempt to make equal increments on an intelligence scale correspond to equal increments of intelligence, but also that the concept of intelligence is so vague that any such accurate quantitative relationship is in practice almost meaningless. We are not, however, at our rope's end.

3. If a psychological unit is not to be achieved we may use a "physical" unit, that is to say, some arbitrarily chosen aspect of an arbitrary scale of measurement. Such units are the year (mental age), the second (mental tests where time is the measure), the item or task (where the number of points is the number

of unit tasks completed, *e.g.*, the U.S. Army intelligence tests), the gram (lifted weights), the syllable (memory experiments), and so on. Every such unit is arbitrary. There is no evidence that equal increments of its scale correspond to equal increments of the psychological entity measured. When we define intelligence, in order to gain definiteness of conception, as ability in some particular test, we are simply substituting a "physical" unit for the ideal but unachievable psychological unit. Now the application of a unit that is not psychological to a quantity that is psychological does not yield a measure of the quantity. It will place the quantity in a given position upon the arbitrary scale and will determine the rank-orders of a number of quantities so placed, but the assumption that rank-orders tell the amount of a given quantity, or, if the zero be unknown, of a given increment, is, of course, unwarranted.

There is one case, of frequent occurrence in the behaviorism of mental tests, where the "physical" and psychological units seem to become identical. Suppose we are studying the learning of typewriting and express our results in the number of words written per minute. Do not words-per-minute truly measure ability in typewriting? Here we are involved in a question of point of view. Words-per-minute measure the product of typewriting. They may perhaps be said to measure ability in typewriting from the point of view of the employer of a stenographic force; they are the ability of his office force over against a given job. A behavioristic psychology that identified behavior with mere product, without any reference at all to the conditions of the product, might take the point of view of the employer; but such a psychology would achieve only a physics, or more likely a common sense, of typewriting. Any definition of behavior as *response to a situation* (cf. Holt, 1916, esp. pp. 153–155) brings in the behaving organism and changes the ground. We can not say that words-per-minute truly measure the behavior of the psychophysical organism or its response to the situation. Does an increment of ten words per minutes mean the same change in ability or in behavior or in response when added to an ability of 50 words per minute as when added to an ability of 100 words per minute? To the employer, yes; but not to the psychologist, or, presumably, to the organism. It is indeed an heroic measure, when we can not make the unit psychological, to attempt to a-psychologize psychology.

4. We are left then with the rank-orders of our psychological quantities, given by reference to a fixed but arbitrary extrapsychological scale; and it is with these rank-orders that we must deal. We are not yet ready for much psychological measurement in the strict sense. It is true that psychophysics may yield a unit and also true that ordinarily it does not. The sense-distance has had only a limited use, and we do not yet know that the stimulus-distance (for it is upon stimulus-distances that the psychometric functions of errors of observation are founded) constitutes a true unit in a behavioristic psychophysics. The case, however, is not so bad as it seems at first. There is nothing new in the contention that mental measurement is impossible (cf. Klemm, 1914, pp. 150–155, 232–267), whereas now we do gain the assurance that rank-orders at least are validly demonstrable. And there is a great deal that can be done with rank-orders. We can deal with frequencies, medians, and quartiles. For example, it is considerable to know of two groups that the lower quartile of the ranks in one overlaps and is practically coincident with the upper quartile of the other. What we must remember, however, is that we are dealing with the statistics of medians, quartiles, contingencies, and correlation ratios; not with the statistics of averages, standard deviations, coefficients of correlation, and linear regressions. All those statistical constants, that imply a scale of equivalent units, violate in use the conditions of the case and lead to a precision of result that is an artifact. The serial constants, that do not presuppose a unit, yield less intricate resultants, but they present a rougher picture that represents truly the rough material which they describe (cf. West, 1918, p. 94).

The initial error in the application of the theory of probabilities was the assumption of the law of insufficient reason. It was wrongly supposed that knowledge could somehow be wrought out of ignorance. This very error, however, has never been routed. It has gone on, multiplying mischief. The substitute for insufficient reason is cogent reason. The more we know of the intimate nature of the entity with which we are dealing the more accurate and complete can our descriptions become. But, if in psychology we must deal—and it seems we must—with abilities, capacities, dispositions, and tendencies, the nature of which we cannot accurately define, then it is senseless to seek in the logical process of mathematical elaboration a psychologically significant precision that was not present in the psychological setting of the problem. Just as ignorance will not breed knowledge, so inaccuracy of definition will never yield precision of result.

References

Bertrand, Joseph. *Calcul des probabilités*. Paris: Gauthier-Villars, 1889.

Boole, George. *An Investigation of the Laws of Thought*. London: Macmillan, 1854.

Boring, E. G. A chart of the psychometric function. *American Journal of Psychology*, 1917, vol. 28, 465–470.

Boring, E. G. The "mnemometric function" and the memory-methods. *Psychological Bulletin*, 1918, vol. 15, 32 f. (Abstract.)

Czuber, Emanuel. *Wahrscheinlichkeitsrechnung und ihre Anwendung auf Fehlerausgleichung, Statistik und Lebensversicherung*. (2nd ed.) Vol. II. Leipzig: B. G. Teubner, 1910.

Edgeworth, F. Y. The philosophy of chance. *Mind*, 1884, vol. 9 (Old Series), 223–235.

Edgeworth, F. Y. The law of error. *Transactions of the Cambridge Philosophical Society*, 1905, vol. 20, 36–65, 113–141.

Fisher, Arne. *The Mathematical Theory of Probabilities*. Vol. I. New York: Macmillan, 1915.

Galton, Francis. *Hereditary Genius*. London: Macmillan, 1869.

Galton, Francis. The geometric mean, in vital and social statistics. *Proceedings of the Royal Society of London*, 1879, vol. 29, 365–367.

Gauss, C. F. *Abhandlungen zur Methode der kleinsten Quadrate*. Berlin: P. Stankiewicz' Buchdruckerei, 1887.

George, S. S. Attitude in relation to the psychophysical judgment. *American Journal of Psychology*, 1917, vol. 28, 1–37.

Holt, E. B. *The Freudian Wish and Its Place in Ethics.* New York: Henry Holt, 1916.

Jevons, W. S. *The Principles of Science.* London: Macmillan, 1883.

Kaufmann, A. A. *Theorie und Methoden der Statistik.* Tübingen: J. C. B. Mohr, 1913.

Keller, Hans. Die Methode der mehrfachen Fälle im Gebiete der Schallempfindungen und ihre Beziehung zur Methode der Minimaländerungen. *Psychologische Studien,* 1907, vol. 3, 49–89.

Klemm, Otto. *A History of Psychology.* (Trans. by E. C. Wilm and Rudolf Pintner.) New York: Charles Scribner's, 1914.

von Kries, Johannes. *Die Principien der Wahrscheinlichkeitsrechnung.* Freiburg: J. C. B. Mohr, 1886.

Laplace, P. S. *Theorie analytique des probabilités.* Paris: V^e. Courcier, 1812.

Lexis, Wilhelm. *Zur Theorie der Massenerscheinungen in der menschlichen Gesellschaft.* Freiburg: F. Wagner, 1877.

McAlister, Donald. The law of the geometric mean. *Proceedings of the Royal Society of London,* 1879, vol. 29, 367–376.

Merriman, Mansfield. *A Textbook on the Method of Least Squares.* New York: John Wiley, 1884.

Miner, J. B. *Deficiency and Delinquency.* Baltimore: Warwick & York, 1918.

Newcomb, Simon. Note on the frequency of use of the different digits in natural numbers. *American Journal of Mathematics,* 1881, vol. 4, 39 f.

Pearl, Raymond. *Variation and Differentiation in Ceratophyllum.* Washington, D. C.: Carnegie Institution, 1907.

Pearson, Karl. Contributions to the mathematical theory of evolution. *Philosophical Transactions of the Royal Society of London,* 1894, vol. 185A, 71–110.

Pearson, Karl. Contributions to the mathematical theory of evolution. II: Skew variation in homogeneous material. *Philosophical Transactions of the Royal Society of London,* 1895, vol. 186A, 343–414.

Pearson, Karl. *Chances of Death.* London: E. Arnold, 1897. 2 vols.

Pearson, Karl. On the criterion that a given system of deviations from the probable in the case of a correlated system of variables is such that it can be reasonably supposed to have arisen from random sampling. *Philosophical Magazine,* 1900, vol. 50 (5th Series), 157–175.

Pearson, Karl. Mathematical contributions to the theory of evolution. X: Supplement to a memoir on skew variation. *Philosophical Transactions of the Royal Society of London,* 1901, vol. 197A, 443–459.

Pearson, Karl. On the inheritance of the mental and moral characters in man, and its comparison with the inheritance of the physical characters. *Biometrika,* 1904, vol. 3, 131–190.

Pearson, Karl. Mathematical contributions to the theory of evolution. XIV: On the general theory of skew correlation and non-linear regression. *Draper's Company Research Memoirs* (Biometric Series), 1905, no. ii.

Pearson, Karl. On the relationship of intelligence to size and shape of head, and to other physical and mental characters. *Biometrika,* 1906, vol. 5, 105–146.

Pearson, Karl. *The Grammar of Science.* (3rd ed.) Pt. i. London: A. and C. Black, 1911.

Pearson, Karl. Mendelism and the problem of mental defect. III: On the graduated character of mental defect, etc. *Questions of the Day and of the Fray*, 1914, no. ix.

Pearson, Karl, and Jaederholm, G. A. Mendelism and the problem of mental defect. II: On the continuity of mental defect. *Questions of the Day and of the Fray*, 1914, no. viii.

Quetelet, Adolphe. *Sur l'homme et le développement de ses facultés, ou essai de physique sociale.* Paris: Bachelier, 1835.

Quetelet, Adolphe (1846). *Letters Addressed to H. R. H. the Grand Duke of Saxe Coburg and Gotha, on the Theory of Probabilities, as Applied to the Moral and Political Sciences.* (Trans. by O. G. Downes.) London: C. & E. Layton, 1849.

Shanks, William. On the extension of the numerical value of π. *Proceedings of the Royal Society of London*, 1873, vol. 21, 318f.

Stumpf, Carl. Ueber den Begriff der mathematischen Wahrscheinlichkeit. *Sitzungsberichte der philosophisch-philologischen und der historischen Classe der Akademie der Wissenschaften zu München*, 1892, 37–120.

Titchener, E. B. *Experimental Psychology: A Manual of Laboratory Practice.* Vol. II. *Quantitative Experiments.* Pt. i. *Student's Manual.* New York: Macmillan, 1905.

Todhunter, Isaac. *History of the Mathematical Theory of Probability.* London: Macmillan, 1865.

Trabue, M. R. *Completion-Test Language Scales.* New York: Teachers College, Columbia University, 1916.

Urban, F. M. *The Application of Statistical Methods to the Problems of Psychophysics.* Philadelphia: Psychological Clinic Press, 1908.

Urban, F. M. Die psychophysischen Massmethoden als Grundlagen empirischer Messungen: Beschreibung der Experimente. *Archiv für die gesamte Psychologie*, 1909, vol. 15, 261–355. (a)

Urban, F. M. Die psychophysischen Massmethoden als Grundlagen empirischer Messungen: Behandlung der Beobachtungsergebnisse bei Voraussetzung bestimmter Annahmen über die psychometrischen Funktionen. *Archiv für die gesamte Psychologie*, 1909, vol. 16, 168–227. (b)

Urban, F. M. The method of constant stimuli and its generalizations. *Psychological Review*, 1910, vol. 17, 229–259. (a)

Urban, F. M. Ein Beitrag zur Kenntnis der psychometrischen Funktionen im Gebiete der Schallempfindungen. *Archiv für die gesamte Psychologie*, 1910, vol. 18, 400–410. (b)

Urban, F. M. Ueber den Begriff der mathematischen Wahrscheinlichkeit. *Vierteljahrsschrift für wissenschaftliche Philosophie und Soziologie*, 1911, vol. 35, 1–49, 145–185.

Urban, F. M. Ueber einige Begriffe und Aufgaben der Psychophysik. *Archiv für die gesamte Psychologie*, 1913, vol. 30, 113–152. (a)

Urban, F. M. Professor Dodge's recent discussion of mental work. *American Journal of Psychology*, 1913, vol. 24, 270–274. (b)

Venn, John. The law of error. *Nature*, 1887, vol. 36, 411 f.

Venn, John. *Logic of Chance*. (3rd ed.) London: Macmillan, 1888.

Weld, L. D. *Theory of Errors and Least Squares*. New York: Macmillan, 1916.

Weldon, W. F. R. On certain correlated variations in *Carcinus moenas*. *Proceedings of the Royal Society of London*, 1893, vol. 54, 318–329.

West, C. J. *Introduction to Mathematical Statistics*. Columbus: R. G. Adams, 1918.

Westergaard, Harald. *Die Grundzüge der Theorie der Statistik*. Jena: G. Fischer, 1890.

Williams, H. D. On the calculation of an associative limen. *American Journal of Psychology*, 1918, vol. 29, 219–226.

Yule, G. U. *Introduction to the Theory of Statistics*. (4th ed.) London: C. Griffin, 1917.

Learning vs. Training
for Graduate Students
1950

After the Second World War clinical psychology expanded enormously and kept on. Eager to maintain high standards that would make the Ph.D. in clinical psychology stand up beside the M.D., those in command argued that the clinical trainees should, in addition to acquiring many other skills and knowledges, receive a broad training in psychology, should indeed be "trained" in experimental psychology. The trainees should take, it was said, "a course" in experimental psychology. A course! I was shocked. The principle was right, of course, but you do not make experimentalists in courses. You get this training to the Ph.D. level and beyond (provided you but have the necessary compulsions) by living a whole life of experimental psychology. I tried to make this point in the following letter which says what it is like to be a prospectively successful graduate student in a laboratory of experimental psychology. This comment went far toward making the phrases "the 80-hour week" and "the 4000-hour year" current. Eighty hours is less than half time. This week provides 168 hours.

We are putting, it seems to me, the cart before the horse with all this talk about "training" graduate students. We psychologists should know that the learning process depends primarily on the active participation of the learner and only indirectly on the trainer. We, the "teachers," "train" graduate students only by

Reprinted with permission from the *American Psychologist,* 1950, vol. 5, 162 f.

providing the facilities—material and verbal—for their ready learning and by setting up the situations most likely to induce motivation.) (Do graduate students learn in courses? They learn some things, though less than the instructor himself who is the more active participator. The best educational strategy would make the taking of courses incidental to the total learning process that terminates in a Ph.D. The way to get a Ph.D., a good one, is to live a life of scholarship and research for three or four years under the conditions most likely to stimulate intellectual development toward a prescribed maturity.

A *curriculum* is a course, a race course, a race that absorbs the total endeavor of the runner until the goal is reached. We distort the meaning of the word *course* when we think of it as a fixed element in the big race, and of the race itself as an *Undverbindung* made up of so many courses glued together. The purpose of this note is to give an alternative picture of the graduate curriculum, the race to the Ph.D. from which so many runners retire winded. I shall speak only about learning to be an experimental psychologist because that is the field I know well. Maybe it is different with the "training" of clinical psychologists—but maybe it is not so different as we are sometimes told.

Suppose, now, I were asked how one hundred A.B. majors, each aspiring to a career in psychology, could best be turned into good experimental psychologists; how would I reply? As I formulate my answer let the reader beware. There is no university which achieves this ideal, not Harvard nor any other place. It is my ideal and some of my colleagues share it, but scarcely all of them. I doubt if all the specifications for this situation can be got into words. When I see this system working—and I often do—I realize that I do not know what makes it work, what catches the loyalty and enthusiasms of the student, what makes him confused about the distinction between work and play.

Let me say also that it is from these limitations that I derive my despair when I am asked the question: How can the clinical psychologist be "trained" in experimental psychology or in scientific method? I do not know how he can. What he needs is to mature by soaking up attitudes about experimental research and he can do that from an atmosphere with which he is identified if he has the time—the years—for it and if he is able enough. How he is to get it as an incident of other "training" I do not know.

Now let us get down to particulars. What should we do first with these hundred A.B. majors? We must begin, certainly, with selection. A thorough personality assessment of the candidates would be desirable, but lacking that, we might be willing to settle for three letters of recommendation, discussing defects as well as virtues, and a score on a test at least as good as the Miller Analogies Test. Let us put the threshold on the MAT at 80, not 70, hoping always for 85 or more. There are not the funds available at present in America to provide opportunity for the average man with an MAT score of 70 to reach the Ph.D. goal in experimental psychology. Let us suppose that we have now cut down the original hundred to forty.

We must assume that considerable motivational selection has already operated. These students would not have become "candidates" without a strong desire for the Ph.D. There would be, however, continued selection after they get into graduate study, and perhaps half of those who started would drop out before the goal is reached.

So now we have forty highly motivated, bright young men to make into experimental psychologists. What do we do next? We separate them into groups and send them to different places. Forty is too many to form the social unit in which learning is optimal.

Ideally no one laboratory would admit more than ten new students a year. Of those ten, perhaps seven would last into the second year and five into the third, presently reaching the Ph.D. goal. In such a group the older students would become as important as the "teaching" staff in imparting information and establishing atmosphere.

The staff must be occupied mainly with research and scholarly pursuits. They would give "courses" because they want intellectual contact with the students, and that helps to systematize the students' development. It is essential that the motivational level of the students be of the 80-hours-a-week, 50-weeks-a-year variety, with holidays and Sundays good fun because they afford a chance to "work." Students who know the difference between "work" and "play" would not last in this atmosphere. The young and vigorous members of the teaching staff would establish the atmosphere. The old chaps in their fifties are likely to have dropped down to sixty hours and to be taking a month off in summer. Fortunately, the tradition would probably carry on in spite of them.

Every graduate student would have access to the laboratories at all times and have a place there to work. A locker is not enough. He must have a chair, a table, and a bookshelf. Half a dozen graduate students packed into a room that was their own would build up an interpersonal situation with more educational (eductive) value than any other factor in that overstressed essential of graduate work called "residence." Such social contact would also have therapeutic value for potential isolates. It goes without saying that these students, each with his personal niche and seat of learning, would have keys to the laboratories. To take away a student's key on account of its misuse would come near to blocking his progress toward the Ph.D. And there must be books available. There ought to be accessible at least a small working library in the laboratories, composed not of specialized or expensive books but of standard volumes for study and reference.

Meanwhile experimentation would go on. A student with an idea would be encouraged to try it out. In such an atmosphere of productivity, experiments and publication by graduate students would not be limited to Ph.D. theses. Here, as with the books, the students would learn by doing.

What you would get in this social unit would be a congeries of older and younger instructors, older and younger graduate students. Every one of them would be available for talk with every other one, and some of the best talk would happen late at night with the talkers sitting on tables. That is the free side of group endeavor. At the same time there would be hierarchy, for the staff must be constantly assessing the graduate students and judging whether they are likely to achieve the precious Ph.D. or whether they should be encouraged to find some other relation to life. There would be courses, but courses are not the essence of residence. There would be examinations, many of them, and the constant process of assessment would be pointed up by performance in these examinations. There might be examinations in courses, in proseminars, sometimes in seminars, in the foreign languages, in statistics, in the general examinations for the Ph.D., all before the final examination of the thesis and the oral defense of it.

The men who had miscalculated their futures would drop out. The first-year ten would become the second-year seven who would become the third-year five. After friendly advice they would try other fields, and only a few would leave bitterly with a sense of having wasted time. Those who reached the goal would have developed. They would not be the same persons who undertook graduate work after an A.B. They now would know something about experimental work, something about scholarship, a great deal about psychology. They would think of the Ph.D. as something very important to them but not as a reason for letting down on research effort. Rather they would see that the Ph.D. frees them for research and for what goes with it—teaching as a rule—and allows them at last to become their own masters in the pursuit of knowledge. The business of graduate study is the acquisition of maturity, the special maturity of the scholar and researcher. It is gained by growing up in the right social and intellectual atmosphere.

The Woman Problem
1951

During the Second World War Alice I. Bryan and I were members of R. M. Yerkes' Survey and Planning Committee, which met for several days at a time and discussed ways in which psychology might contribute to America's war effort. Personal matters kept coming up and Dr. Bryan and I soon found that we disagreed about the feminist problem, or at least about what you should actually do to be fair to women. I then had the idea—which I now know to be impractical—that honest intelligent persons who disagree should always by intimate discussion either come into agreement or become aware of the nature of the a priori values that separate them. For this reason I suggested to Dr. Bryan that she and I collaborate on a study of the status of American women psychologists. We published three joint papers under the general title "Women in American Psychology" (*Psychological Bulletin,* 1944, vol. 41, 447–454; *American Psychologist,* 1946, vol. 1, 71–79; 1947, vol. 2, 3–20) and we even got a prize for a summary of this work, but we did not reshape our values into a single pattern, and, when we faced admonitory conclusions, we had to compromise or retreat to description of fact. My plan had not worked. Four years later I thought: Let me write the truth now just as I see it. It will do me good, my own personal uncompromised "truth." Here it is.

Dr. Mildred B. Mitchell (1951) has pointed out that women do not hold administrative and honorific positions in the APA

Reprinted with permission from the *American Psychologist,* 1951, vol. 6, 679–682.

[American Psychological Association] "in proportion to their numbers and qualifications" and that especially do they fail of election to "top level" offices, being frequently chosen for the more laborious job of secretary.

Dr. Mitchell is right, of course. Women are accorded less recognition than men in the professions and in public life. We hardly need more statistics to prove that. The APA has had only two woman presidents out of its 59, one in 1905, one in 1921, and none in the last half of its existence when its increasing size makes election so much more difficult. Only about 8 per cent of the persons listed in *American Men of Science* (1933 edition) were women. Less than 6 per cent of the 127 psychologists starred in the first seven editions of this directory were women. The National Academy of Sciences had in 1950 among its 461 members only three women. The American Philosophical Society [in the same year], not limited to science, had among its 486 members only eight women. Neither of these societies has any women among its honorary foreign members. Less than 8 per cent of the entries in *Who's Who in America* are for women. There can be no question that professional women acquire less prestige than professional men "in proportion to their numbers," but *why?* Is it not time to stop confirming this obvious fact and to attmept to get some understanding of the underlying social dynamics?

Certainly the Woman Problem is not solely a problem for and about women. It will be comprehended best when it is considered in relation with similar problems of social dynamics.

The Woman Problem is, for instance, related to the Great Man problem. Do science and thought and history, we may ask, advance step-wise by the successive contributions of great men, or is intellectual progress more or less continuous? Does history perhaps merely select the names of certain men as indices of advances in thought and knowledge, while neglecting the antecedent, the contemporaneous, and the subsequent events that are necessary for getting a great discovery ready to be made and then afterward getting it accepted as truth? The Great Men of history are the men who achieved great prestige, some of them while living, others posthumously. It appears, moreover, that prestige is gained or lost, not only by achievement, but also by such other reinforcers and inhibitors as the timing of the discovery, the inertia of contemporaneous thought, the way in which the discovery is promoted or advertised, and the prestige of the discoverer—for prestige begets prestige; it has positive feedback. When a man has first emerged from inconspicuousness, his subsequent acts gain attention more readily than before and his prestige tends to build itself up, especially if it is continuously supported by good work. The point here is that prestige is no simple function of merit. Neither men nor women gain prestige simply "in proportion to their qualifications" (in Dr. Mitchell's phrase). Thus it comes about that an understanding of the psychodynamics of the history of science will help in an understanding of the Woman Problem, for it is not only women who complain of history's injustice (Boring, 1950).

The Woman Problem is also similar to the Youth Problem. On the average, men make their greatest contributions to knowledge at the ages of 30–45, becoming less effective, less frequently productive, as they grow older. Harvey Lehman (1936; 1942; 1943; 1944; etc.) has plotted these productivity curves. The cause of decreasing frequency of original contributions by aging men is not yet known; perhaps it is wholly motivational. In general, prestige and the culture tend to preserve the status of once important men as they grow older, and in the American success-culture men often maintain prestige by slipping over into administration from the field of discovery. To some extent the past status of the old is supported by our culture, but that is not nearly so true here in the occident as it has been in the orient. As a rule the young men in their thirties and forties are ready to take over from the oldsters, and to a considerable extent they do. Someone once proposed establishing a "Society of ExperimentING Psychologists" for men under forty, an active group free of the prestige inhibitions which were supposed to limit election to the Society of Experimental Psychologists—and indeed the new society was formed although under a different name. Now the grim reaper of middle age harvests the members of the younger society into the older—at age forty or even sooner. We must not, however, forget the existence of this Youth Protest, comparable to the Woman Protest in being directed against the fixed prestige of older men. The chief difference here is that the young grow old, and change their views, whereas women never quite turn into men.

For men there is a standard operating procedure about the acquisition of prestige. It runs—for psychologists—something like this: First you get a Ph.D. Then you manage some good research and publish it. In that way, you get some recognition. You keep on with research, now accepting also some administrative responsibilities. If you continue to impress your profession with the quality of your performance, you are likely to develop intellectual claustrophobia. You find yourself presently seeking larger perspectives. Perhaps you write a book, a book that, bringing together the researches of others, affords you the needed scope for broad interpretation. Or you may get over into the administration of research or of other professional activities. You may even find psychology too confining and become a dean or a college president. All this is standard for psychologists. It applies approximately to every past president of the APA. I am not sure that it holds for theoretical physicists who seem to be able to find scope for broad interpretation within their science and thus may not need to escape from research to book-writing or administration. Nor am I sure that the rule applies to European scientists, for abroad custom supports the prestige of the older men in greater security than is the case in America. Nevertheless, if a woman wanted to be president of the APA, this would be the course for her to follow, except that in this curriculum she had better aim at writing a book than at being a dean. For its top honors the APA looks askance at administrators.

It seems probable that this standard course for the evaluation of prestige is connected with the normal American success-culture. Prestige springs from power and leads to more power, but not much power is required for dealing with little things. It is the book-writer and the administrator who handle the large theories and the broad policies, thus maintaining and enhancing their prestige as they gather in the fruits of success. It is my impression that it is at this upper level that women are most often blocked in the pursuit of prestige. If a woman wants power and prestige as an administrator, she runs up against the man-made world. It is not the APA which keeps women down, but the universities, industry, the government, the armed services. With top level administrative jobs so hard for her to get, why then does she not write books? Sometimes she does, but the book that brings prestige should deal with broad generalities, and there is some indication that the women of our culture are more interested in the particular, and especially, if I may lift terms from Terman and Miles (1936, pp. 400 f.), in the young, helpless, and distressed. Rogers, the only clinical psychologist who until now had been president of the APA, came to fame through a general theory of therapy and a book about it. Scott, in applied psychology, came in through administrative success with personnel testing in the First World War. The exceptionally skillful practitioner—be he or she clinical psychologist, college teacher, or general physician—gains at most a local recognition which almost never admits him to the dictionaries of biography.

Another important contributor to prestige is job-concentration. Beardsley Ruml has spoken humorously of the 168-hour week for the fanatic who lives primarily for his job—he who eats, sleeps, and finds recreation only because he wishes to work better. These compulsive persons are very common among successful professional men and in business and statecraft. Such persons can undertake any job at any time in any place on earth, provided only it seems important enough. Now it has been remarked that these people make poor parents, and presumably they usually do. Thus

it comes about that the Woman Problem is found to be affected
by philosophy of living. Inevitably there is conflict between professional success and success as a family man or a family woman.
That is not to say, of course, that a man of exceptional ability
cannot save time from his profession to spend on his family,
nor that maximal concentration is always maximally efficient in
producing prestige; nevertheless the fact remains that you can
not often do two things at once and that limited time is one of
the factors that prevent achievement. Thus it is true that ambitious professional mothers have a grievance, for custom gives
them greater responsibility for the children than it gives their
husbands. It would have been desirable for Dr. Mitchell, had
it but been possible, to separate in her statistics the married from
the unmarried women, discarding the negligible unmarried men
altogether. It would have been still better for her to have
ignored sex and marital status, and to have used as a basic param-
eter measures of job-concentration for every member of the
APA. What we are after is knowledge of the effects of professional fanaticism.

Now against this background of social dynamics, let us see
what must usually happen to the ambitious woman member of
the APA.

I do not believe that sex prejudice operates against women in
APA elections to top level offices. I can not prove this faith, but
I think that on the average and given everything else equal, a
male psychologist will vote for a woman in preference to a man—
or for a member of any minority group that he thinks is under-
privileged or discriminated against. Everything else is, however,
not often equal and women are usually not preferred for the top
level jobs because some of their male competitors have more
prestige.

Intelligence and special abilities will count for their possessor,
man or woman, all through. Let that not be forgotten. It is only
when a woman loses out in competition to a man of presumably
equal intelligence and special skill that the Woman Problem
emerges.

When the professional woman starts out on her career, she can be imagined as having two choices to make—although in fact it is doubtful that she really can do very much to choose her personality. She can not, of course, choose her level of intelligence, but she might perhaps attempt a decision about job-concentration and whether to work with particulars or generalities, in technology or in science. If she chooses less job-concentration in order to be a broader person, a better wife, or a better mother, then she is perhaps choosing wisely but she is not choosing the maximal professional success of which she would be capable. She is in competition with fanatics—the 168-hour people —and she had better accept that bit of realism about job-concentration. Certainly she is less free than a man to choose work that deals with the large generalizations, because those jobs are associated with basic research, and the top positions in the universities are not as freely open to women as to men, whereas basic research under government auspices has not yet settled down into any permanent pattern.

All along the question of marriage interferes with the woman's assured planning. Can a woman become a fanatic in her profession and still remain marriageable? Yes, she can, for I know some, but I think a woman must be abnormally bright to combine charm with concentration. These women make the synthesis by being charmingly enthusiastic. The Woman Problem comes up again after the professional woman has acquired a husband and a couple of children, with the culture pressing to give her a heavy responsibility in the home, with her husband noting, perhaps, that his own success demands his own job-concentration. A couple can compromise and work out a fairly proportioned scheme for the good life as they see it, and some do just this. Perhaps two spouses, each on half-concentration, are better than one on full concentration, but the pair would not be elected president of the APA. Some women readers will undoubtedly think me callous to the frustration of others, but I am asking only for realism. Do you work at your profession 20, 40, or 80 hours a week? It makes a difference in competition, though it is not the only thing to make a difference; and the Woman Problem exists because there is this competition and invidious comparison.

There are about as many married as unmarried women in the APA (Bryan and Boring, 1947, p. 14). Why not let the older unmarried women give up the thought of marriage and compete on equal footing with the men? Part of the answer to that question is that they will not be on equal footing. Nearly all the men are married, and a married man usually manages to make his marriage contribute to his success and prestige. Most of the married women do not receive the same professional support from their husbands and the unmarried women have no husbands. The only exception in favor of marriage for professional women is that those women who look for success in the psychology of interpersonal relations and not for great prestige often believe that their marriages make better psychologists of them (Bryant and Boring, 1947, pp. 15 f.). In general, marriage is not an asset for most professionally ambitious women psychologists.

When the unmarried woman seeks prestige at the upper levels, she finds that the administrative posts are not fully open to women. Nevertheless, she is free to seek public success by working with some kind of large generalities. That approach to prestige generally means writing a definitive discussion of an important topic in a book. You would think that ambitious women would take to book-writing more than they do, although it must be admitted that writing a book is more work than those who do not write them think. Still this is the right advice to give the women who seek prestige under our present cultural limitations. If they do not take the advice, perhaps the reason lies in Terman and Miles' observation that women are more concerned with the particular than the general.

Here then is the Woman Problem as I see it. For the ICWP [International Council of Women Psychologists] or anyone else to think that the problem can be advanced toward solution by proving that professional women undergo more frustration and disappointment than professional men, and by calling then on the conscience of the profession to right a wrong, is to fail to see the problem clearly in all its psychosocial complexities. The problem turns on the mechanisms for prestige, and that prestige, which leads to honor and greatness and often to the large salaries, is not with any regularity proportional to professional merit or the social value of professional achievement. Nor is there any presumption that the possessor of prestige knows how to lead the good life. You may have to choose. Success is never whole, and, if you have it for this, you may have to give it up for that.

References

Boring, E. G. Great men and scientific progress. *Proceedings of the American Philosophical Society*, 1950, vol. 94, 339–351.

Bryan, A. I., and Boring, E. G. Women in American psychology: prolegomenon. *Psychological Bulletin*, 1944, vol. 41, 447–454.

Bryan, A. I., and Boring, E. G. Women in American Psychology: statistics from the OPP questionnaire. *American Psychologist*, 1946, vol. 1, 71–79.

Bryan, A. I., and Boring, E. G. Women in American Psychology: factors affecting their professional careers. *American Psychologist*, 1947, vol. 2, 3–20.

Lehman, H. C. The creative years in science and literature. *Scientific Monthly*, 1936, vol. 43, 151–162.

Lehman, H. C. Optimum ages for eminent leadership. *Scientific Monthly*, 1942, vol. 54, 162–175.

Lehman, H. C. Man's most creative years: then and now. *Science*, 1943, vol. 98, 393–399.

Lehman, H. C. Man's most creative years: quality versus quantity of output. *Scientific Monthly*, 1944, vol. 59, 384–393.

Mitchell, M. B. Status of women in the American Psychological Association. *American Psychologist*, 1951, vol. 6, 193–201.

Terman, L. M., and Miles, C. C. *Sex and Personality.* New Haven: Yale University Press, 1936.

Human Nature vs. Sensation:
William James and the Psychology
of the Present
1942

William James was born on 11 January 1842, and in 1942 the
Department of Philosophy and Psychology at Harvard University
planned a centennial celebration, a symposium of papers about
James and his influence, a symposium that was never held because travel was restricted during the Second World War. Nevertheless I published my paper and this is it. There is a basic dichotomy in systematic psychology, a dichotomy in which James was
on one side and I (especially then) on the other. It was natural,
however, for me to resort to the theme that has been with me
these many years, the theme that the progress of thought and
discovery depends to some extent upon the personalities of the
thinkers and the discoverers. Thus I suggest here that the issue
between Jamesians and modern positivists may not require resolution, that psychology's great scientific endeavor needs not only
division of labor but also the division of personality that makes
complementary and even incompatible activities essential for
progress. Or, if I did not say just that, at least this paper represented progress in my own thinking toward that subsequent
opinion.

WILLIAM JAMES ON SENSATION

William James and the psychology of sensation: that is my
topic. Yet the outstanding thing about James in this connection

Reprinted with permission from the *American Journal of Psychology*,
1942, vol. 55, 310–327.

is that he did not like sensation as a chapter in psychology and neglected it as much as he could. Disliking it, he nevertheless entertained it with his usual conscientiousness, while he disapproved withal the labors of most of its sponsors. Their researches, from 1860 to 1890, seemed to him for the most part unimportant and the controversy which they aroused futile, although they were, nevertheless, the *raison d'être* of the new experimental psychology. For all that it is James's picturesque disparagement of them that is remembered and quoted by every student of his *Principles*. His apt *bons mots* have outlived the memory for their occasions.

At first glance James's attitude seems to present us with a contradiction. The new experimental psychology of 1870 and thereabouts was, for the most part, made up of the researches of Weber, Fechner, Helmholtz, Wundt, Aubert, Mach, and Vierordt —all investigations of sensation: Weber and the cutaneous *Ortsinn:* Fechner and the psychophysical methods; Helmholtz on vision and hearing; Wundt on the visual perception of depth; Aubert on light and color; Mach on vision and time; Vierordt on the *Zeitsinn*. This was the new physiological psychology which James had first heard about and then read, which he chose as his *Fach* in the early '70's. If it captured his thought then, why had he turned against it by 1890? He wrote then in the *Principles:*

Within a few years what one may call a microscopic psychology has arisen in Germany, carried on by experimental methods, asking of course every moment for introspective data, but eliminating their uncertainty by operating on a large scale and taking statistical means. This method taxes patience to the utmost, and hardly could have arisen in a country whose natives could be *bored*. Such Germans as Weber, Fechner, Vierordt and Wundt obviously cannot; and their success has brought into the field an array of younger experimental psychologists, bent on studying the *elements* of the mental life, dissecting them from the gross results in which they are embedded, and as far as possible reducing them to quantitative scales. The simple and open method of attack having done what it can, the method of patience, starving out, and harassing to death is tried; the Mind must submit to a regular *siege,* in which minute advantages gained night and day by the forces that hem her in must sum themselves up at last

into her overthrow. There is little left of the grand style about these
new prism, pendulum, and chronograph-philosophers. They mean business, not chivalry. What generous divination, and that superiority in
virtue which was thought by Cicero to give a man the best insight into
nature, have failed to do, their spying and scraping, their deadly
tenacity and almost diabolic cunning, will doubtless some day bring
about. (James, 1890, vol. I, pp. 192 f.)

If that is what James thought about the new psychology, why
did he ever enlist under its banner?

The answer to that question has two parts. In the first place,
James was not a man to enlist under any banner. He never wanted
to join any movement. His curiosity and imagination had been
captured by the possibilities of the new psychology, not by its
achievements, and he saw in it, moreover, a means whereby he
could remain secure in physiology, where he had had his training
and held a post, and yet cultivate philosophy without assuming
the full responsibilities of that more difficult discipline, as he
conceived it to be. Others in those days had to make similar decisions. Wundt, starting in as a physiologist, had argued himself
into his own synthetic brand of experimental philosophy—a
chair of philosophy in a psychological laboratory, an experimental
journal called *Philosophische Studien*, a set of systematic handbooks on physiological psychology, logic, ethics, and systematic
philosophy. Stumpf, who loved music most and had been con-
verted by Brentano to the rigors of philosophy, chose psychology
for his *Fach*, because it was the only field, besides esthetics,
where he could philosophize by experimenting with music. Like
James he grew up into philosophy and away from the laboratory.

That is the second point about James's relation to the new sensory psychology: He grew away from it, and it grew away from
him. In 1872, when James was only thirty, when Fechner's *Psychophysik* was only twelve and Wundt's *Physiologische Psychologie*
was not quite born, James's imagination could be caught by the
possibilities of a new science. Eighteen years later, when the
Principles was published, James had been disillusioned enough to

write the passage that I have quoted. Everyone knows how he said of Fechner and psychophysics:

> But it would be terrible if even such a dear old man as this could saddle our Science forever with his patient whimsies, and, in a world so full of more nutritious objects of attention, compel all future students to plough through the difficulties, not only of his own works, but of the still drier ones written in his refutation. (James, 1890, vol. I, p. 549.)

There lay the trouble. Patient whimsies. Unnutritious objects of attention. This new psychology, a promising adolescent in 1870 was growing up into a dull intolerant bigot in 1890, or so it seemed to James. Where then lies the truth? Was James at fault, or the new psychology, or both or neither? Just how much more nutritious could the new psychology have been? Wundt's meat was James's poison. Was James's Wundt's?

In the first place, let it be said that James hated sham and that there was a very considerable amount of false scientification in this period when the new psychology was being formed. Someone has said that the members of a community could not manage to subsist by taking in each other's washing, and for similar reasons science cannot live by mutual criticisms alone. If the scientific process is not kept wet from the fountain of empiricism, it shrivels and dries up. James called Fechner's law "an 'idol of the den,' if ever there was one," because the respect shown it in both attack and defense was out of all proportion to the validating evidence for it. It became, in fact, an Institutional Principle, which psychologists preserved by characterizing all its refutations as its exceptions. James was right about these idols, but, being so close to them, he failed to see what use it is that idols have.

The point here is that the new psychology was not, *an und für sich,* a discovery, but a movement. If it had been a discovery, it would have been hailed for what it was, have been doubted by some critical skeptics, and have stimulated a flurry of other lesser discoveries which grew out of the facts of the first or else used the method of the first. There was, in fact, a great deal of this sort of fertile discovery by Helmholtz, Fechner, and the others, but it was not in itself what made the new psychology into a movement. The movement was formal. It had a name: *Physiologische Psychologie*. It claimed status as a science and thus definitely set itself off against the nonexperimental empiricism of philosophy. Wundt wrote a handbook to demonstrate its nature and adequacy as a new science, and was the first to found a psychological laboratory, for James's laboratory three years earlier was not founded: it came into being because his instruction in psychology required demonstration. Wundt also founded a journal. A movement is thus more than an idea because it needs all these impedimenta. It does not merely grow; it marches against opposition.

A formal movement is thus a protest and the psychological reason for protest is, of course, insecurity. No established science feels insecure or protests, for, being secure, it turns to work without attention to itself. But the new psychology of James's day was insecure, self-conscious, protestant, and full of the business of founding itself. It exaggerated the immediate importance of its tools and methods, and, in a way, it had to, because that is the state of mind of a new science. It was aggressive, and the aggression got into the experiments and into the publications. Out of this situation there arose among the "new" psychologists a strong faith in the validity of certain basic experimental methods like psychophysics and introspection, and in the reality of certain hypostasized entities like the mental element, apperception, and feeling. These were the idols to which James objected.

In short, James objected to time spent on pseudo-problems. To decide whether feeling is an attribute of sensation, or an element, and whether it has attributes of its own, is to learn nothing new about man (Perry, 1935, vol. II, p. 123). To argue as to whether the magnitude of a sensation is given by the number of j.n.d. by which its stimulus is above the threshold is equally futile when one does not know whether all j.n.d. are equal and when sensations seem to introspection to have no magnitude. Of such matters, James, upholding no school and furthering no movement, was impatient, necessary as they may have been to make the movement move. They were indeed the impedimenta. It is easy for us today to sympathize with James's impatience, to see why he felt they were not "nutritious objects of attention." Was that the only reason for his dissatisfaction with the new psychology that was so predominantly sensory?

No.

A sense-physiologist could find within the same literature, after all the carapace of argument and systematic artifact has been removed, no end of "nutritious objects of attention"—all the facts about color and tone with which Helmholtz's treatises were packed, for instance. Were not Newton's laws of color mixture nutritious—that absurd and unbelievable discovery that white is not simple but is a mixture of colors? And was not this a law of psychology since white has no physical existence and Newton knew nothing of retinal physiology? Yet James did not mention color mixture in the *Principles,* and put the topic into the *Briefer Course* only under protest (Perry, 1935, vol. II, p. 125). If it was the broader generalizations that James wanted and not mere facts, then he had such things as Helmholtz's resonance theory of hearing, which had in it a bit of genius, a lot of scientific precision, and enough nutriment to feed to generations of the sort of psychologists who can thrive on such a diet. Not James, however. The laboratory psychology disappointed him. It was accurate, but its program made it look so "small" (Perry, 1935, vol. II, p. 122). He wanted a functional psychology, which could discover the forces that govern the moral and religious life and bring them under control (Perry, 1935, vol. II, pp. 121 f.). In fact, the whole conception of a functional psychology is that it considers the adjustment of the total living organism to its environment, and is not primarily concerned with the description of the functioning of small parts of its mechanism.

In other words, what you find nutritious depends on what

kind of digestion you have—a physiologist's or a philosopher's. James had a philosopher's. Many of his contemporaries who called themselves psychologists had the physiologist's kind. A psychologist could turn out to need one diet or the other, but no stomach could prosper on both. Let us, therefore, examine more closely this dichotomy, where James made a choice. And let us consider it in the contemporaneous situation, where we may be able to understand it more easily. We do not have to go far from home to find what I take to be the Jamesian preference still expressed.

[¶ Here are omitted the discussions of Wolfgang Köhler's defense of values, W. E. Hocking's complaint about modern experimental psychology's dealing only with near-minds, and H. A. Murray's propaganda for the centering of dynamic psychology upon needs. These three positions seem to be good modern equivalents of what James wanted psychology to be.]

MODERN POSITIVISM

At this point we ought, it seems to me, to introduce that confused and dangerous word *positivism*. Mach was a positivist. James at times favored positivism—of the Machian kind. Recently, however, the Vienna circle have been the positivists, and modern psychology, influenced more by behaviorism and Bridgman's operational definitions than by Schlick and Carnap, often likes to express fealty to "logical positivism" or to what it sometimes calls "operationism." It is plain that the modern positivists are descended from the older positivists in two ways: both groups are antimetaphysical and both believe in the reduction of constructs to the more primary data involved in observation. There is, however, a difference in the nature of the ultimates of reduction. For Mach experience was ultimate. To achieve safety and understanding one reduced the scientific entities to the basic data of observation which is experience. Thus Mach fits into the phenomenological tradition and can properly be regarded as a grandparent of Gestalt psychology. The Machian descendants seem, however, to constitute a Kallikak family, for Mach is also grandparent to the logical positivism which seeks reduction, not to experience, but to the operations of the observing process. Modern positivistic psychologists, instead of regarding phenomenal experience as ultimate, ask for a definition to be expressed in terms of the processes by which experience is observed. No longer do they believe that to have an experience is in itself to know about it.

The consequence of this change in the atmosphere of positivism has been that phenomenology, instead of finding support in positivism as it could with Mach, is now utterly opposed to the current brand of positivism. Listen to Köhler in the preface of *The Place of Value in a World of Facts*.

Never, I believe, shall we be able to solve any problems of ultimate principle until we go back to the sources of our concepts—in other words, until we use the phenomenological method, the qualitative analysis of experience.

At this point one might, thinking of Mach, put Köhler down as a good positivist. But read his next sentence.

In this our Positivists show hardly any interest. They prefer to deal with concepts which have acquired a certain polish in the history of scientific thought, and they think little of topics to which these concepts can not be directly applied. (Köhler, 1938, p. vii.)

That sentence shocked me when I first read it, for it completely reversed the accepted meaning of positivism. The concepts polished by much use in scientific thought are what one finds in metaphysics which all positivists have agreed to eschew. Positivism tries to get back to the simple data or processes of observation. How can Köhler charge it was using only the popular shopworn articles? He can, though, and does. His book, moreover, makes clear what he means. Phenomenology and positivism parted company early in the present century, and now they can hardly speak to each other. Köhler is on the side of phenomenology and I think James would have been too.

The problem whether to choose values or facts [Köhler],

minds or near-minds [Hocking], needs or sensations [Murray] is in itself a matter of relative values. Köhler is at pains to point out that the modern positivists are not incorrect but merely insufficient. What is correct may not, however, be enough, he notes; and if one asks, enough for what? the answer has already been given. Enough for the understanding of man and for what man thinks is most important about man.

PHENOMENOLOGY AND REDUCTION

It might be possible simply to leave the whole problem here, to say that there are in the world both phenomenologists and reductionists, that neither gives the whole picture and both together are more complete than either alone. Such a view implies a certain symmetry between the two positions. It asserts that, if something of the whole is lost by reduction, then the whole itself must lack what reduction adds. Certainly a case could be made for emotional symmetry between the two positions. The phenomenologists, it is true, are thoroughly disturbed by the failure of conventional science to leave the values alive when dealing with man, but then conventional science has itself been often disturbed by the way in which the phenomenologists leave the values in. Anyone who is familiar with the history of the way in which science first and psychology later—from Copernicus to John B. Watson—accomplished the reduction of man's irreducible values knows that science has felt neither complacent nor assured about its value of valuelessness. Both parties to this controversy must have felt insecure, else they would have lacked the motive for the aggression of moral judgment and apt invective. Perhaps the best solution of this dilemma is to admit the existence of an individual difference, describe it, approve it, and rest content with the interesting fact that one man's meat is another's poison. Certainly such a solution is easiest. Nevertheless let us see if we cannot come to some understanding of this difference in the value of value.

The difference is old. For instance, Goethe, the phenomenologist, denounced Newton, the experimentalist (Boring, 1942, pp.

28–34, 49 f., 112–117, 123 f.). This animadversion of Goethe's had nothing to do with man, but I bring up the matter because I think that the issue between James and Wundt, between phenomenologists and positivists, is more fundamental than Köhler makes it. Newton was cautious; Goethe was bold. Newton had the insight that the moon is forever falling to the earth, but he delayed publication for many years while he tried to get his calculations to confirm his insight. Goethe had the insight of the metamorphosis of homologous parts as he examined the sheep's skull on the Lido and that was enough for him. Newton demonstrated by a few simple experiments with prisms that white is a mixture of colors, and Goethe with a prism in hand but no experiment impeached Newton as having denied the obvious. Perhaps this instance is not fair since it exhibits Goethe wrong and thus at a disadvantage, but there is hardly any other event which shows so clearly that the phenomenologist must have faith in himself and his own observation, whereas the experimentalist mistrusts himself and is forever looking to controls and mediacies to correct his own errors.

Starting with Newton we can come on down the line of history. Goethe derided Newton because he used experiments to distort the obvious. Helmholtz ridiculed Goethe as a victim of his own vain obstinacy. James (1879, p. 10) found that Helmholtz's "indefinite and oracular statements about the part played by the intellect [in perception] have momentarily contributed to retard psychological inquiry." Sully objected to the "dazzling effect" of James's *Principles* as obscuring "the sharp boundaries of scientific thought" (Perry, 1935, vol. II, p. 104). Since then there has been the opposition between Watson and McDougall, and between behaviorism and Gestalt psychology. The most famous opposition of this nature was, however, the mutual disapproval of Helmholtz and Hering, each for the other, an antagonism that gives us at once the key to the difficulty, for Helmholtz was an empiricist and Hering a nativist. In this dichotomy James, of course, belongs on the side of Hering as do also all the Gestalt psychologists.

It is usual to refer to the issue of nativism *vs.* empiricism as a dead and futile controversy of the late nineteenth century, but now we begin to see that the controversy is alive and still with us. The dislike of the Gestalt psychologists for Helmholtz is based upon his empiricism, his constant appeal to past experience for the explanation of present phenomena. Similarly the phenomenologists mistrust operationism because it goes beyond the given to the conditions of givenness, asserting that the given is not ultimate since the giving of it has to be understood. These operationists do not take experience as self-validating; they want to know what experience is and they answer their own question by submitting the process of observation to description. So there lies the issue: nativism *vs.* empiricism; Hering, Stumpf, and James *vs.* Lotze, Helmholtz, and Wundt; phenomenology *vs.* reductionism. Are we to give up the problem with the admission of the existence of a difference in tastes, or can we say something more about it?

In the course of the development of this opposition the initiative would seem to have passed from the nativists to the reductionists. If such an individual difference in respect of values is given, what nativist could question the validity of a given? The reductionist, on the other hand, might reasonably be asked to do something more than to describe the difference. What is it that he could say, with James, Hocking, Murray, and Köhler all speechless now that they have discovered the primary fact of this difference in nutritious diets? Not much, I fear; yet I, who was born to feel safer with Helmholtz than with Hering, venture a first step along the path of reduction. Since the path is known to be an infinite regress, no one must expect me to approach its end.

NOTHING BUT AND SOMETHING MORE

In the first place, let me say, then, that Nothing But is also Something More. The phenomenologist takes the given and rests. Even Lotze said that nativism is not a theory of space because it does nothing but accept space. The reductionist takes the given and asks for Something More about it. The argument for Nothing But is merely that the Something More is always in the same general direction—Something More is Nothing But the same direction of reduction. Is that poverty or is it riches? That question need not, perhaps, be answered; yet there is a fact in psychology that suggests the answer, suggests that the answer may depend in part upon an individual difference as to what provides a presentation, meaningless in itself, with an adequate meaning.

What happens in perception? What is the general rule? It is that a stimulus gets the focus of attention, is completed or built upon by the organism until it is adequately meaningful, and then is allowed to make room for a next comer. Most potential stimuli have no effect, and nearly all of those which are effective remain marginal—like the words on a page which is quickly read and easily understood. If, however, you confront the perceiving mind with a sensory pattern that lacks adequate meaning and get that pattern focal, then the inevitable result is that the perceptual core gets further specification by the organism. The strange is what lacks sufficient meaning and the business of perception is to make the strange familiar. That is, if you like, the context theory of meaning, and nothing is surer than that the organism, faced with too little meaning for a focal core, will manage to find some context to add, enough to give itself a sense of competence and security. If the core is a face, then a name may be sufficient context. If the core is a face that floats in air without a body, then the context may be "magic" or "hallucination." That is the manner in which mere classification seems to the organism to provide understanding.

There will not be much objection to my insistence that accrual of context supplies meaning, but I have been speaking here of adequate meanings. When is a meaning adequate or sufficient?

Thirty years ago Jacobson (1911) and Titchener (1912, esp. pp. 174–181), working on the problem of meaning and understanding, found—at least Titchener found it in Jacobson's data—an individual difference as to what constitutes sufficiency of meaning. Jacobson gave his observers letters, words, and sentences, asking them to state the meaning. Now what is the meaning of a letter *A* presented in a visual exposure apparatus? One observer in particular—Titchener called him "logical"—was obsessed with the difficulty of knowing where to terminate a meaning. The letter *A* is a letter—black—typed—on white paper— in an apparatus—in a psychological experiment—at Cornell— where *Bewusstheiten* can be analyzed—and where there is criticism of Würzburg—which is Külpe's school—and not Wundt's. Altogether there is an infinite number of infinite regresses that can be used to explicate the context of the original core. How much of how many of them constitutes a meaning for *A*? Even this observer found with practice that he did not have to go along the path of explication forever in order to get *the* meaning; he could recognize what was too much meaning or too little though he never felt sure just where the proper boundary lay. Other observers, however, had no difficulty in stating meanings. They seemed to intuit how much Jacobson wanted in the way of meaning and were not troubled by the logical problem of indefinite explication. Titchener called these observers "subjective," because they ignored the logic of the situation to do what the experimenter wanted of them, to give a simple determinate verbal meaning.

Although this ancient experiment proves nothing by itself, it serves as an illustration of the nature of one kind of meaning and of its indeterminacy. To understand something is to do something more than to accept it. One must make specifications about it, bring in into relation with other somethings. One must, moreover, know when to stop, to know when enough meaning is enough. All that seems clear and simple. Now let us apply the context theory of meaning to the question of nativism *vs.* reductionism.

TASTES IN SCIENTIFIC MEANINGS

The nativist accepts the given, takes what comes. He has every right to say that there must be primaries, that acceptance of the given without further specification is the normal process of perceiving. Mostly the mental life is too busy for the accrual of contexts to its multitudinous cores. Most perceptual items remain marginal. The reductionist, on the other hand, finds himself insecure in the mere acceptance of a focal item. Understanding for him is something more than acceptance or even description. The object must be put into relation to other objects, and, the larger the relational system into which he can introduce the object, the more secure he feels. Reductionists tend to be physicalists because they have a sure technique for reducing all mental concepts to physical by specification of the mechanisms of observation, the defining operations. The physical system, being a large system, thus furnishes for them maximal security. Reduction does not, however, have to be physical. As one studies the empiricism of the theories of space in the late nineteenth century, one is struck with the satisfaction which the authors felt at being able to *do* something about space. A nativist *as nativist* has nothing to do but accept the given. The only way in which nativists got any fun out of their theories was by becoming geneticists enough to show how complex space is built up out of the native givens—as James's discussion of theory of space shows so clearly.

The choice between modern phenomenology and modern positivism would seem thus to be of this kind. The positivist finds phenomenology empty. There is not enough to it. He wants Something More. The phenomenologist, on the other hand, finds physicalism too full, too full of the wrong things. He objects to Nothing But. The phenomenologist holds that the positivist's reduction is unrepresentative and, therefore, a false surrogate for the real thing. The positivist says that he cannot understand aspects of the real thing except in so far as they can be put into relation with something else, that relating is never destructive, and that the unrelatable is a useless mystery. Yet even he has to quit relating at some point in the relational process, and it might be argued that he could have stopped at the start, with the phenomenologist. It is all a question as to how much context it takes to make a scientific entity understandable, and on that matter scientists do indeed seem to differ.

There is little more for me to say. In leaving you thus with an unreduced individual difference on your hands, with the mere assertion of its existence, I am, of course, playing the nativist. The empiricist should ask: How is nativism generated, and how empiricism? Perhaps some future empiricist will, indeed, solve the problem, will show that a phenomenologist must have had a happy childhood with love and security to spare, a childhood in which it was natural to accept the givens without demanding accounts of their origins. The empiricists and reductionists would then turn out to be the insecure children, who learned early to look beyond the given, suspecting a catch in what is free. If to this remark the phenomenologist replies that positivism is, therefore, founded on nothing better than the sensed inferiority of the positivists, these latter are still free to assert that sensed insecurity in nevertheless the sanction for science itself.

In all this discussion we have not really gotten away from James except in respect of chronology. It is a century since his birth and half a century since the *Principles*, which he wrote during the decade in which I was born. Although some of the problems were different then, others have stayed with us. Their permanence seems to argue that they are fundamental and perhaps referable, at least in part, to the relative permanences of human temperament, rather than that they are questions of right and wrong in science. It was the reductionists—Helmholtz and his kind—who first caught James's interest for the "new science." He refused, however, to go along with these founders. His drive derived not from his concern with the processes of understanding but from his concern with the mystery of human nature. A reductionist might say that James would be unimpressed by an understanding of a mystery that removed the mystery, since a mystery can be described, though not understood, without loss of its charm. Certainly it is plain where James would stand in the controversies of today. He would stand, of course, now as always, on his own feet. In general, however, he would take a position on the side of the Gestalt psychologists and phenomenologists. He would belong with Hocking and Murray and Köhler and all those distinguished others whom I have not named. The psychology of sensation has, nevertheless, advanced more than the psychology of motivation during the last fifty years. Just think what has happened to the scientific knowledge of the mechanism of hearing in the 1930's alone! Yet James still would not like sensation. He would approve of it and call it presumably, as others do now, "physiology." He would still be the nativist, accepting the given; nor would he even now wish to "saddle our Science forever" with the psychophysiology of sensation, when he could see before him "a world so full of more nutritious objects of attention." After all, even a rat knows how to choose his own vitamins.

References

Boring, E. G. *Sensation and Perception in the History of Experimental Psychology.* New York: Appleton-Century, 1942.

Jacobson, Edmund. On meaning and understanding. *American Journal of Psychology*, 1911, vol. 22, 553–577.

James, William. Are we automata? *Mind*, 1879, vol. 4, 1–22.

James, William. *The Principles of Psychology.* New York: Henry Holt, 1890. 2 vols.

Köhler, Wolfgang. *The Place of Value in a World of Facts.* New York: Liveright, 1938.

Perry, R. B. *The Thought and Character of William James.* Boston: Little, Brown, 1935. 2 vols.

Titchener, E. B. Description *vs.* statement of meaning. *American Journal of Psychology*, 1912, vol. 23, 165–182.

A History of Introspection
1953

In 1952, when Wayne Dennis was about to take over the editorship of the *Psychological Bulletin*, he asked me if I would not write a bibliographical article on the subject of what became of introspection. It did seem odd. Before 1927 when Titchener was still alive, it was as if psychology in America were divided between introspectionism (Titchener and his satellites) and behaviorism (everybody else). Mostly from 1875 to 1905 in Germany and America introspection was said to be psychology's sole or principal method, although practice often differed from this theory. How could introspection disappear entirely? Of course, it had not gone. What was good persisted under other names. This article says how I thought that piece of history had happened.

A proper but cumbersome title for this article would be "The History of the Availability of Consciousness to Observation in Scientific Psychology." If conscious experience can be said to exist, then the question arises as to whether modern psychology ought not to take into consideration its data, as indeed it used always to do. Thus my paper might even be called "What Became of Introspection?" One common answer to that question would be that introspection was not viable and so gradually became extinct. Another answer, however, is that introspection is still with us, doing its business under various aliases, of which *verbal report* is one. The former statement about the failure of

Reprinted with permission from the *Psychological Bulletin*, 1953, vol. 50, 169–189.

introspection is approximately true of that introspection which flourished under Titchener at Cornell in 1900–1920, whereas the latter statement about camouflaged introspection is accepted by the modern positivists who hold that the concept of conscious experience has meaning only when it is defined operationally.

DUALISM

The belief in the existence of conscious mind in man is very old, as old as philosophy and as old as the belief in the immortality of the soul, the immortality of that part of a person that is not his mortal body. Thus it has come about that something conscious is usually one term in a dualism, like mind *vs.* matter, the rational *vs.* the irrational, or purpose *vs.* mechanism. There have been psychological monists, like La Mettrie (1748), the materialist, who argued that man is a machine and who got himself consequently into theological trouble, but even he was more concerned with reducing to their bodily bases the mental states that dualism had already established than in describing man without benefit of dualism.

Inevitably the doctrine of immortality and the old-time importance of theology played a role in psychology. The words for soul and mind are not distinguished in French and German (*l'âme, Seele*) nor are the Greek and Latin words (*psyche, nous; anima, mens*) as distinct as the English translations. It was the faculty of reason that carried with it the right to immortality, and Descartes (1649), a devout Catholic, gave men rational souls, made of unextended immortal substance, and maintained that animals are mortal irrational automata. Thus Descartes became an important ancestor in both the dualistic (conscious, introspective) line of descent, and in the objective (mechanistic, reflex, tropistic) line.

British empiricism fixed dualism and the concept of consciousness upon psychology. Locke, Berkeley, Hume, Hartley, Reid, Stewart, Thomas Brown, the two Mills, and Bain, all were concerned in different ways with how the mind gets to know about the external world. Thus they recognized the basic mind-matter dichotomy. Presently there came also into the hands of these philosophers the doctrine of association which dealt with the synthetic relations among the items of mind or consciousness (Boring, 1950a, pp. 157–245). There never was—nor is there now—a good word for this immaterial term of the mind-matter dichotomy. James was complaining about that in 1890 (vol. I, pp. 185–187). Mostly the word was either *mind* (*Seele*) or *consciousness* (*Bewusstheit*). Nineteenth century psychology formulated the dichotomy as psychophysical parallelism, and that doctrine was so firmly impressed upon psychological thinking that the American operational revolution of the present century came about only with the greatest difficulty.

It would not be profitable to go into great detail here about the history of the belief in what we are calling *consciousness*. The existence of consciousness seemed for many centuries to be an obvious immediate datum, the basic undeniable reality of one's own existence. "Cogito, ergo sum," said Descartes. James (1890, vol. I, p. 185) summed the matter up:

> *Introspective Observation is what we have to rely on first and foremost and always.* The word introspection needs hardly to be defined— it means, of course, looking into our own minds and reporting what we there discover. *Every one agrees that we there discover states of consciousness.* So far as I know, the existence of such states has never been doubted by any critic, however skeptical in other respects he may have been. That we have *cogitations* of some sort is the *inconcussum* in a world most of whose other facts have at some time tottered in the breath of philosophical doubt. All people unhesitatingly believe that they feel themselves thinking, and that they distinguish the mental state as an inward activity or passion, from all the objects with which it may cognitively deal. *I regard this belief as the most fundamental of all the postulates of Psychology,* and shall discard all curious inquiries about its certainty as too metaphysical for the scope of this book.

In general the philosophers, physiologists, and physicists who founded the new experimental psychology in 1850–1870—Fechner, Lotze, Helmholtz, Wundt, Hering, Mach, and their associates

—were psychophysical parallelists who would have subscribed to this view of James's (Boring, 1950a, pp. 261–356). Psychology—even the new "physiological psychology"—was essentially the study of consciousness, and its chief method was introspection. Physiology came in because these parallelists believed in "no psychosis without neurosis" (Huxley, 1874) and thus could employ the apparatus of the physiological laboratory to control stimuli and to record the effects of neural events.

About introspection (*innere Wahrnehmung*) there was, however, some question. There is a long history of opinions on the manner in which the mind observes its own processes, one that begins with Aristotle and Plato and carries on to the present. Eisler has abstracted the views of eighty-four writers on the subject, from Aristotle to the beginning of the present century (Eisler, 1910, vol. III, pp. 1735–1742). Locke (1690), founding empiricism, held that all ideas—that is to say, the contents of the mind—come from experience either by sensation, which provides knowledge of the external world, or by reflection, which is the inner sense and provides knowledge of the mind's own operations. Neither sensation nor reflection, however, was regarded by the early empiricists as a process subject to error. The belief grew up that to have conscious experience is also to know that you have it, and thus ultimately Wundt (1896, pp. 1–6), basing his new systematic physiological psychology upon British empiricism, defined introspection as immediate experience. The facts of physical science, he thought, are mediated and derived by inference from immediate experience, which in and of itself is immediately given and constitutes the subject matter of psychology. This view suggests that Wundt thought that introspection cannot lie, but actually there was an inconsistency there, for the Wundtian laboratory put great emphasis upon training in introspective observation and in the accurate description of consciousness.

Brentano wrote in 1874 (vol. I, pp. 131–203): "The phenomena inwardly apprehended are true in themselves. As they appear

. . . so they are in reality. Who then can deny that in this a great superiority of psychology over the physical sciences comes to light?" Against this view, James (1890, vol. I, p. 189) remarked: "If to *have* feelings or thoughts in their immediacy were enough, babies in the cradle would be psychologists, and infallible ones." The classical objection to the *ipso facto* adequacy of the immediate was raised by Auguste Comte (1830–42, vol. I, pp. 34–36), the founder of positivism, who noted that introspection, being an activity of the mind, would always find the mind introspecting and never engaged in the great variety of its other activities. Actually Comte's argument was, however, much more than this quibble, which could have been answered by the statement that introspection is not a procedure but merely the recognition that knowledge, when given, exists as knowledge. Comte was complaining, as did twentieth century behaviorists, that introspection is unreliable, that it results in descriptions which often cannot be verified, and that in many other ways it fails of the positive character that science demands.

J. S. Mill answered Comte's quibble by asserting that introspection is a process and requires training for reliability. It is not strictly immediate, Mill (1882, p. 64) thought, for it involves memory—immediate memory, perhaps; yet immediate memory is not the datum itself and comes with a chance for error in it. On this whole matter, see James's (1890, vol. I, pp. 187–192) excellent discussion. Mill's point is reinforced by the modern realization that it is almost impossible to distinguish between anesthesia and immediate anterograde amnesia: a man whose memory lasts only one second is so crippled in capacity for introspection as to be practically as unconscious as any reacting organism or machine.

CLASSICAL INTROSPECTION

We may regard that introspection as classical which was defined by fairly formal rules and principles and which directly emerged from the early practices in Wundt's laboratory at Leipzig. Of course, there were no immutable rules for introspection. The great men kept disagreeing with one another and changing their minds. Nevertheless there was a body of opinion which was in general shared by Wundt, by Külpe before he left Leipzig, by G. E. Müller at Göttingen, by Titchener at Cornell and by many other less important "introspectionists" who accepted the leadership of these men. Stumpf at Berlin held to less constrained principles, and Külpe's later doctrine of introspection after he had gone to Würzburg was opposed by Wundt and Titchener.

Classical introspection is the common belief that the description of consciousness reveals complexes that are constituted of patterns of sensory elements. It was against this doctrine that Külpe at Würzburg, the behaviorists under Watson and the Gestalt psychologists at Wertheimer's initiative revolted. Introspection got its *ism* because these protesting new schools needed a clear and stable contrasting background against which to exhibit their novel features. No proponent of introspection as the basic method of psychology ever called himself an *introspectionist*. Usually he called himself a *psychologist*.

Wundt, undertaking to establish the new psychology as a science, turned to chemistry for his model. This choice landed him in elementism, with associationism to provide for synthesis. The psychological atoms were thus sensations and perhaps also feelings and images. The psychological molecules were perceptions and ideas (*Vorstellungen*) and the more complex combinations (*Verbindungen*). Because Wundt changed his views from time to time about images and feelings, the sensation became the example of the sort of stuff that appears in a good description of consciousness. Thus, half a century later, we find Titchener (1929, pp. 259–268) concluding that *sensory* is the adjective that best indicates the nature of the contents of consciousness. In this way Wundt fixed both elementism and sensationism upon introspection, and introspectionism in the proper laboratories always yielded sensory elements because that was "good" observation. It seems reasonable to suppose that laboratory atmosphere and local cultural tradition did more to perpetuate this value than did any published admonitions about observation.

Although Wundt (1888; 1896, pp. 1–6) defined the subject matter of psychology as immediate experience, he did distinguish introspection (*Selbstbeobachtung*) from inner perception (*innere Wahrnehmung*). Inner perception might be self-validating, but it was not science. Wundt insisted on the training of observers. Even in the reaction experiment Leipzig observers had to be trained to perform the prescribed acts in perception, apperception, cognition, discrimination, judgment, choice, and the like, and to report when consciousness deviated from what had been called for. Thus it is said that no observer who had performed less than 10,000 of these introspectively controlled reactions was suitable to provide data for published research from Wundt's laboratory. Some Americans, like Cattell, had the idea that the minds of untrained observers might also be of interest to psychology, and later a bitter little quarrel on this matter developed between Baldwin and Titchener (Boring, 1950a, pp. 413 f., 555). For all that, Wundt's notion of what constitutes proper introspection was much more liberal than is generally supposed, for he left room in formal introspection for retrospection and for indirect report. He was much less flexible in respect of the elements and their sensory nature.

What happened next to introspection was the acceptance of the conception that physics and psychology differ from each other in points of view but not in fundamental materials. Mach (1886) argued that experience ("sensation") is the subject matter of all the sciences, and Avenarius (1888–90) a few years later, that psychology views experience as dependent upon the functioning of the nervous system (he called it the "System C") and physics as independent of the action of the nervous system. Presently, after the two men had agreed that they agreed, they had great influence upon Külpe and Titchener who were both then at Leipzig. In his textbook of 1893 Külpe (pp. 9–13) accepted this distinction by point of view, but Titchener is the person who emphasized it most. In 1910 (pp. 1–25), he was saying that the data of introspection are "the sum-total of human experience considered as dependent upon the experiencing person," and later he could write the formula:

$$\text{Introspection} = \text{psychological (clear experience} \rightarrow \text{report),}$$

which means that introspection is the having of clear experience under the psychological point of view and the reporting upon it also under the psychological point of view (Titchener, 1915a, pp. 1–26). Substitute physical for psychological, and you have the formula for physics. The stock example for introspection is the illusion, the case where perception differs from stimulus-object in some respect. For perception experience is regarded just as it comes, dependent upon the perceiving of the perceiving person and thus upon the action of his nervous system. For the physical account of the object, however, the perceiver must be abstracted from and the physicist has resort to measurement and other physical technics. Titchener (1929, pp. 259–268) held to this distinction by point of view all his life.

It was Külpe (1893, pp. 30–38) who split Wundt's psychological atom, analyzing sensation into its four inseparable but independently variable attributes: quality, intensity, extensity, and duration. Titchener later held to this view which served to tighten rather than to loosen the contraints of atomism upon introspective psychology (Boring, 1933, pp. 17–35).

One of the most thorough discussions of introspection was provided by the erudite G. E. Müller (1911, pp. 61–176). Müller was more liberal than Wundt and left room for all the indirect and retrospective forms of introspection. Being primarily interested in the application of introspection to memory, he distinguished, for instance, between the present recall of the past apperception of a past event and the present apperception of the present recall of a past event—an important distinction, since present apperception can be interrogated as to detail whereas past apperception has become fixed and no longer subject to exploration.

It was Titchener who placed the greatest constraints upon introspection by his requirement that the description of consciousness should exclude statements of meaning. At first Titchener had perception in mind and called the report of meanings the *stimulus-error,* insisting that trained observers by taking the psychological point of view would describe consciousness ("dependent experience") and attempt no statements about the stimulus-objects ("independent experience" as given by the point of view of physics) (Boring, 1921; Titchener, 1910, pp. 202 f.). After Külpe had claimed to find imageless (nonsensory) thoughts in the consciousnesses of judgment, action, and other thought processes, Titchener (1912a) broadened his criticism to an objection against the inclusion of any meanings at all in the data of introspection. He was arguing that straight description (*Beschreibung, cognitio rei*) would yield the kind of sensory contents that had become standard in classical introspection, and that inferences about conscious data (*Kundgabe, cognitio circa rem*) are meanings which do not exist as do the observed sensory processes (Titchener, 1912b; 1912c). Thus his psychology has even been called *existential psychology,* because he believed that the meanings, occurring as inferences, lack the positive character of sensations and images, the existential data (Titchener, 1929, p. 138).

It was never wholly true that introspection was photographic and not elaborated by inferences or meanings. Reference to typical introspective researches from Titchener's laboratory establishes this point (Hayes, 1906; Nakashima, 1909; Geissler, 1909; Pyle, 1909; Okabe, 1910; Clarke, 1911; Jacobson, 1911). There was too much dependence upon retrospection. It could take twenty minutes to describe the conscious content of a second and a half, and at the end of that period the observer was cudgeling his brain to recall what had actually happened more than a thousand seconds ago, relying, of course, on inference. At the Yale meeting of the APA in 1913, J. W. Baird with great enthusiasm arranged for a public demonstration of introspection with the trained observers from his laboratory at Clark, but the performance was not impressive. Introspection, with inference and meaning left out as much as possible, becomes a dull taxonomic account of sensory events which, since they suggest almost no functional value for the organism, are peculiarly uninteresting to the American scientific temper.

Classical introspection, it seems to me, went out of style after Titchener's death in 1927 because it had demonstrated no functional use and therefore seemed dull, and also because it was unreliable. Laboratory atmosphere crept into the descriptions, and it was not possible to verify, from one laboratory to another, the introspective accounts of the consciousnesses of action, feeling, choice, and judgment. It is not surprising, therefore, that Külpe, Watson, and Wertheimer, all within the decade 1904–1913, reacted vigorously against the constraints of this idealistic but rigid pedantry.

DESCRIPTION OF THE IMPALPABLE

What came to be called *systematic experimental introspection* developed at Würzburg in 1901–1905 under Külpe's leadership (Boring, 1950a, pp. 401–410, 433–435). Külpe, influenced like Titchener toward positivism by Mach, had gone from Leipzig to Würzburg with the conviction that experimental psychology ought to do something about thought. The new experimental psychology could handle sensation, perception, and reaction, and Ebbinghaus in 1885 had added memory to its repertoire. Wundt had said that thought could not be studied experimentally, but Külpe, a positivist, was convinced that all you had to do was to get observers thinking under controlled conditions and then have them introspect upon the thought process.

There followed a brilliant series of papers by Külpe's students: Mayer and Orth on association (1901), Marbe on judgment

(1901), Orth on feeling (1903), Watt on thought (1905), Ach on action and thought (1905). Every one of these investigators found what we have called classical introspection inadequate to his problem. Mayer and Orth (1901) could describe the associated trains of images that run on in thinking but could discover from introspection no clue as to how thought is directed toward a goal. Marbe (1901) found judgments forming readily in terms of images, but got from introspection no hint as to how or why they were formed. Feeling resisted Orth's introspective analysis and he was obliged to invent a vague term, *conscious attitude,* to describe the affective life. Certainly feelings did not appear as sensations or images to his observers (Orth, 1903). Watt and Ach worked independently and came to mutually consistent conclusions. Watt, to make introspection more efficient, invented fractionation. He split up the psychological event under investigation into several successive periods and investigated each by itself, thus reducing the amount of memory and inference that were involved in the introspective report. Still the essential in thought eluded him, until he realized that the goal-directedness of thinking is predetermined by the task or instruction—the *Aufgabe* he called it—which the observer accepted before the individual thought process got under way (Watt, 1905). Ach developed the concept of the *determining tendency* as the unconscious guide which steers the conscious processes along a predetermined course to solve whatever problem thought is directed upon. He also elaborated fractionation with chronoscope control and coined the phrase *systematic experimental introspection.* The determining tendency itself is unconscious, but the conscious processes which it directs seemed to Ach's observers not to be describable in the terms of classical introspection, that is to say, in images and sensations. Ach (1905) therefore invented the term *awareness* for these vague and elusive contents of consciousness and his observers learned to describe their consciousnesses in terms of impalpable awarenesses (*unanschauliche Bewusstheiten*).

The Würzburgers thought they had discovered by introspection a new kind of mental element, but the *Bewusstheit* never gained the accepted status of a sensation or an image. Instead the Würzburgers were said to have discovered imageless thought, and many persons argued that the school had failed because its finding was negative: thoughts were not images, but what actually were they? Titchener, however, believed he knew. He said that these Würzburg thoughts were in part conscious attitudes which are vague evanescent patterns of sensations and images, and in part meanings and inferences which ought to be kept out of psychology as the *Kundgabe* which is not true description (Titchener, 1912a). We, with the perspective of forty years upon us, see that the main contribution lay in the realization of the importance of the unconscious *Aufgabe* and determining tendency. The course of thought is unconsciously determined: that is a conclusion which fitted the *Zeitgeist* of the period of its discovery, when Freud too was discovering that motivation is ordinarily not available to introspection.

Külpe's conclusion was, however, different. He believed that the impalpable awarenesses had been established as valid data of consciousness and he called them *functions* to distinguish them from the sensations and images of classical introspection, which he called *contents* (Külpe, 1920). *Funktionen* and *Inhalte* are two kinds of conscious data that make up what has been termed the bipartite psychology of Külpe's later days. In this choice Külpe was combining the introspection of Wundt with the introspection of Brentano. He was also making easier the coming protest of Gestalt psychology against Wundtian introspection.

AWARENESS OF MENTAL ACTIVITY

Meanwhile nearly all the philosophers and psychologists were dualists and most of the psychologists were also psychophysical parallelists. If you believe in conscious events as dependent upon brain events but wholly separate and different from the brain events, then you must believe in some kind of introspection or inner perception whereby you obtain your evidence about the mental events. The behavioristic monism of the twentieth century was unknown in the nineteenth. A belief in some kind of introspection was general in psychology and also in common sense.

The appeal to introspection was especially important in the case of act psychology, which claimed that a careful and unbiased examination of the mind shows that it does not consist of stable contents like images and sensations, but of acts directed intentionally upon an object or of activities striving purposively toward a goal (Boring, 1950a, pp. 439–456, 715–721). We have already seen that Brentano defended introspection as self-validating. He was the representative of intentionalistic act psychology who was contemporary with Wundt, and who thus posed the dilemma between Wundt's contents and his own acts (Brentano, 1874), a dilemma of which Külpe, as we have just noted, seized both horns. Brentano influenced the philosopher James Ward (1918) in his subject-object conative psychology of 1886, revised in 1918, and Ward influenced McDougall (1923), who, in spite of having once defined psychology as the science of behavior, elaborated a purposive psychology in 1923, a system that made purpose and striving a characteristic of all mental activity.

In Germany Stumpf, stimulated by Brentano's sponsorship of psychic acts and by Husserl's (1901) argument for phenomenology as the simplest description of experience, came to the conclusion that Wundt's kind of introspection yields the data of phenomenology but that psychology proper consists rather of Brentano's acts or, as Stumpf (1906) called them, *psychic functions*. Thus it is correct to say that by 1915 both Stumpf and Külpe believed in two kinds of introspective data: on the one hand, Stumpf in phenomena and Külpe in contents, and, on the other, both of them in functions (acts). Külpe (1920, pp. 42–45) was inclined to think that the functions were observed retrospectively (*rückschauende Selbstbeobachtung*), the contents immediately (*anschauende Selbstbeobachtung*).

Except for Titchener and his satellites, American psychology tended all along to be practical and functional in the Darwinian sense. As such it was destined to become behavioristic. It is interesting, therefore, to note that early American functional psychology of James, Dewey, Angell, and the Chicago school was introspective. Organisms have acquired consciousness because of its adaptive function, the argument ran. When the smooth course of habitual action is interrupted by external events, then "in steps consciousness," said James Angell (1907; Boring, 1950b, pp. 276–278), to solve the organism's problem. It is because functional psychology regarded the data of consciousness as essential to an understanding of the adjustment of man to his environment that Watson, founding behaviorism, declared that he was as much against functional psychology as against introspectionism.

PHENOMENOLOGICAL DESCRIPTION

The next protest against the constraints of classical introspection came in connection with the founding of Gestalt psychology —by Wertheimer (1912), we generally say, in his paper on seen movement. Wertheimer was working on the conditions of visually perceived movement. You can see movement when no stimulus object moves, as when stimulus displacement is discrete. Seen movement is thus a conscious, not a physical, event. Classical introspection would have required the description of perceived movement with reference to conscious contents, or mental processes, or images and sensations, or perhaps the attributes of sensation. Wertheimer thought, however, that any such reference or analysis would be a supererogation. Perceived movement can be recognized as itself and its conditions studied; why bother then with the Leipzig hocus-pocus? Since seen movement can thus be accepted immediately as an identifiable phenomenon, Wertheimer called it *phi*—the "*phi*-phenomenon." In

1912 the notion of phenomenology was in the air. Husserl (1901) had used the term for the free unbiased description of experience ("being") and Stumpf (1906) had picked it up. Thus Köhler and the other Gestalt psychologists came always to speak of the data of direct experience as *phenomena,* avoiding all the words that were associated with classical introspection. Later it was such *phenomenological observation* that became a technic to displace *introspection* (Boring, 1950a, pp. 601–607).

This Magna Carta of phenomenology presently released a great deal of good research, most of it on problems of perceptions. In G. E. Müller's laboratory Katz's (1911) work on brightness constancy had even preceded Wertheimer's, and Rubin's (1915) classical study of figure and ground came soon after. There began a long series of investigations of the laws of perceived form, studies which introduced new descriptive concepts for the phenomena, like *organization* and *articulation,* and new functional concepts, like *closure, transposition,* and *object constancy* (Boring, 1950a, pp. 611–614).

Nearly all these perceptual studies have been performed in an atmosphere of dualism. You try to find the stimulus conditions or else the brain pattern that is necessary and sufficient for the perception. Wertheimer, Köhler, and Koffka have all supported the concept of *isomorphism,* the hypothesis that the field pattern of the perception corresponds topologically to the field pattern of the underlying events in the brain, and, while neither Gestalt psychology nor experimental phenomenology requires isomorphism as a basic concept, nevertheless isomorphism requires some kind of dualism, and thus the phenomena become one term in its psychophysiological correlation. Köhler's (1920) great book on *Physische Gestalten* supported this view.

As Gestalt psychology waxed, classical introspection waned. Wertheimer's paper on phenomenal movement was in 1912. Külpe died in 1915. Köhler (1917) worked with apes on the island of Teneriffe during World War I and applied the new phenomenological principles in the description of their psychology. Koffka's students were busy publishing papers on perception. Wundt died in 1920, the year that Köhler published *Physische Gestalten*. In 1922 Köhler went to Berlin to succeed Stumpf. The Gestalt psychologists had started a new journal devoted to their interests in 1921, *Psychologische Forschung*, and Wertheimer (1921; 1923) used its early pages to make the case against classical introspection. Koffka restated the case in English for Americans in 1922. Titchener died in 1927. Köhler's *Gestalt Psychology* appeared in 1929, and Koffka's *Principles* in 1935. It is reasonable to say that phenomenological observation had won out over classical introspection by 1930.

Under Hitler's influence the Gestalt psychologists who remained productive all came to America. There the victory of phenomenology, made easier by Titchener's death, was no great triumph, for other strong forces were operating to swing American psychology toward behavioristics. Nevertheless, phenomenology remained, not only respectable, but stimulating and useful in initial attacks upon many psychological problems, as Gibson's (1950) recent phenomenological study of the visual world shows. So here we come to a case where introspection, under an alias, can be said to be still practiced, provided the word *introspection* is not restricted to its Leipzig-Cornell meaning.

PATIENTS' PROTOCOLS

The emphasis which modern psychopathology places on the unconscious creates for it a complementary concern with the conscious. Thus psychoanalysis stresses the importance to therapy of bringing repressed ideas from the unconscious into consciousness. The analysand, bubbling free associations on the couch, is certainly giving the analyst information about his consciousness (*Kundgabe*) though he remain far from the use of classical introspection. When and how, we may ask, did psychopathology get itself concerned with the content of consciousness?

Nearly always the first evidence of what we now call mental

disease lies in abnormal conduct, in maladaptive behavior. The abnormal person, witch, or patient as the case may be, first calls attention to himself by queer or alarming conduct. The obvious symptoms that require social action, remedial or protective, are usually not reports of visions or complaints about voices, but such deviations from standard behavior as inconvenience others. Nevertheless psychopathology, which grew up surrounded by a belief in dualism, was never primarily behavioristic. There was for it always the presumption that a witch is conscious, even though the devil might have taken possesson of her will, and later that the hallucinations and delusions of the hysterical patient are conscious phenomena. Subjectivism, always implicit in these symptoms, was not very often explicit before the end of the nineteenth century.

Zilboorg's (1941; White, 1948) account makes it clear how the idea of mental derangement began in the conception of demoniacal possession. For these possessed people and for the fools, except in those cases where they were honored, the therapy consisted of discipline, threats, fetters, and blows, none of which actually had much value except to relieve those who administered the punishment. Even the Renaissance, which is said to have "discovered man," did not free these unhappy victims of an intolerant theological self-assurance, until at last the reaction toward humane treatment arrived with Pinel and his successors early in the nineteenth century. During the seventeenth and eighteenth centuries you get as subjective data the reports of melancholy (sometimes ending in suicide), of passions, of deliriums ("errors of reason"), of fantasies, of cholers, humors and madness, of spleen, vapors and hysterical distempers, of love as a cause of mental disability. An incubus might be a woman's hallucination, delusion, or wish projection, or else a fiction of other people's belief about her. The reforms of the nineteenth century toward the humane treatment of the insane and the rise of the concept of mental disease (Pinel, 1801) did not go far toward the subjectivization of psychopathology.

Braid's (1843) theory of hypnosis, as the scientific successor to mesmerism was called, was based on suggestion as a principle, a mentalistic but not a conscious entity. Liébeault (1866) cured a patient of sciatic pain by hypnosis; is a patient who says he feels pain introspecting? Liébeault was a dualist, for the title of his book asserts that he was studying *l'action de la morale sur le physique:* a treatise on psychosomatic medicine in 1866. Later Charcot (1886–90, vols. III and IX) worked out the stigmata of hysteria and thus, as he thought, of hypnosis, but most of the stigmata were not described in conscious terms, being phenomena like anesthesias, amnesias, and catatonias. Kraepelin, Wundt's onetime student, whose classical system of mental diseases reached maturity about 1896, established the basic dichotomy between manic-depressive psychoses and dementia precox. Thus he recognized elation, depression, and hallucinations as symptoms of mental disease, but that is a far cry from saying that his psychiatry was based on some kind of introspection.

Nevertheless this last decade of the nineteenth century was the decade for psychopathology to turn truly psychological. It marked the emergence of Janet first, and then of Freud. Janet's classical study of the symptoms of hysteria appeared in 1892, and Freud's great book on the interpretation of dreams in 1900. Janet's theory of hysteria in terms of dissociation and the retraction of the field of attention was a psychological theory, although not an introspective one. Freud in his association with Breuer discovered the "talking cure" out of which psychoanalysis has emerged (Breuer and Freud, 1895). The effect of psychoanalysis upon psychiatry has during the present century been profound. Not only has psychiatry taken over psychoanalytic concepts while rejecting the total system, but the psychiatric interview has been arranged to assay consciousness, as well as to bring to consciousness those forgotten materials whose absence constitutes a symptom of mental disorder. Nowadays the interview and the couch are used as tools for a special kind of introspection, one which inventories consciousness and seeks to bring forgotten memories up to and across the threshold of introspection.

One of the most definite claims for the use of introspection by abnormal psychology was made by Morton Prince (1905; 1914), Janet's complement in America, long a student of dissociated and alternating personalities, and later insistent upon the simultaneous functioning of coconscious personalities. Prince once suggested that introspections might be obtained simultaneously from two coconscious personalities, even though they had but one set of receptors and effectors between them. You might, he thought, be able to question one personality with written questions shown to the eye and get the protocols spoken by the voice, while the other personality received spoken questions by ear and replied by writing on a pad. This is a difficult form of dissociation and, when it has been tried, the protocols tend to become habituated clichés or nonsense (Solomons and Stein, 1896); yet Prince's suggestion carries the point that patients' protocols are, after all, a kind of introspection. The operationist can, of course, translate protocols into discriminative response, for any consciousness that yields public data can be described in behavioristic terms; yet that fact does not alter the feeling of reality that the psychopathologists have about both consciousness, got by introspection, and unconsciousness, observed by more inferential technics.

PSYCHOPHYSICS

It was the prevailing nineteenth century dualism of mind and body, and thus of spiritualism and materialism, that led Fechner (1860), concerned with combating materialism and in establishing a spiritualistic monism, to invent psychophysics. By measuring both the physical stimulus and the psychical sensation and by showing how the magnitude of the latter is dependent upon the magnitude of the former, he believed that he was bringing mind and matter into a single system of relationships. The effect of Fechner's success in devising or standardizing the classical psychophysical methods which are still in use was to support the current psychophysical parallelism—although that is not what Fechner intended. For psychophysics the stimulus was available as an independent variable. The sensations, or the relative magnitudes of two sensations, or the sense-distances between two sensations, were available to introspection and so constituted a dependent variable in the psychophysical experiment. This kind of introspection has remained scientifically useful in experimental psychology for a full century and persists in good status today, although of course operationism has the necessary formulas for transforming it into behavioristic terms.

Before Fechner the experimental attack on sensory problems was apt to be psychophysical. Investigators determined both absolute and differential thresholds. When Bouguer in 1760 (pp. 51 f.) measured the differential threshold for brightness, he relied on the observer's judgment as to when a shadow on a screen becomes only just noticeable. Weber's formulation of his psychophysical law in 1834 (pp. 44–175) depended on the same kind of judgment. Sensory phenomenology was stimulated by the discovery of the law of the spinal nerve roots (1811, 1822) which showed that the sensory nerves present a set of problems of their own. Johannes Müller's (1826, pp. 44–55; 1833–40, vol. II, p. v) doctrine of specific nerve energies was, in a sense, psychophysics, since it distinguished between sensory quality and the property of the stimulus which arouses the quality. Many of these early instances of psychophysics, especially the quantitative ones, have been discussed by Titchener (1901–05, vol. II, pt. ii, pp. xiii–cxvi). There is no need to labor the point that parallelism was the accepted doctrine of the century and that psychophysics consisted in the observation of correlations, many of them quantitative, between the two correlated terms of mind and body. No one doubted that you can observe mind as sensory experience.

For at least half a century (1860–1910) psychophysics flourished along with classical introspection and came under some of its constraints. It was thought, for instance, that observers need special training in order to give reliable results. Titchener (1910, pp. 202 f.; Boring, 1921), as we have already seen, warned against the stimulus-error, and both Wundt and Titchener believed that control stimuli (*Vexirversuche*) were improper. For instance, in determining the limen of dual impression upon the skin, you vary the separation of the esthesiometer points according to some standard procedure, but you do not throw in single points as controls—not if you are a classical introspectionist. The control lies in training the observer to avoid the stimulus-error. If he says *two* when he has only one, he is not wrong, for introspection cannot lie—or at least it was thought that good introspection of trained observers cannot lie very much, and in any case to argue that a one-point stimulus cannot give rise to a two-point perception is to prejudge the experiment which seeks to find what it is that you do for every value of the stimulus.

The same point about introspection appears in Wundt's method of identical series for the investigation of recognition (Reuther, 1905, pp. 24–30). In this method you give the observer a series of stimulus-objects, and later you give him in the test the identical series again, having him state which items he recognizes. You do not introduce new items as controls. He knows the series are the same, but you trust him in his introspection. He will not report recognition for an item unless he experiences recognition, and no one but the observer himself can publish the privacy of his own consciousness. If you place all this responsibility on the observer, no wonder training becomes important.

This kind of incontrovertible psychophysical introspection did not last long in the functional atmosphere of American psychology. Perhaps it has not now been heard of for thirty years.

For the half century after Fechner the psychophysicists always talked about observing and measuring sensation, but actually they were observing, reporting upon, and measuring, not complete sensations, but sensory attributes. From Fechner on, the psychophysical methods were applied to judgments of the quality, intensity, extensity, or duration of sensory experience, and Külpe (1904), after he broke away from Wundt, suggested that you never actually do observe a whole sensation, but only separately its attributes, out of which you build the sensation up as a scientific construct. Later Rahn (1914), a student of Külpe's, reinforced this comment, and Titchener (1915) ultimately adjusted his views to meet the contention.

Külpe in 1893 (pp. 30–38) had argued that the attributes of sensation are (*a*) inseparable from the sensation (if any attribute becomes zero, the whole sensation ceases to exist) but (*b*) independently variable with respect to each other (you can change one and keep the other constant). Later this view turned out to be wrong, for there are separate attributes, like the pitch and loudness of tones and the hue and brightness of spectral lights, which cannot easily be varied independently by controlling their stimulus. Stevens (1934a; 1934b; Boring, 1935) solved this problem by an appeal to the concept of invariance. You have, he said, an independent attribute if it remains invariant when the dimensions of the stimulus are varied in accordance with some unique determined function. This concept results in plotting isesthetic contours on a stimulus diagram, *e.g.*, in plotting isophonic contours for pitch and loudness against stimulus frequency and energy, or isochromatic contours for hue, brightness, and saturation against stimulus wavelength and energy. Sensory equality becomes the crucial datum, but subjective equality is computed from the same basic introspective data that Fechner used—judgments of *greater* and *less* or of some similar complementary categories.

Modern psychophysics is also engaged in the determination of sensory interval scales and ratio scales, and for this purpose observers report on the relation of one sense-distance as greater or less than another (interval scale) or on the ratio of one sensory attribute to another (ratio scale) (Stevens, 1951, pp. 23-30). Such introspection is reliable and receives general approval, even in behavioristic America.

There are other less quantitative kinds of psychophysics which still make successful use of reports on sensory experience and which can be properly classified as modern introspection. An excellent example is Crocker's (1945) work on the analysis and assessment of flavors by trained panels of judges, persons who are really introspectors especially trained to appreciate and analyze tastes and smells. They estimate the degree of the various olfactory and gustatory components in a flavor, check judgments against one another, working as a cooperative team with high motivation and enthusiasm. Such a trained panel may be sent out from the parent laboratory to some industrial plant to savor and calibrate its product, and then may later be brought back to the parent laboratory for checking in introspective reliability and also, when necessary, for analytic recalibration. Crocker's account of how attitudes are fixed and judgments rendered uniform in these panels is reminiscent of the atmosphere of Wundt's laboratory in all respects, except that Crocker's laboratory lacks the authoritarian control of Wundt's.

Another recent example of the modern use of the report of sensory experience is the book on pain by Hardy and his associates (1952). This book sets forth the psychophysics of pain, having regard, among other things, to the different qualities of algesic experience, and to establishing a sensory scale of pain by the subjective equation of algesic sense-distance.

The lesson to be learned from psychophysics is, therefore, that, in respect of the observation of sensory experience, introspection has thrived for a hundred years and is still in style.

ANIMAL CONSCIOUSNESS

In denying rational souls to animals, Descartes had made the problem of animal psychology relatively unimportant, but Darwin (1872), with his evolutionary argument that the forms of both mind and body show continuous development from lower species to man, changed all that. You began then to hear from Romanes (1883) about mental evolution and the evolution of intelligence. Romanes coined the term *comparative psychology* for the study of the nature of mind in different species. By giving the animal mind the benefit of the doubt, he was able to represent animal intelligence as not so far below man's. Lloyd Morgan (1894), writing a comparative psychology, sought to temper Romanes' enthusiasm with the principle of parsimony: do not interpret an action as the outcome of the exercise of a higher psychical faculty, he said, if it can be interpreted as the outcome of one that stands lower in the psychological scale. Lloyd Morgan warned against "anthropomorphism" in assessing animal behavior—meaning, of course, anthropopsychism. Loeb (1890), establishing the concept of tropism and the unconscious action of lower animal forms, suggested that consciousness emerges in the course of evolution as it becomes needed for more adaptive action and that the faculty of associative memory constitutes a criterion of it. Experiments on animal intelligence began, notably Thorndike's in 1898. In the decade 1900–1910 there was marked activity in experimental comparative psychology, a great deal of it concerned with the measurement of animal intelligence for which the maze was regarded as a very useful instrument.

Although there had already been argument put forward in favor of an objective animal psychology (Beer *et al.*, 1899), comparative psychology got under way in a period when a psychology with consciousness left out was generally regarded as psychology without its psyche—a branch of physiology perhaps. American functional psychology kept consciousness inside the fold, and the comparative psychologists settled on a formula for the observation of animal consciousness which might well have been called *animal introspection.* Nowhere has this problem been more clearly stated than by Washburn in her handbook of 1908 (p. 13) on the animal mind. She wrote:

If an animal behaves in a certain manner, what may we conclude the consciousness accompanying its behavior to be like? . . . At the outset of our discussion . . . we are obliged to acknowledge that *all psychic interpretation of animal behavior must be on the analogy of human experience.* We do not know the meaning of such terms as perception, pleasure, fear, anger, visual sensation, etc., except as these processes form a part of the contents of our own minds. Whether we will or no, we must be anthropomorphic in the notions we form of what takes place in the mind of an animal.

There is an implication here that you learn about human consciousness by direct observation of it in introspection, but that animal consciousness is known only indirectly by analogical inference. Not everyone held to that difference, however. Max Meyer (1921) put forward what he called the psychology of "the other one," an argument that your own personal consciousness is not material for science, being particular and not general, and that psychology studies always other organisms—other people, other animals. In this sense both the animal's conduct and man's words are introspection if they are taken as meaning something about the subject's consciousness. Even Titchener (1910, pp. 30–36) can be found saying of this argument from analogy: "The animal is thus made, so to say, to observe, to introspect; it attends to certain stimuli, and registers its experience by gesture."

It is interesting to see how Watson, before he had thought out behaviorism, accepted the current belief of this first decade of experimental animal psychology that knowledge of animal consciousness is the ultimate goal in comparative psychology. Watson was still at Chicago, the home of systematic functional psychology, which held that consciousness is to be understood psychologically in terms of its use to the organism. He had entitled his monograph of 1907 (pp. 90–97): *Kinaesthetic and Organic Sensations: Their Role in the Reactions of the White Rat to the Maze.* In this investigation he eliminated vision, hearing, taste, smell, and certain cutaneous factors from the repertoire of the rat who still remembers how to run the maze, and he concluded that "intra-organic sensations—the kinaesthetic sensations coupled with the organic probably, and possibly with the static" are what the rat uses in following the correct path. Watson even discussed the possibility of the rat's use of visual imagery, which "in our own case would play a preponderating role." He suggested that success for the rat as it runs may re-assure it: "If the turn is made at the proper stage (and it has been shown that blind rats deprived of their vibrissae can make these turns without allowing their bodies to touch the edges of the openings at the turns), the animal may be supposed thereby to get a 'reassuring feeling' which is exactly comparable to the experience which we get when we touch a familiar object in the dark."

Later, of course, Watson repudiated this supererogatory con-cern with consciousness and asked psychologists to get closer to their data of stimuli and responses. That was a move toward positivism, but Watson did not think of that. Indeed, it is pos-sible to regard animal behavior as a kind of language which means something about consciousness, just as it is also possible to strip introspection of its meanings and regard it as mere verbal motion. Certainly, if Max Meyer's "other one" can introspect, the animals can too and did before behaviorism made their con-sciousness unimportant.

VERBAL REPORT

Watson's reaction (1913), away from the pedantry and unre-liability of introspection, as he saw it, toward the more positive psychology of stimulus and response, was an attempt, not so much to create behaviorism as a new psychology with conscious-ness left out, as it was to reformulate the old psychology in new terms. For the imagery of thinking, he suggested that we can substitute incipient subvocal movement. Feeling, he believed, might turn out to be endocrine. Association had already been shown by Pavlov to be a conditioning of reflex responses and not necessarily a connection among ideas. Watson (1919) formally ruled introspection out of psychology but he left in the more reliable results of introspection, notably in psychophysics. Thus it was necessary for him to leave in introspection as verbal report. Did he thus embrace the bath with the baby? Is introspection anything more than verbal report?

Actually there is a difference. Verbal report viewed simply as behavior is capable of physical specification in which the writing and speaking of words appear as very different kinds of movements until they have been shown to be equivalent in an experimental situation. On the other hand, verbal report as introspection is not response but observation and description and therefore reference, an indication of objects of observation in the sense of the meanings of the words used.

Another way of expressing this same matter is to write two formulas:

[1] Introspective observation: $E \rightarrow O = S \rightarrow$ facts of consciousness
[2] Behavioristic observation: $O = E \rightarrow S \rightarrow$ facts of psychology

The corresponding sentences are: [1] In introspective observation, the experimenter notes the facts of consciousness which the observer, who is the subject, has observed. [2] In behavioristic observation, the observer, who is the experimenter, observes the behavior of the subject in respect of its implications for the facts of psychology. In classical introspection the subject is the observer. He has responsibility for the correctness of his descriptions of conscious data and thus he had at Leipzig, Cornell, and elsewhere to be trained, for introspection is more than having experience. Behaviorism shifts the locus of scientific responsibility from an observing subject to the experimenter who becomes the observer *of* the subject. In this way it is possible to bring to psychological observation irresponsible and untrained subjects— animals, children, the feebleminded, the mentally ill, and also the untrained normal human adult. Thus all the mental tests come into psychology because mostly they involve verbal responses from naive subjects. And the animal experiments come in because ordinarily the discriminative behavior of the animals is a language devised by the experimenter and taught to the animal so that he can tell the experimenter about his abilities and capacities. Are we to say that the animal is not introspecting because he is not communicating to himself what he is communicating to the experimenter? Perhaps. The important thing is to see that Watson, in attacking introspection, was objecting, not to the use of words by the subject, but to trusting the subject to use the words only with those meanings that the experimenter wishes the words to have.

INTROSPECTION AS AN OPERATION

Watson, in substituting verbal report for introspection, was moving in the positivistic direction, but the culmination of this movement came later with the acceptance of operational definitions as providing the most secure specification for psychological concepts. Operationism is perhaps a movement toward greater precision in scientific thinking, but it is not a school. American psychologists first picked up this modern form of the old positivism from the physicist, P. W. Bridgman (1927), who was using the technic to explain relativity theory. Then it was found that logical positivism, as the movement came to be called later, was developing at the same time among the logicians in Vienna (Frank, 1949, pp. 1–52). Presently it became clear that the two movements were logically the same. Stevens (1939) undertook to be the expositor to American psychologists. Bridgman was content to let operational definition go back ultimately to experience, but for psychologists that regression would not do at all. For them experience was a concept in special need of definition, since the availability of consciousness to scientific observation was the main problem dividing the schools (Stevens, 1935a; 1935b). The effect of a great deal of discussion along these lines in the 1930's was a change in the status of consciousness from (*a*) the reservoir of experience upon which all empirical science draws to (*b*) a concept based upon observation and specified by the observational operations that make conscious data available to science. That is a large change from the introspection that cannot lie because the having of experience is the knowing that you have it.

Nowadays the word *introspection* has dropped out of use. *Consciousness* or *phenomenal experience* or *sensory datum* or some other equivalent mentalistic term indicates a psychological construct which is got by inference *from* the observations. A comparable concept is the *intervening variable,* and a case could be made for Tolman (1936) as a phenomenological operationist, directly observing purpose and kindred entities in his data. Do you truly observe consciousness or an intervening variable? Do you observe any construct, or do you infer it? Do you look at the ammeter and observe the strength of the current or is what you observe merely a pointer on a scale?

Thus the answer to the question "What became of introspection?" seems to be this. Introspection as a special technic has gone. The object of introspection—sometimes called *consciousness,* sometimes something else—is a construct like an ability, or an intervening variable, or a conditioned response, or any of the other "realities" out of which a general psychology is formed. The modern equivalent of introspection persists in the reports of sensory experience in psychophysics, in the protocols of patients with psychological difficulties, in the phenomenological descriptions of perception and other psychological events as provided notably by Gestalt psychologists, and also in a great deal of social psychology and psychological philosophy where the Cartesian dualism is still found to be convenient.

UNCONSCIOUSNESS

Any study of the history of the availability of consciousness to scientific observation, like the present one, gains significance as we consider also the availability of unconsciousness to science. *A* is specified clearly only with respect to *not-A.* It would not, however, be proper to undertake now the consideration of all the means whereby a knowledge of unconscious psychological events has been brought into science. Nevertheless we may use a paragraph to list the outstanding fields which contributed to what nowadays we call psychology and which got along, nevertheless, without any observation that might be called *introspection*.

The *reflex* was thought almost from its discovery to be unconscious, largely because it could occur without the brain, although Pflüger was of the opinion that its purposiveness implies that it is conscious. Was Lotze, who disagreed with Pflüger, relying on introspection to be sure that reflexes are unconscious? *Instinct* was ordinarily opposed to intelligent action and often supposed to be unconscious. Unconsciousness, however, was not ordinarily involved in its definition; the criterion for instinct was that it was unlearned and usually involuntary. Loeb's *tropism* was defined with consciousness irrelevant. Herbart's *ideas in a state of tendency* were defined as unconscious, as were Fechner's *negative sensations*. Although the Würzburg school was developing systematic introspection, it seems clear now that its great discovery was the existence and effectiveness of unconscious tendencies—the *determining tendency*, the *Aufgabe*, etc. Freud made the concepts of the unconscious familiar to everyone and also started the development of the technics of observation that now replace introspection, but the test of unconsciousness (suppression, repression) remained in part introspection, the fact that ideas that might have been expected to be in mind were conspicuously absent. Thus dynamic psychology carries on with the basic assumption that you cannot trust the subject's personal belief (introspection) for the true assessment of his motives.

In all these cases consciousness is seen to have been important in a negative manner, for its absence is a matter of interest and sometimes even an essential specification—as would, indeed, be expected in a psychology that was originally formed on the dualism that *consciousness* has a distinctive meaning.

CONCLUSION

Now let the writer say what he thinks has become of introspection.

There have been in the history of science two important dichotomies that have been made with respect to introspection. (*a*) The first is animal psychology *vs.* human psychology: human beings are supposed to be able to introspect, and animals are not. (*b*) The second is the unconscious mind *vs.* the conscious mind, with introspection the means of observing consciousness. These two dichotomies reduce, however, to one: inference *vs.* direct experience.

Operational logic, in my opinion, now fuses this single dichotomy because it shows that human consciousness is an inferred construct, a concept as inferential as any of the other psychologists' realities (James, 1890, vol. I, p. 184), and that literally immediate observation, the introspection that cannot lie, does not exist. All observation is a process that takes some time and is subject to error in the course of its occurrence.

Introspection's product, consciousness, appears now in the bodies of its progeny: the sensory experience of psychophysics, the phenomenal data of Gestalt psychology, the symbolic processes and intervening variables employed by various behaviorists, the ideas, the manifest wishes, the hallucinations, delusions, and emotions of patients and neurotic subjects, and the many mentalistic concepts which social psychology uses. The newest usage is this latter one, social perception, a term which refers both to the perception of social phenomena, like anger and danger, and the perceptions which are understood by reference to their social determinants; but here the introspection is not different in kind from the phenomenological description that the Gestalt psychologists still use. In general, however, it seems to the writer that there is no longer to be found any sharp dichotomy setting off the introspectable from the unconscious. That once fundamental distinction disappeared with the dissolution of dualism. Consciousness nowadays is simply one of many concepts which psychology employs, usually under some other name, whenever it finds the category useful for the generalization of observations.

References

Ach, Narziss. *Ueber die Willenstätigkeit und das Denken.* Göttingen: Vandenhoeck & Ruprecht, 1905.

Angell, J. R. The province of functional psychology. *Psychological Review,* 1907, vol. 14, 61–91.

Avenarius, Richard. *Kritik der reinen Erfahrung.* Leipzig: Fues & Reisland, 1888–90. 2 vols.

Beer, Theodor, Bethe, Albrecht, and von Uexküll, J. Vorschläge zu einer objektivirenden Nomenclatur in der Physiologie des Nervensystems. *Biologisches Centralblatt,* 1899, vol. 19, 517–521.

Boring, E. G. The stimulus-error. *American Journal of Psychology,* 1921, vol. 33, 449–471.

Boring, E. G. *The Physical Dimensions of Consciousness.* New York: Century, 1933.

Boring, E. G. The relation of the attributes of sensation to the dimensions of the stimulus. *Philosophy of Science,* 1935, vol. 2, 236–245.

Boring, E. G. *A History of Experimental Psychology.* (2nd ed.) New York: Appleton-Century-Crofts, 1950. (a)

Boring, E. G. The influence of evolutionary theory upon American psychological thought. In Stow Persons (Ed.), *Evolutionary Thought in America.* New Haven: Yale University Press, 1950. Pp. 269–298. (b)

Bouguer, Pierre. *Traité d'optique sur la gradation de la lumière.* Paris: Guerin & Delatour, 1760.

Braid, James. *Neurypnology; or, the Rationale of Nervous Sleep; Considered in Relation with Animal Magnetism.* London: Churchill, 1843.

Brentano, Franz. *Psychologie vom empirischen Standpunkte.* Leipzig: Duncker & Humblot, 1874.

Breuer, Joseph, and Freud, Sigmund. *Studien über Hysterie.* Leipzig and Vienna: Deuticke, 1895.

Bridgman, P. W. *The Logic of Modern Physics.* New York: Macmillan, 1927.

Charcot, J. M. *Oeuvres complètes.* Paris: Bureaux du Progrès médical, 1886–90. 9 vols.

Clarke, H. M. Conscious attitudes. *American Journal of Psychology,* 1911, vol. 22, 214–249.

Comte, Auguste. *Cours de philosophie positive.* Paris: Bachelier, 1830–42. 6 vols.

Crocker, E. C. *Flavor.* New York: McGraw-Hill, 1945.

Darwin, Charles. *Expression of the Emotions in Man and Animals.* London: Murray, 1872.

Descartes, René. *Les passions de l'âme.* Paris: Le Gras, 1649.

Eisler, Rudolf. *Wörterbuch der philosophischen Begriffe.* Berlin: Mittler & Sohn, 1910.

Fechner, G. T. *Elemente der Psychophysik.* Leipzig: Breitkopf & Härtel, 1860.

Frank, Philipp. *Modern Science and its Philosophy.* Cambridge, Mass.: Harvard University Press, 1949.

Freud, Sigmund. *Die Traumdeutung.* Leipzig: Deuticke, 1900.

Geissler, L. R. The measurement of attention. *American Journal of Psychology,* 1909, vol. 20, 473–529.

Gibson, J. J. *The Perception of the Visual World.* Boston: Houghton Mifflin, 1950.

Hardy, J. D., Wolff, H. G., and Goodell, Helen. *Pain Sensations and Reactions.* Baltimore: Williams & Wilkins, 1952.

Hayes, S. P. A study of the affective qualities. *American Journal of Psychology,* 1906, vol. 17, 358–393.

Husserl, E. G. *Logische Untersuchungen: Untersuchungen zur Phänomenologie und Theorie der Erkenntnis.* Halle: Niemeyer, 1901.

Huxley, T. H. On the hypothesis that animals are automata, and its history. *Fortnightly Review,* 1874, vol. 22 (New Series 16), 555–580.

Jacobson, Edmund. On meaning and understanding. *American Journal of Psychology,* 1911, vol. 22, 553–577.

James, William. *Principles of Psychology.* New York: Henry Holt, 1890.

Janet, Pierre. *L'état mental des hystériques.* Paris: Rueff, 1892.

Katz, David. Die Erscheinungsweisen der Farben und ihre Beeinflussung durch die individuelle Erfahrung. *Zeitschrift für Psychologie,* 1911, Ergbd. 7.

Köhler, Wolfgang. Intelligenzprüfung an Anthropoiden. *Abhandlungen der Preussischen Akademie der Wissenschaften (physikalisch-mathematische Klasse),* 1917, nr. 1.

Köhler, Wolfgang. *Die physischen Gestalten in Ruhe und im stationären Zustand.* Braunschweig: Vieweg & Sohn, 1920.

Köhler, Wolfgang. *Gestalt Psychology.* New York: Liveright, 1929.

Koffka, Kurt. Perception: an introduction to Gestalt-Theorie. *Psychological Bulletin,* 1922, vol. 19, 531–585.

Koffka, Kurt. *Principles of Gestalt Psychology.* New York: Harcourt, Brace, 1935.

Kraepelin, Emil. *Psychiatrie.* (5th ed.) Leipzig: Barth, 1896.

Külpe, Oswald. *Grundriss der Psychologie.* Leipzig: Englemann, 1893.

Külpe, Oswald. Versuche über Abstraktion. *Bericht über den I. Kongress für experimentelle Psychologie,* 1904, vol. 1, 56–68.

Külpe, Oswald. *Vorlesungen über Psychologie.* Leipzig: Hirzel, 1920. (Posthumous)

La Mettrie, J. O. *L'homme machine.* Leiden: Luzac, 1748.

Liébeault, A. A. *Du sommeil et des états analogues, considérés surtout au point de vue de l'action du moral sur le physique.* Paris: Masson, 1866.

Locke, John. *Essay concerning Human Understanding.* London: Basset, 1690.

Loeb, Jacques. *Der Heliotropismus der Thiere und seine Uebereinstimmung mit dem Heliotropismus der Pflanzen.* Würzburg: Hertz, 1890.

Mach, Ernst. *Beiträge zur Analyse der Empfindungen.* Jena: Fischer, 1886.

Marbe, Karl. *Experimentell-psychologische Untersuchungen über das Urteil.* Leipzig: Engelmann, 1901.

Mayer, André, and Orth, Johannes. Zur qualitativen Untersuchung der Association. *Zeitschrift für Psychologie,* 1901, vol. 26, 1–13.

McDougall, William. *Outline of Psychology.* New York: Charles Scribner's, 1923.

Meyer, Max. *Psychology of the Other One.* Columbia: Missouri Book Company, 1921.

Mill, J. S. *Auguste Comte and Positivism.* (3rd ed.) London: Trübner, 1882.

Morgan, C. L. *Introduction to Comparative Psychology.* London: Scott, 1894.

Müller, G. E. Zur Analyse der Gedächtnistätigkeit und des Vorstellungsverlaufes, I. *Zeitschrift für Psychologie,* 1911, Ergbd. 5.

Müller, Johannes. *Zur vergleichenden Physiologie des Gesichtssinnes.* Leipzig: Cnobloch, 1826.

Müller, Johannes. *Handbuch der Physiologie des Menschen.* Coblenz: Hölscher, 1833–40. 3 vols.

Nakashima, Taizo. Contributions to the study of the affective processes. *American Journal of Psychology,* 1909, vol. 20, 157–193.

Okabe, Tamekichi. An experimental study of belief. *American Journal of Psychology,* 1910, vol. 21, 563–596.

Orth, Johannes. *Gefühl und Bewusstseinslage.* Berlin: Reuther & Reichard, 1903.

Pinel, Philippe. *Traité médico-philosophique sur aliénation mentale.* Paris: Richard, Caille & Revier, 1801.

Prince, Morton. *The Dissociation of a Personality.* New York: Longmans, Green, 1905.

Prince, Morton. *The Unconscious.* New York: Macmillan, 1914.

Pyle, W. H. An experimental study of expectation. *American Journal of Psychology,* 1909 ,vol. 20, 530–569.

Rahn, Carl. The relation of sensation to other categories in contemporary psychology. *Psychological Monographs,* 1914, vol. 16, no. 1 (Whole No. 67).

Reuther, Fritz. Beiträge zur Gedächtnisforschung. *Psychologische Studien,* 1905, vol. 1, 4–101.

Romanes, G. J. *Mental Evolution in Animals.* London: Kegan Paul, Trench, 1883.

Rubin, Edgar. *Synsoplevede Figurer.* Copenhagen: Gyldendal, 1915.

Solomons, L. M., and Stein, Gertrude. Normal motor automatism. *Psychological Review*, 1896, vol. 3, 492–512.

Stevens, S. S. The attributes of tones. *Proceedings of the National Academy of Sciences*, 1934, vol. 20, 457–459. (a)

Stevens, S. S. Volume and intensity of tones. *American Journal of Psychology*, 1934, vol. 46, 397–408. (b)

Stevens, S. S. The operational basis of psychology. *American Journal of Psychology*, 1935, vol. 47, 323–330. (a)

Stevens, S. S. The operational definition of psychological concepts. *Psychological Review*, 1935, vol. 42, 517–527. (b)

Stevens, S. S. Psychology and the science of science. *Psychological Bulletin*, 1939, vol. 36, 221–263.

Stevens, S. S. Mathematics, measurement and psychophysics. In S. S. Stevens (Ed.), *Handbook of Experimental Psychology*. New York: John Wiley, 1951. Pp. 7–49.

Stumpf, Carl. Erscheinungen und psychische Funktionen. *Abhandlungen der Preussischen Akademie der Wissenschaften (philosophisch-historische Klasse)*, 1960, nr. 4.

Thorndike, E. L. Animal intelligence. *Psychological Monographs*, 1898, vol. 2, no. 4 (Whole No. 8).

Titchener, E. B. *Experimental Psychology*. New York: Macmillan, 1901–05. 2 vols., 4 pts.

Titchener, E. B. *A Text-Book of Psychology*. New York: Macmillan, 1910.

Titchener, E. B. Description *vs.* statement of meaning. *American Journal of Psychology*, 1912, vol. 23, 165–182. (a)

Titchener, E. B. Prolegomena to a study of introspection. *American Journal of Psychology*, 1912, vol. 23, 427–448. (b)

Titchener, E. B. The schema of introspection. *American Journal of Psychology*, 1912, vol. 23, 485–508. (c)

Titchener, E. B. *A Beginner's Psychology*. New York: Macmillan, 1915. (a)

Titchener, E. B. Sensation and system. *American Journal of Psychology*, 1915, vol. 26, 258–267. (b)

Titchener, E. B. *Systematic Psychology: Prolegomena*. New York: Macmillan, 1929. (Posthumous)

Tolman, E. C. Operational behaviorism and current trends in psychology. In *Proceedings of the Twenty-Fifth Anniversary Celebration of the Inauguration of Graduate Studies at the University of Southern California*. Los Angeles: University of Southern California Press, 1936. Pp. 89–103.

Ward, James. *Psychological Principles*. Cambridge, England: University Press, 1918.

Washburn, M. F. *The Animal Mind*. New York: Macmillan, 1908.

Watson, J. B. Kinaesthetic and organic sensations: their role in the reactions of the white rat to the maze. *Psychological Monographs*, 1907, vol. 8, no. 2 (Whole No. 33).

Watson, J. B. Psychology as the behaviorist views it. *Psychological Review*, 1913, vol. 20, 158–177.

Watson, J. B. *Psychology from the Standpoint of a Behaviorist.* Philadelphia: Lippincott, 1919.

Watt, H. J. Experimentelle Beiträge zur einer Theorie des Denkens. *Archiv für die gesamte Psychologie,* 1905, vol. 4, 289–436.

Weber, E. H. *De pulsu, resorptione, auditu et tactu: annotationes anatomicae et physiologicae.* Leipzig: Koehler, 1834.

Wertheimer, Max. Experimentelle Studien über das Sehen von Bewegungen. *Zeitschrift für Psychologie,* 1912, vol. 61, 161–265.

Wertheimer, Max. Untersuchungen zur Lehre von der Gestalt, I. *Psychologische Forschung,* 1921, vol. 1, 47–58.

Wertheimer, Max. Untersuchungen zur Lehre von der Gestalt, II. *Psychologische Forschung,* 1923, vol. 4, 301–350.

White, R. W. *The Abnormal Personality.* New York: Ronald Press, 1948.

Wundt, Wilhelm. Selbstbeobachtung und innere Wahrnehmung. *Philosophische Studien,* 1888, vol. 4, 292–309.

Wundt, Wilhelm. *Grundriss der Psychologie.* Leipzig: Engelmann, 1896.

Zilboorg, Gregory. *A History of Medical Psychology.* New York: Norton, 1941.

Edward Bradford Titchener: 1867-1927
1927

Titchener had far more influence upon me than any other person in my professional life, the brilliant, erudite, magnetic, charming Titchener, who interested himself in the details of your research and writing and in how your wife cooked the mushrooms, helping in big and little things, but demanding loyalty, deference, and adherence to the advice so freely offered.

In the last twenty years of his life Titchener had few contemporary friends and remained surrounded by younger disciples. Was I one? I used to call myself a "heretic," being more aware of my dissents from Titchener than of my agreements, but in fundamentals I was as a psychologist Titchener-formed in habits of thoroughness, in belief in historical orientation, and in the aspiration to write English well. Only for a short period was this heretic a good introspectionist. Yet Titchener, the erudite egoist, remained always a fascinating subject, and the stories about him and how he ran his laboratory and the lives of those who crossed his orbit can even now hold an audience when told by an erstwhile enthusiastic disciple.

On 3 August 1927, the impossible happened. Titchener died. It was as if the Ten Commandments had suddenly crumbled, and I, recognizing at once the historical magnitude of this catastrophe, went into action. I wrote this paper in time for it to appear ten weeks later in the October number of the *American Journal of Psychology*, of which Titchener had until near the end been editor. I corresponded with his mother and with C. S. Myers, both in England, with the New York numismatist to find out how good

Reprinted with permission from the *American Journal of Psychology*, 1927, vol. 38, 489–506.

Titchener had made himself in this field, with American psychologists galore. I worked out the data from local records. My manifest reason for immediate publication seemed to be to honor Titchener, but that does not now make good sense. Now I think that I was moved by the suppressions of seventeen years of ambivalence, enthusiasms mixed with frustrations, with here at last a chance to tell the whole story, honestly and candidly, as befits the description of a scientist by a scientist. At last it could all be said with the sanction of scientific objectivity. A maturer man would have waited, let the writing get cold, have looked at it again, but I at forty was not yet mature, seven years before my psychoanalysis, and my frustrations had waited a long time.

This reprinting omits the many comments and anecdotes in footnotes, about a quarter of the total original article.

After thirty-five years of continuous service to psychology at Cornell University, Edward Bradford Titchener, the dean of experimental psychology in America (cf. Holt, 1911, p. 25), died unexpectedly in Ithaca, New York, on August 3, 1927, at the age of sixty. The death of no other psychologist could so alter the psychological picture in America. Not only was he unique among American psychologists as a personality and in his scientific attitude, but he was a cardinal point in the national systematic orientation. The clear-cut opposition between behaviorism and its allies, on the one hand, and something else, on the other, remains clear only when the opposition is between behaviorism and Titchener, mental tests and Titchener, or applied psychology and Titchener. His death thus, in a sense, creates a classificatory chaos in American systematic psychology.

Titchener was born on January 11, 1867, at Chichester, England, an old Roman town with walls still standing, about seventy miles south of London and not far from the coast. There is an insistent historicity about this little town that accords well with the historical cast of Titchener's mind in adulthood. The Titcheners were an old Chichester family. In 1532 John Tychenor was the headmaster of the Prebendal School in Chichester, which our Titchener attended in boyhood. William Titchener, the great-grandfather, was mayor of Chichester in 1832, and lent money to the city in return for which he received a lien on the regalia of the city. His son Edward (the grandfather) was a distinguished lawyer, according to a long list of appointments which he held. He is said to have run through several fortunes and to have died relatively poor, having been obliged to move from a residence in an old abbey, Greyling Wells, to a smaller house. He had two sons, William and John; and John was the father of our Titchener. John was the second son, but anyway, there was no longer a fortune for him to inherit. He went on an adventure to America at the time of the Civil War, and returned to England after fighting with the Confederate army. In 1866, he married Alice Field Habin of Kingsham, which is not far from Chichester, and in 1867 Edward Bradford was born. John Bradford died not many years afterward while still in his thirties. Edward Bradford Titchener therefore had his own way to make. There was no parental assistance forthcoming for him; he had, so far as his family was concerned, simply the consciousness of a very respectable descent.

When he was about fourteen he went on a scholarship to Malvern College, an important English public school, then about twenty years old. The college is in Worcestershire, over a hundred miles from London and very near Wales. There he spent four years.

After Malvern he went to Oxford in 1885, and became a member of Brasenose College. For four years he was senior scholar of Brasenose in classics and philosophy and senior Hulmian "exhibitioner" (a term applied to the holder of what, in America, is called a scholarship). In his fifth year he became a research student of physiology under Burdon-Sanderson, either because of the attraction of the subject or of the man, or perhaps because of both. He always expressed a great admiration for Burdon-Sanderson and acknowledged an intellectual debt to him. His first book he dedicated to him. He received the A.B. degree from Oxford in 1890, when he was twenty-three years old.

The conjunction of philosophy and physiology in Germany had produced physiological psychology and it is not strange that the combination of these two interests at Oxford should have led Titchener toward the new psychology. It was really quite new, much newer than the thirty years since Fechner's *Elemente* might lead one to suspect. [Wilhelm] Wundt's laboratory at Leipzig had been in existence only eleven years. On the other hand, interest was growing rapidly. Wundt's *Philosophische Studien* was in its sixth volume; the *Zeitschrift für Psychologie* had just been begun; Stumpf was completing the *Tonpsychologie;* Ebbinghaus' experiments on memory were five years old; G. E. Müller had begun on psychophysics; there was plenty to read in German. America was beginning to follow suit. Hall had opened the first formal laboratory at Hopkins, based on the German model, had gone to Clark and had begun another there. Cattell, back from Germany, was experimenting at Pennsylvania. Three other American laboratories had started and three more were about to be gotten under way. *The American Journal of Psychology* had reached its third volume. Ladd's *Physiological Psychology* was three years old, and James's *Principles* was to appear in the fall. The year before there had been the first International Congress of Psychology at Paris with one hundred and twenty psychologists in attendance. England was slow to learn from Germany, but the founding of *Mind* by Bain in 1876 had been in a sense a recognition of the birth of a new psychology. It was at such a time that Titchener, trained in philosophy and physiology, went to Wundt at Leipzig to study experimental psychology.

At Leipzig he found Külpe, as *Dozent,* Meumann, Kirschmann, Kämpfe, and Pace, Scripture, and Frank Angell from America. This was the beginning of a lifelong friendship and mutual regard between Titchener and Angell, based upon similar tastes and Angell's admiration for Titchener's "impersonal frankness." The second year Pace, Scripture, and Angell left and Witmer and Warren came. Titchener roomed with Meumann. Like the graduate students of any laboratory the world over, this group was much together in informal psychological discussion. Külpe was planning and writing his *Grundriss* which he published in 1893 and which Titchener translated into English in 1895. The thought was somewhat communal, and Titchener published in 1896 his *Outlines* on a similar plan. Some of the discussion, I have been told, hinged upon the fundamental methodological issue. Wundt had separated psychology and physics by reference to immediate and mediate experience, but younger men are always anxious to improve upon the master. Mach's *Analyse* had appeared in 1885; Avenarius had brought out the first volume of the *Kritik* in 1888 and the second in 1890. We all know that these books formed the basis of Külpe's and Titchener's definition of psychology. Külpe, as the more philosophical of the two, is said to have been especially concerned with Avenarius; Titchener, perhaps already turning from philosophy to science, preferred Mach, for whom his enthusiasm was never dampened.

The contact with Wundt was not personally intimate. Wundt was thirty-five years older than Titchener. He had not yet reached the height of his fame, but he was already the great man, expecting and receiving deference and homage, and capable of becoming "white and trembling with anger when some of his 'Zuhörer' . . . slipped out of a lecture on philosophy shortly before its close." With the graduate students "he dealt . . . somewhat autocratically, and prescribed the lines and methods of research . . . minutely" (Various, 1921). Probably Titchener's work on the *Erkennungsact* (Titchener, 1892a) and the doctoral dissertation, *Ueber binoculare Wirkungen monocularer Reize* (Titchener, 1892b), were arbitrarily assigned in this way.

But if Titchener's intercourse with Wundt was not intimate personally, it was, nevertheless, both intimate and effective academically. The similarity between Titchener and Wundt may be partly merely a coincidence that they were similar personalities, though one was an Englishman and the other a German. Nevertheless this fact is not enough to explain all of the many overt items of resemblance. At least a dozen attitudes of Titchener's he got from Wundt. There is his own autocracy in the Cornell Laboratory, not only in the matter of theses, less obvious perhaps than Wundt's, but, supported by his dominating personality, equally effective. There is his persistent assumption that all the men of the Cornell Laboratory represent a single intellectual endeavor, opposed to an uninitiated outer world. There are both his tolerance in self-criticism and his inflexibility in polemics. There is his constant effort to demonstrate that psychology is a science. There is his consequent belief in formal psychological apparatus, and the need of "building up" a laboratory by the collection of standardized pieces. There is his conviction that the elementary lectures should be accompanied by experimental demonstration, and also his habit (but here he excelled Wundt) of dramatizing his lectures. One device was his invariable custom of lecturing in an Oxford master's gown: "It confers the right to be dogmatic," he said. Another was the tradition under which the members of his staff have always attended the elementary lectures—and listened often, let it be said, with suppressed excitement to hear how, after some new discovery at Cornell, he would alter the familiar treatment of the subject. Could the picture be more like Leipzig and less American or English?

Actually then there were only two years of Wundt. In 1892, when twenty-five years old, Titchener received the degree of Doctor of Philosophy and returned to England. Here the record shows that he was an extension lecturer in biology at Oxford for a few months, a very natural arrangement in view of his relation to [the famous physiologist] Burdon-Sanderson, and of the fact that he had already since 1889 published ten articles in general biology, all of them in *Nature*. Titchener would have liked to stay on at Oxford, but Oxford has never, then or now, adequately recognized psychology, and experimental psychology as a science would have had there a particularly hard row to hoe. At any rate on leaving Leipzig he had already agreed to go to America.

Frank Angell, his Leipzig friend of 1890–91, had gone back to

America to Cornell to open a psychological laboratory initiated by a benefaction that phrenology is said to have inspired. After his first year at Cornell he was called, at its inauguration, to Stanford University, and he recommended Titchener for his Cornell post. "In those days a laboratory was a laboratory," Titchener has often said; and this young laboratory psychologist, still only twenty-five years old, hurried to Ithaca, New York, with its laboratory, as an assistant professor of psychology. He never left Cornell; and within psychology Cornell and Titchener have become almost interchangeable words.

Ithaca was certainly a remarkable change from Oxford and Leipzig. The scenic beauty of the Cornell campus, between two deep gorges, was then, except for mud, as it is now; but the university, architectually at least, was raw. Nevertheless Titchener had his laboratory. The first years were strenuous ones. The six-room laboratory in White Hall had to be equipped with bought standard pieces and with homemade apparatus. He married in 1894, Sophie K. Bedlow of Portland, Maine, and she helped him greatly in the laboratory and later with drawings for the books. He may have been discouraged, for in 1893 he applied for the post at Toronto, and his effort to leave so soon after he had come was not looked upon with favor by the University.

He plunged immediately into scientific work and writing. His list of publications contains sixty-two articles, long and short, from 1893 to 1900 inclusive (Foster, 1917). He began to put the master into English. With [J. H.] Creighton he translated Wundt's *Human and Animal Psychology* in 1894, and revisions of the succeeding editions in 1896 and 1901. With [J. E.] Gulliver he translated the first volume of Wundt's *Ethics* in 1897 and the revisions in 1902. He had actually translated the entire third edition of the *Physiologische Psychologie* at Oxford, and, after revising it at Leipzig, took it to Wundt, only to find that its publication was prevented by the fact that the fourth edition was then ready to appear. In Ithaca he translated the fourth edition, and, holding it for last revisions, found it in turn displaced by the publication of the much enlarged fifth edition. Not discouraged, he began again on the fifth and published immediately in 1902 the first six of its twenty-two chapters when his work on the *Manuals* took him away. He translated [Oswald] Külpe's *Grundriss* for publication in 1895, and with Pillsbury he translated Külpe's *Introduction to Philosophy* for publication in 1897. In addition to all this he wrote his own *Outline of Psychology* in 1896, his *Primer of Psychology* in 1898, and began the *Experimental Psychology*, of which the first two volumes appeared in 1901, and which we shall return to presently. It was a remarkable accomplishment, even as great men go.

Meanwhile he was "settling in." He was made a full professor in 1895, when still only twenty-eight years old. Graduate students were beginning to work in the laboratory, which was moved to larger quarters in Morrill Hall in 1896. Miss [Margaret Floy] Washburn was his first Ph.D. in 1894. [W. B.] Pillsbury took his degree in 1896, Miss [Eleanor A. McC.]Gamble and [Madison] Bentley theirs in 1898, [G. M.] Whipple his in 1900. Titchener spent much time on his lectures and insisted, even against the President, upon not lecturing more than once a day. He took over the introductory lectures from President [J. G.] Schurman in 1895 and succeeded with them at once. They remained extremely popular until he relinquished them for a time in 1909.

It was during this period that Titchener began to draw away from the philosophers. He was a member of the Sage School of Philosophy, but science, he thought, had nothing to do with philosophy—or at least with philosophers, for he always made the distinction. In all it was a struggle of fifteen years or more, but Titchener finally won his fight for a separation and a division of the spoils of scholarships and fellowships.

With all his working and fighting, the Titchener of the nineties found time for society. He was a member of a congenial group, and I am told he was the "lion" of many social occasions. He was then, as always, an unusual mixture of decorum and of informal, intimate, sympathetic friendliness. He always felt respect for men much older than himself; and he always expected and even exacted it from young men, no matter what the degree of intimacy. Although he was outspoken in criticism of his friends, there was nevertheless underneath a persistent strain of loyalty, and his antagonism to those who had once transgressed his code was lasting.

The total picture in America is not so easy to draw, nor is it so important. A foreigner settling in a new country is not always welcomed, particularly when necessities of life like laboratories are scarce. Especially may this be true of a dominating personality. Yet Titchener seemed always ready to respond to friendship. Angell had moved across the continent, but [E. C.] Sanford, he felt, welcomed him, and until Sanford's death there remained a warm cordiality between these two men. With Sanford he joined Hall on the staff of *The American Journal of Psychology* in 1895. In general, however, Titchener felt repulsed and isolated, and thus he let his colleagues alone, except in controversy. He was probably not constituted for teamwork.

His relation to the American Psychological Association was typical. The twenty-six charter members elected Titchener and Münsterberg at the meeting for organization at Clark University in the summer of 1892. Titchener was present at the first regular meeting the next winter, but he shortly resigned over a difference of opinion that had arisen about some action which he thought a matter of honor. He was host at the Ithaca meeting in 1897, but not a member. He joined again in 1910, but I do not think he ever went to a meeting after 1897. When the Association again met in Ithaca in 1925, he was still a member but did not attend, although he held court for a continuous stream of visitors at his house. The next year he allowed his membership to lapse.

Thus the lines between America, on the one hand, and Titchener, on the other, became sharply drawn. Clark University, because of Sanford and *The American Journal of Psychology*, remained within his world and was later definitely to affect it. The *Psychological Review* was still in the camp of the enemy;

naturally Titchener stuck to *The American Journal of Psychology* as the mouthpiece for Cornell, following here a well established German tradition. Until 1917 he never published in any of the Psychological Review Publications except once briefly in 1902 and thrice again briefly in controversy in 1910 and 1912. The record shows clearly that he avoided these journals and found less obvious places when *The American Journal of Psychology* seemed unavailable.

The controversy with [J. M.] Baldwin over reaction times in the middle nineties was partly an ordinary scientific controversy but also a symptom of something beneath the surface. It is interesting to see now that it hinged on a fundamental national difference that was to become more obvious as American psychology developed. Titchener was saying: we must study the generalized human mind, even if it can be done only with elaborately trained observers; this was the German view. Baldwin was saying: we want to know about all sorts of minds, even if some of them are untrained in laboratory work. It is a similar opposition that developed later between the "pure" scientific psychology of the generalized, normal, adult, human mind (Titchener) and functional psychology, the psychology of individual differences, mental tests, applied psychology, and lastly, behaviorism.

Thus it was in the late nineties that Titchener (1898; 1899; cf. Dallenbach, 1915, esp. p. 483) used James's phrase "structural psychology" in opposition to functional psychology. The latter had come to be applied to the Chicago product (John Dewey, A. W. Moore, and James R. Angell), although philosophically the American tradition, including Columbia and William James, is functional. In the ebb and flow of discussion and controversy the Cornell school thus came for a decade and even longer to be called "structural." Titchener himself, however, always disliked labels as pinning one down and impeding progress. He soon abandoned the word, and more recently "introspectional" has been substituted for it without the least acquiescence from Titchener. The younger men, who in general like sharp dichotomies, might think of themselves as "structuralists" or "introspectionalists," but not so Titchener. I never heard him refer to his school by any other word than "we."

We are now, however, passing into the first decade of the new century. Here Titchener's publication fell off for he was engaged in a great undertaking, the preparation of the four volumes of the *Experimental Psychology,* popularly known as "Titchener's Laboratory Manuals." Some one once said that this is the most erudite psychological work in the English language, and I am inclined to agree, not even excepting James (whose *Principles* Titchener called "theory of knowledge" and not psychology!). What Titchener wanted to do was to establish psychology as a science by the exhibition of its scientific nature and by the introduction of laboratory "drill courses" (as he always called them) into university instruction. Sanford's *Course* of 1894–98 was not enough; the project needed to be prosecuted upon a larger scale. Titchener worked out all these experiments in the laboratory first. It was not sufficient for him to have the reports of research. He had to devise clean-cut procedures which would require but simple apparatus (for laboratory appropriations were small) and then to see whether students could get univocal results with them. If they did not, instructions could be changed, cautions could be added, procedure could be modified. A tremendous amount of careful, laborious work in the laboratory was necessary. The relation of the volumes to the psychological literature is more obvious. In this respect they are encyclopedic and also astonishingly accurate. While there must be errors in typography and references, I have still to find one. When the *Quantitative Manuals* were almost completed, G. E. Müller's *Psychophysische Methodik* appeared in 1904, and Titchener had to revise all the way through. However, he never shirked responsibility of this sort and these *Manuals* were published the next year. The *Qualitative Manuals* had appeared in 1901.

It was about this time that Titchener's separatism showed itself in another fashion. Titchener was spiritually, as well as actually, outside of the American Psychological Association. It did not always follow in "the straight scientific path," which was of course experimental psychology in the narrower sense in which that phrase is still used. He wanted a group where there could be intimate discussion and constructive criticism of laboratory research then in progress. Later, perhaps even then, he dwelt upon the importance of the attendance at such meetings by graduate students, who thus would hear their seniors in friendly debate. So in 1904 he organized at Cornell a group which has ordinarily been called "the Experimentalists." Nothing could have been more informal in organization. Certain laboratories were to constitute the group, and Titchener always, even up to the time of his death, thought of a laboratory in Wundtian fashion as a man with his staff, his students, and his problems as the common property of all. The "Experimentalists" have met every spring at different laboratories twenty-four times, omitting only the year of the War. They never had a president, a secretary, a record, a program, or with a few exceptions, even a printed notice in the journals. There was only, every year, a "host," with Titchener of course as *deus ex machina*. The principle was ideal, especially in overorganized America. Many of us who have attended have felt that these meetings were the most stimulating of the year. As time went on, with Tichener's vigorous personality creating enemies as well as friends, the group became more limited. The bonds were between men and not laboratories; and only those who knew Titchener can realize how completely these meetings centered about him, and why they thus belong, not in a history of their own, but in his biography.

With the *Manuals* out of the way, Titchener's interest in systematization came to the fore. It had never lapsed since the Leipzig days, but in so far as it found its way into print it was more often for the sake of removing an objection than from a pure interest in construction. [Ernst] Mach and [Richard] Avenarius were necessary to prove psychology a science. "Structural psychology" was intended as an antidote to "functional psychology." The doctrine of the sense-distance in the *Quantitative Manuals* was Delboeuf's and was meant by Titchener to overcome the "quantity objection" to mental measurement. Now, however, Titchener, almost forty, was ready to cope with the problems of attention, feeling, and thought. There were three years (1905–07) of preparation with little productivity. Then in February, 1908, Columbia University asked him to deliver a series of lectures; he gave the *Lectures on the Elementary Psychology of Feeling and Attention* and published them in the same year. It was feeling and attention that he held to be "elementary"; the lectures are not. Attention was then (as now, alas!) a difficult concept. It seemed to imply activity, and "scientific introspection" shows only content in the mind. How was science to deal with it? Titchener sought to settle the problem of attention by declaring its status as an attribute of sensation. Feeling too was an uncomfortable item. Wundt's theory was not believed, and feeling was always becoming either sensation or, like attention, activity. Tichener sought to give it, as far as possible, independent elementary status, thus preserving for an elementaristic system an additional term with which to work.

The next year he was invited for a lecture series at the University of Illinois. Külpe had slipped from the path that led straight from Wundt, and Külpe's school of "imageless thought" at Würzburg, while it brought thought into the laboratory as Wundt would not attempt to do, introduced into psychology a fourth element (sensation, image, feeling, thought) which Tichener could not, in the experiments of his graduate students, find. At Illinois Titchener gave the *Lectures on the Experimental Psychology of the Thought-Processes*, which were published the same year. Here he analyzed and combated Külpe's school, seeking to reduce thought to the sensory and imaginal conscious attitudes. Perhaps the most important thing in this book is the context theory of meaning, which psychologizes the supposedly imageless thoughts in a way that explains why they seem to be imageless.

All this while the graduate students in the laboratory were very active, mostly upon problems related to Titchener's then primary interest. Titchener himself was also preparing the *Text-book of Psychology,* intended for instruction in elementary courses, but really a systematic work in brief compass. The first half of it appeared in 1909 and the whole in 1910. It is the only thorough account of Titchener's psychology that we have in single covers. It was printed seventeen years before his death and to the psychological world at large still represents Titchener, for there has come from him nothing else comparable.

Titchener kept on thinking, reading, and working. The system of 1910 was old in 1915, and it has, perhaps several times, been again outgrown. The language of his laboratory changed, and a graduate three years absent had on returning to learn psychology again—not entirely, but some fundamental thing that shot through the entire structure and bobbed up at every point of a discussion. Naturally the Cornell group felt that it was far in advance of psychology in general and of the Titchener who was known outside. There is, however, a striking change in the objective record. The change is not so much in the number of titles in Titchener's bibliography as that there are no books except the *Beginner's Psychology* in 1915, begun as a revision of the old *Primer,* but characteristically written entirely anew. On the surface then there is a difference between the first and the last halves of the thirty-five years in America. Can it be explained?

First, we must note that in 1909 Clark University, then a virgin university for research and graduate instruction only, called Titchener on Sanford's elevation to the presidency of Clark College. Cornell responded by appointing Titchener to a professorship in the Graduate School, thus relieving him of all undergraduate instruction. The laboratory was divided. In 1912, however, when Bentley went to Illinois, Titchener resumed command of both halves of the laboratory (so closely integrated that it had never been really divided), and he also returned to the elementary lectures by way of a special additional appointment.

The result of these changes was the creation of a life of academic retirement. Let me picture Titchener from 1913 to 1917 when I was his "underling."

In the first semester on Tuesday and Thursday at eleven he lectured to the undergraduates in the new lecture room in Goldwin Smith Hall, the room with a psychological demonstrational laboratory and an office built off it, and with the pitch of the seats determined by Titchener's stature. The demonstration was set out the hour before, and Titchener arrived shortly after ten to inspect it. Later the staff gradually gathered in his office. When the time of the lecture arrived, he donned his gown, the assistant brushed his coat for fear of ashes from the ever-present cigar, the staff went out the door for apparatus and took front seats, and Titchener then appeared on the platform from the office door. The whole rite was performed pleasantly and sometimes jokingly; yet it was scrupulously observed. After the lecture the staff gathered in Titchener's office for an hour for talk and at one o'clock dispersed for lunch. The laboratory was across the campus in Morrill Hall and Titchener never went near it during the first semester. That he was able from his house, nevertheless, to determine some of the smallest details of its operation is a tribute to a personality that could impress its will, generally without resentment, upon others.

In the second semester the lectures ceased and the seminary began on Monday evenings in the laboratory. Invitation to attend was an honor. The staff were always there as a matter of course. The seminary brought Titchener to the laboratory and there was the chance for the lucky graduate to persuade Titchener to look at his apparatus, but he did not always succeed. The seminary ran on, with prandial entertainment provided in rotation by its members, until late—often until after midnight when gas light had to be substituted for electricity.

In June Titchener came to the laboratory for doctors' examinations, but I do not think that in seven years (perhaps seventeen) he was once in the laboratory between June and February. Graduates saw him at the house and not often. On my dissertation I conferred with Titchener twice, once when the problem was planned, once eighteen months later when he had gone over the finished manuscript. He had a special assistant and no one else ever saw him in the mornings (except at the lectures in the first semester). Telephoning, for others than the assistant, was taboo except in great emergencies.

In those days Titchener played tennis daily in the summer. During the rest of the year he would on occasion go down town to shop, but otherwise lived almost entirely in the house. He had, I think, absolutely no social engagements except with the laboratory group and with the little orchestra of his family and students that he conducted at home on Sunday evenings. His old-time friends had been much older than himself and were dead or removed from Ithaca. Professors who had long been at Cornell had never seen Titchener. They could not even get into his lectures, for the room was full of sophomores and no one else was admitted.

In the last decade there were changes in this routine, but they do not greatly alter the picture. In 1918 Titchener began to lecture in the summer school for financial reasons. His tennis dropped off at the same time. Some (but not all) graduate students with doctoral research in hand, went to the house weekly for the most careful oversight and instruction.

In 1911 Titchener gave the Lowell lectures (never published), but thereafter he traveled only with great reluctance. He went to the "Experimentalists" in the spring. At the time of the [First World] War he broke his rule to lecture, so that he might contribute to the Prince of Wales Fund for war widows and orphans. He lectured at Wesleyan in 1922 and at the opening of the new Princeton Laboratory in 1925, both in connection with attendance upon the meetings of the "Experimentalists." He had planned this present fall to participate in the opening of the new laboratory at Wittenberg College, for he still felt that the founding of a psychological laboratory was the most important physical thing that could happen in psychology.

Now this life of retirement ought to have led to increased

productivity. It did not on the record. Is the record at fault?

Perhaps it is in the beginning of the period. From about 1912 to 1917 Titchener was energetically engaged in writing a systematic psychology. His friends supposed then that it was to be a work of several volumes like Wundt's *Grundzüge*. In 1917 the first volume was done all but the last chapter. Had the first volume of a great work appeared in 1918, I suppose we should say that the preceding period was merely one of incubation; but it did not appear. In 1921–22, having become sole editor of *The American Journal of Psychology*, he printed therein two of the chapters (Titchener, 1921a; 1921c; 1922). About this time he seems to have decided not to attempt to continue the work beyond this volume of systematic prolegomena, and also to rewrite the volume in part without again printing these chapters. The book was advertised by the publishers. Titchener's friends urged him to complete it, but there was always some excuse. When an anonymous benefactor offered, in behalf of the book, to relieve him of teaching in the summer of 1927, he hesitated, agreed, but deferred acceptance until 1928. He died without publishing.

I can not presume to say anything of the growth of Titchener's psychology since 1917, but must leave that to some intimate colleague of these years. Already in 1917 there had been a shift in the doctrine of sensation and the attribute (Titchener, 1915). The doctrine of dimensions came later, as did also the stress on phenomenological observation as distinguished from introspection. There have been hints of the "newest" psychology in theses, but none that are clear to the uninitiated. Only his manuscript or some laboratory intimate of the last few years, who has lived in the community built around the "system," can tell us.

The best key to Titchener's life, I think, lies in the fact that he emulated Wundt—how consciously I do not know. We have already seen the superficial evidence of the Leipzig impress, but I think the influence goes deeper. Often when Titchener wrote about Wundt, he seemed to be writing about himself. Often when he defended Wundt in print, he used phrases which he has used in defense of himself (cf. Titchener, 1921b).

Titchener (1921b, pp. 163–169) urged that there were three interests and corresponding periods in Wundt's life, concerned successively with the establishment of experimental psychology, with the creation of a scientific metaphysics, and with the development of *Völkerpsychologie;* and he was most emphatic in his insistence that those interests constitute, not three programs of work, but a single, closely integrated program. The parallel in Titchener holds for the first two periods. He began with the further establishment of experimental psychology as a science (1892–1905); he went on to systematization, that made many say he was no longer an "experimentalist" (1905–1927); he had always a keen interest in anthropology, and a few of his friends had wondered if he would not turn to anthropological writing when he retired from his active professorship. Yet these interests were not successive, but continuous; he had never been without them all; the dates mean only the dominance of one in personal publication. Titchener thought of them as an integrated whole and defended the unity of the plan in Wundt. He was at pains to show that Wundt foresaw the entire plan of his life in 1862 (Titchener, 1921b, esp. p. 163), and just so might Titchener's tripartite psychology be traced from 1892.

In this article on Wundt, Titchener protested against the belief that "social psychology was Wundt's first and fondest love, and that all his life, up to about 1890, was spent in clearing intruders out of the way, that he might ultimately return to it." "I should not accept this legend," he wrote, "if it came with Wundt's own subscription; I should mistrust an old man's memory" (Titchener, 1921b, p. 169). Strong words! Could Titchener have been anticipating the criticism that he was not at heart an experimentalist should he presently turn, in his writings, to anthropology? Or could he have been thinking of the criticism that his interest in system called in question the primary nature of his experimentalism?

Then there is the discussion of Wundt's fluidity. James (1920, vol. I, p. 263) once said of Wundt: "Cut him up like a worm, and each fragment crawls; there is no *noeud vital* in his medulla oblongata, so that you can't kill him all at once." Titchener dissented vigorously from this sort of criticism, which is not unlike complaints that were sometimes made of him. Wundt was, he said, "as honest as the day," but his work was always "at once systematic and provisional" and "he held his theories far more loosely than his readers ordinarily suppose"; "his greatest reverence was for fact" (Titchener, 1921b, pp. 169–171). Titchener based his assurance in this matter on Wundt's assertions to him in conversation; what intimate of Titchener's is there who has not heard him use almost identical phrases about himself?

There is also what Titchener (1921b, pp. 171 f.) said of the necessity that Wundt should not be taken externally and superficially and "that students of Wundt must read his books in series, and can never hope to understand him fully from any single presentation of his thought." How often Titchener used this same argument in reply to criticism!

Most of the other similarities between Titchener and Wundt we have already noted as lying in the more objective record. There remains only his editorial attitude. Titchener wanted a journal of his own, like Wundt's *Philosophische Studien*. He never had it, although he practically secured it in 1921 when he became sole editor of *The American Journal of Psychology*. When he found in 1925 that it was not easily possible in America to do what used to be the rule in Germany, he resigned. However, he discovered that the continued *American Journal* and the Psychological Review Publications were to him what the *Archiv* and the *Zeitschrift* were to Wundt in 1902. He thought of a Cornell series, analogous, I suppose, to Wundt's *Psychologische Studien*, started under similar circumstances. Actually he finally arranged to participate in the founding of a new journal—a project still incompletely realized at the time of his death.

The evaluation of Titchener's psychology can be left to posterity, and such was his wish, often expressed. He said of Wundt's plan of life: "As to the ultimate significance of that task, it would be the part of wisdom to keep silence; we stand too near to

Wundt to see him in a just perspective" (Titchener, 1921b, p. 176). Certainly Titchener was a remarkable personality and a great psychologist. That his influence has been so effective in spite of his personal isolation from psychologists and his intellectual isolation from the national trend is, I take it, a test of greatness. A century hence it will be possible to say just where his psychology belongs in the history of the science.

References

Dallenbach, K. M. The history and derivation of the word "function" as a systematic term in psychology. *American Journal of Psychology*, 1915, vol. 26, 473–484.

Foster, W. S. A bibliography of the published writings of Edward Bradford Titchener, 1889–1917. In *Studies in Psychology: Contributed by Colleagues and former Students of Edward Bradford Titchener*. Worcester, Mass.: Louis N. Wilson, 1917. Pp. 323–337.

Holt, E. B. Titchener's psychology: review of *A Text-Book of Psychology*, by Edward Bradford Titchener. *Psychological Bulletin*, 1911, vol. 8, 25–30.

James, Henry (Ed.). *The Letters of William James*. Vol. I. Boston: Atlantic Monthly Press, 1920.

Titchener, E. B. Zur Chronometrie des Erkennungsactes. *Philosophische Studien*, 1892, vol. 8, 138–144. (a)

Titchener, E. B. Ueber binoculare Wirkungen monocularer Reize. *Philosophische Studien*, 1892, vol. 8, 231–310. (b)

Titchener, E. B. The postulates of a structural psychology. *Philosophical Review*, 1898, vol. 7, 449–465.

Titchener, E. B. Structural and functional psychology. *Philosophical Review*, 1899, vol. 8, 290–299.

Titchener, E. B. Sensation and system. *American Journal of Psychology*, 1915, vol. 26, 258–267.

Titchener, E. B. Brentano and Wundt: empirical and experimental psychology. *American Journal of Psychology*, 1921, vol. 32, 108–120. (a)

Titchener, E. B. Wilhelm Wundt. *American Journal of Psychology*, 1921, vol. 32, 161–178. (b)

Titchener, E. B. Functional psychology and the psychology of act, I. *American Journal of Psychology*, 1921, vol. 32, 519–542. (c)

Titchener, E. B. Functional psychology and the psychology of act, II. *American Journal of Psychology*, 1922, vol. 33, 43–83.

Various. In memory of Wilhelm Wundt, by his American students. *Psychological Review*, 1921, vol. 28, 153–188.

Lewis Madison Terman: 1877-1956
1959

My friendship with Terman dates from late 1918 after the Armistice in the First World War, when R. M. Yerkes brought both Terman and me to Washington to work on the report of the Army intelligence testing. Terman liked me. He helped get me appointed secretary of the American Psychological Association. In 1921, after I had gone to Clark University, he had me out at Stanford for a twelve weeks' summer quarter and I fell in love with Stanford—partly because I had for lecture use the data on systematic psychology, collected at Cornell and later used in my *History of Experimental Psychology*. All this material was new to the graduate students at Stanford and they flocked to hear me. In 1922 Terman was back of my being called to Stanford to be the experimental psychologist there, and I would have loved to go; yet I chose Harvard for complicated reasons discussed elsewhere in this book. After that the close friendship persisted until Terman's death. Yerkes and Terman and I—they were respectively ten and nine years my senior—formed a vague triangle with correspondence about mutual interests going on along all three sides.

When Terman died, his son, like his father a member of the National Academy of Sciences, asked me to write the Memoir for the Academy. He was sure that his father would have liked this best, and I think he was right. So this is that Memoir. Advisers examining the accounts I have written of Titchener, Yerkes, Dallenbach, Lashley (a history of his thought only), and Terman, concluded that this biography was my best. Titchener's person-

Reprinted with permission from the *Biographical Memoirs of the National Academy of Sciences*, 1959, vol. 33, 414-440.

ality gave vivid color to what I wrote of him, but the Terman
sketch, written in my seventies, is a more mature attempt to
understand a man.

Lewis Madison Terman, for fifty years one of America's
staunchest supporters of mental testing as a scientific psychological technique, and for forty years the psychologist who more than
any other was responsible for making the IQ (the intelligence
quotient) a household word, was born on a farm in Johnson
County, Indiana, on January 15, 1877, and died at Stanford
University on December 21, 1956, a distinguished professor
emeritus, not quite eighty years old (Terman, 1932; Hilgard,
1957; Sears, 1957).

When a biographer seeks to find causes for the events in the
life that he is describing, he is apt to find himself facing the
nature-nurture dilemma, uncertain whether, in order to account
for the traits of his subject, he should look to ancestry or to environment. Terman (1932, pp. 297–305 *et passim*), as it happens
—when he wrote his own biography at the age of fifty-five in
1932—faced exactly this problem in accounting for himself. In
his choices he must indeed have been influenced by the *Zeitgeist*,
for, as the weight of scientific opinion shifted from hereditarianism toward environmentalism, his judgment shifted too throughout the forty years (1916–1956) during which this issue remained
vital to him.

In 1916 Terman published what came to be called the Stanford
Revision of the Binet test of intelligence, a test that measured
intellectual growth in youth from three years of age to adult
intelligence, which seemed to be reached at sixteen years or
perhaps a little sooner. The measure of intelligence that was supposed to remain invariant with age is the intelligence quotient,
the ratio of mental age (average intellectual test performance
for a given age) to chronological age (times 100). That idea
had been William Stern's in 1912 (esp. pp. 25–29), but Terman,
by improving the tests for mental age, was able to demonstrate

that the IQ is indeed fairly constant with changing age, at least when cultural influences are also constant. If the IQ is constant from an early age, then adult intelligence is predictable from childhood, and it becomes easy to suppose that the intelligence measured is an invariant fixed at birth and quite possibly at conception by the genes. Terman was supported in this view by the growing realization at this time that feeble-mindedness cannot be greatly altered by training, and by the definition of *feeble-minded* in terms of the invariant IQ. The IQ was, of course, not strictly constant, but its variability and its regression toward mediocrity with advancing age could be laid to imperfections in the tests, perhaps to their lack of validity in measuring the fixed underlying intelligence in which so many had come to believe.

In the teens and twenties liberal opinion fought this view of a biologically elite intelligentsia, focusing attention on such changes in the IQ with age, education, and socioeconomic status as were discovered. Terman, nevertheless, stuck to his original view. His initiation in 1921 of his genetic studies of genius, studies that were still being continued with the examination of the same group of gifted persons at the time of his death thirty-five years later, was based on his belief, which he got from Francis Galton, that the brains of the country are one of its great resources and that they can be selected with scientific procedures and used to advance the national welfare and civilization. Thus in 1932 (pp. 329 f.), when he ventured to lay down eighteen articles of faith in a credo that he printed at the end of his autobiography, his eighth belief was "that the major differences between children of low and high IQ, and major differences in intelligence test scores of certain races, as Negroes and whites, will never be fully accounted for on the environmental hypothesis."

As time went on this faith of Terman's in a basic invariant intelligence for every person weakened a little. The evidence that test scores for intelligence depend on socioeconomic status increased. By the time of the Second World War the use of factor analysis to establish separate primary abilities, especially L. L. Thurstone's work (1938), had cast doubt on the unitary nature of intelligence. The I, as well as the IQ, was getting into trouble. Terman in his personal copy of his autobiography wrote in the margin opposite the sentence just quoted about Negroes and whites, "I am less sure of this now (1951)!" and later, "And still less sure in 1955!" (Hilgard, 1957, p. 478). On the other hand, his continuing study of the gifted children, at last grown up after twenty-five years, reinforced his belief—in spite of a certain small regression of the top group toward mediocrity as age advanced and the realization that achievement depends on motivation as well as on intelligence—that there is in society under its ordinarily constant conditions an intellectual elite who need to be identified and specially trained and encouraged for the promotion of civilization.

It is hard to say whether Terman's faith in the importance of heredity made him, when he came in 1932 to assess the causes of his own success, discount the effects of environment, or whether, unable to see anything in his circumstances as a poor farm boy that could have led him into an intellectual life of national importance, he looked to heredity for an explanation because, being inscrutable, it could not disappoint him. Certainly he then seemed at pains to show that there was nothing either in the commonplace of his rural youth nor in the agricultural lives of his immediate forebears that could explain the intellectual avidity that made him ultimately successful in the scientific world. Nor would his belief that heredity must be of great importance be weakened when his own son, F. E. Terman, was also elected to the National Academy of Sciences. Lewis Terman must have believed that intelligence was there in his ancestors, undisplayed because the environment failed to yield or permit the necessary motivation.

Whatever their origin, this biographer sees two important characteristics that, appearing early in the life of Lewis Terman, supported him to the end. In the first place, he had tremendous drive and persistence that lasted in his pursuit of knowledge from the time he entered the Central Normal College in Danville, Indiana, at the age of fifteen, all through his life, in spite of setbacks with tuberculosis, being burned in a fire, breaking a hip, and other disabilities. Always he returned indefatigable and enthusiastic to his work. His views of it might change or the facts of nature might force a change; still he followed obstinately the same track, not with a dour stubbornness, but in a friendly, sympathetic, social activity in his contacts with colleagues, students, and his "gifted children." There is something special there that is part of his success.

The other characteristic that marked his life was his inextinguishable desire for reading, which began when he was about ten years old, at which time his brother bought a book on phrenology. (The man who was selling the book had felt Lewis's bumps and predicted great things for him.) Lewis read the *Britannica* in his father's library and most of the other tenscore books that his father owned. At the Central Normal College when he was sixteen and seventeen, he was reading John Dewey's *Psychology,* Darwin's *Origin,* Huxley's *Lectures,* and other books of that sort. He read William James's *Principles of Psychology,* quite new then, surreptitiously because his instructor disapproved of the book's literary flavor. Later, when he got to Indiana University, came under the influence of W. L. Bryan, E. H. Lindley, and J. A. Bergström, and decided to become a psychologist, his reading of the "right" things continued. While at Indiana he also mastered French and German so that, when he went to Clark University later, he could read adequately for Stanley Hall's seminar in three languages. This addiction to the use of books persisted until the end. Lewis Terman was a well-read man and not only within his special field.

Enthusiasm and tenacity, plus wide and well-chosen reading, seem to have been important factors in Terman's career. Nevertheless the autobiographer, as well as the biographer, faces an inevitable dilemma when he looks for causes of how his subject came to achieve eminence. If the biographer can find an environmental explanation he is apt to accept it *faute de mieux*. Often the acceptance of the alternative hereditarian explanation is due merely to the failure to find an environmental one, nor is the case proved by marshaling a few bright ancestors when all the other forebears have disappeared in the obscurity of the past.

With Terman it is possible to make a case for his inordinate will to achieve as a compensation for a frustrated youth, but that does not account adequately for his love of learning. Had he read only what would immediately promote his success, we could suggest that early frustration could be at work here too, but the fact is that he read more broadly, seemingly just for the joy of it, than his professional advancement ever required. Terman himself inclined toward an hereditarian explanation of himself, noting proudly his son's eminence. What he failed to note in this connection was the fact that his two older brothers did not rise so high, that his married sisters did not manage, in choosing their mates, to mark themselves off as exceptionally gifted, in the way that the bright girls of Terman's own "gifted group" did when they married. You have to take Terman as a fact. Considered alone he is not a good instance of environmental effect or of heredity.

Now let us see what are the facts that belong on this central core of the intellectual endeavor that is the key to an understanding of Terman's life.

YOUTH AND EDUCATION

Lewis M. Terman was the twelfth child among the fourteen children of James William Terman and Martha P. Cutsinger. James Terman was a farmer, the son of a Virginia farmer of Scotch-Irish descent who was born in 1794, fought in the War of 1812, migrated on horseback to Ohio about 1820, moved on to Indiana in 1846, taking James with him, and died there in his

seventies shortly after the Civil War. This Terman, Lewis's grandfather, had married a woman named Jones of Welsh extraction.
They had twelve children, of whom James was one of the
youngest.

Martha Cutsinger, Lewis's mother, was the daughter of a Penn-
sylvania-German farmer who went from Pennsylvania to Ken-
tucky and thence to Indiana. He married a woman named
Deupree of Huguenot origin, As a young man James Terman
went to work for Cutsinger, married his daughter in 1855, and
then moved away to a farm of his own in another part of the
same county. Lewis, as we have noted, was born in 1877, after
his parents had been married twenty-two years.

In this all-agricultural environment it would have seemed a
safe prediction in 1890, say, when Lewis was thirteen, that he
would become a farmer, marry young, have a large family who
were destined to become farmers and farmers' wives except for
a couple who would be schoolteachers, an alternative rural
possibility. Lewis worked on his father's farm for five or six
months every year from the time he was eleven until he was
eighteen. He fitted easily into the work and did not dislike it,
yet his avidity for knowledge was beginning to show and presently made the difference between a farmer and an intellectual.
From the age of five to the age of thirteen he attended a one-room
rural school of about thirty children and one teacher. He stayed
on for a year after he had finished the eighth grade and apparently spent the next two years on the farm. Perhaps this was
the crucial moment, or at least what Terman himself would have
regarded as the crucial moment, when he was led to decide that
he wanted something that the farm would not provide, something that he could get at the Central Normal College at Danville.

Terman must later have come to believe that his success in the
intellectual world of science meant that he himself was a "gifted
child" in the phrase that he later coined in his genetic study of
genius, that he had superior intelligence that could nevertheless
have remained submerged under the routine of a farmer, where

industry is repetitious and originality is confined to those small inventions that never emerge to alter even slightly the course of civilization. No wonder he believed so firmly that genius needs to be discovered, directed, and reinforced.

In 1892, when Lewis was fifteen, his parents sent him to the Central Normal College. He stayed two years, for thirty weeks the first year and twenty weeks the second. Then he taught a one-room rural school for a year and went back to the Central Normal College the next year for forty-eight weeks to complete the "scientific course" and receive the degree of B.S. After that he taught a rural school again and went back to the College, this time for eighteen weeks to complete the course in pedagogy and receive the B.Pd. degree. Still his eagerness for more and more education was not satisfied, so now, without stopping to earn more money, he borrowed enough to spend forty-eight additional weeks at Danville, thus completing the "classical course" to receive an A.B. Altogether he had spent one hundred sixty-four weeks at the Normal College, had three degrees to show for his work, yet remained vague as to what the future held for him.

Terman was now twenty-one years old. For the next three years he was principal of a township high school where he taught all the courses to about forty pupils. After the first year he married Anna B. Minton, a teacher whom he had met at Danville. Their son Frederick was born the next year. Both Lewis and Anna were sure that Lewis needed more schooling.

By this time Terman had decided that he wished to prepare himself to teach pedagogy and psychology, and he looked to Indiana University where W. L. Bryan, the Stanley Hall-trained psychologist from Clark University, was teaching. Indiana University was only fifty miles from his home. His friends advised him to go there to get a better A.B. than the Normal College could confer. To do so he had to borrow money again, though living in Bloomington was relatively cheap.

At the University he found, besides Bryan, E. H. Lindley and

J. A. Bergström, both of them, like Bryan, Clark Ph.D.'s. After Terman's first year Bryan became President of the University and was lost to Terman. Bergström was not so easy to know, but Terman came after a while to appreciate him and also to realize that experimental psychology, Bergström's *Fach,* was not for him. Terman was awkward with apparatus and never could learn to adapt himself to the mechanical phases of psychology's then new experimentalism. Especially Terman liked Lindley, who presently was steering him in the direction of Stanley Hall and Clark.

At Indiana, Terman improved his French and German so that he could read the literature in psychology without great difficulty. He became quite excited over the new scientific movement in German psychology, even though he was not prepared himself to become an experimentalist. He read a great many more books, received a solid Indiana A.B. at the end of his first year, an A.M. at the end of his second, and borrowed $1,200 more to go on to Clark University and a Ph.D. with Stanley Hall. Hall was still one of the giants of the new American psychology, a contemporary of James's, almost twenty years older than Cattell and Baldwin, the founder of the first American psychological laboratory and the second in the world. No wonder Terman's ambition soared at the thought of a Ph.D. with Hall.

It was in the spring of 1903 that the Termans had their second child, a daughter, Helen (now Helen Terman Mosher and living in Stanford). Little Fred was then almost three. Yet neither Terman nor his wife demurred about taking this family of four to Clark on a borrowed $1,200 for a Ph.D. which turned out to be two years away. Terman owed his success not only to his own courage and ambition, but also to his wife's courage and her identification with his ambition.

The two years at Clark, when Terman was twenty-six to twenty-eight years old (1903–1905), were wonderful years for the farm boy so avid for education and now at last within sight of a Ph.D. He wrote of the University:

The Clark of my day was a university different in important respects from any other that ever existed in America—. . . in spirit much akin to the German university yet differing from it because of the small student body. It enrolled in all its departments only about fifty full-time students. . . . Possibly thirty of the fifty were there primarily for psychology, philosophy, and education. The informality and freedom from administrative red tape were unequalled. The student registered by merely giving his name and address to President Hall's secretary. He was not required to select formally a major or minor subject. There was no appraisal of credentials for the purpose of deciding what courses he should take. *Lernfreiheit* was utterly unrestricted. There were professors who proposed to lecture and there were students who proposed to study; what more was necessary? The student could go to three or four lectures a day, or to none. No professor, so far as I could see, kept a class list. Attendance records were, of course, unheard of. No marks or grades of any kind were awarded at the end of the year or semester. One could attend a course of lectures all year without being required or necessarily expected to do the least reading in connection with it. There were no formalities about candidacy for a degree. The student was allowed to take his doctor's examination when the professor in charge of his thesis thought he was ready for it. No examination except the four-hour doctor's oral was ever given. (Terman, 1932, p. 313.)

Yet *Lernfreiheit* was not quite so easy as it sounds. Terman described the intense motivation generated by the demand for a report in Hall's famous Monday evening seminar. The reporting student who did not weather the storm of criticism from his peers, reinforced as it might be by the deliberate and recondite negatives of the seminar's famous moderator, might go home for a week in bed, and one in Terman's day had a nervous breakdown when he realized his failure.

At Clark, Terman had contact with E. C. Sanford, the experimentalist, but it did not make him apparatus-apt. He sat under W. H. Burnham and heard his polished lectures on education and educational psychology, and he learned to perceive the beauty of an English style that Hall did not have. (Perhaps his own later facility as a clear and interesting writer owes something to Burnham.) From every quarter he felt the influence of

European psychology as it went on in Germany with the new laboratories, in France with Binet and the measurement of intelligence, in England with Galton and the mental tests. Hall was, of course, his chief stimulus, though Hall did not support Terman in the two subjects of his special interest: the mental tests and the study of superiorly intelligent children. Hall was, however, never coercive, and Terman chose for his thesis the comparison of seven dull with seven bright children by the use of a great number of tests of Terman's own devising. Earlier Terman had presented to Hall's seminar a survey of the history of belief about bright children, how they had come to be looked down upon and regarded as instable and abnormal, likely to be a weight upon society instead of an aid to it. This view Terman intuitively opposed, and he set himself to test it by devising tests for bright children. Thus his principal life endeavor began at Clark in 1904. He took his Ph.D. under Hall in 1905, when he was twenty-eight years old.

MATURITY

Terman's life is so associated with difficulties of health and accident that inevitably a biographer pauses to wonder whether the effort to overcome the obstacles may not indeed have encompassed other activities and have been one of the causes of his success. At any rate the road to achievement, after he had obtained the Ph.D. at Clark, was no easier than the road he had already traversed.

The chief enemy was tuberculosis. There had been hints of it in 1899 and 1900, but the first serious hemorrhages occurred in the summer of 1904, in between the two years at Clark. He rested a few weeks and then took special care of himself during his second and last Clark year. He knew he needed to find a position in the south or southwest, but that requirement did not daunt him, for Stanley Hall was so closely identified with what was then the modernization of education under the impact of the new psychology that many of his Ph.D.'s took administrative or teaching positions in normal schools or high schools. That kind of position could be found where the climate would be favorable, as might not have been the case for a university post. Within three days Terman had opportunities to go to Florida, Texas, and San Bernardino, California. He chose the last, going there as a high school principal. He had another hemorrhage a few weeks after the term began, but he rested for eleven days and was soon back at work. What he regarded as a successful year ended with an offer of a professorship of child study and pedagogy at the Los Angeles State Normal School, an offer which he accepted.

He was at Los Angeles for four years (1906–1910). The library was good. The work was interesting. There were other psychologists there who stimulated him—Arnold Gesell and Beatrice Chandler, who later married each other. There grew up a friendship with E. B. Huey, an old Clark man. In the summer of 1907 the Termans, the Gesells, and Huey were together on vacation. Later, when Huey was working in Adolf Meyer's clinic at Johns Hopkins, and Terman was about to move to Stanford, Huey urged Terman to undertake work with the new 1908 Binet scale for measuring intelligence—and Terman did, publishing the Stanford revision six years later.

Bergström, by whom Terman had been taught at Indiana, was called to Stanford in 1909 as a psychologist in the Department of Education, but he died before the year was over. Stanford then asked Huey, who decided, however, to stay with Adolf Meyer a little longer. After that Stanford turned to Terman, a third Stanley Hall man, and he accepted.

Terman went to Stanford in 1910 as an assistant professor of education in E. P. Cubberley's department, and was promoted to be an associate professor in 1912 and a full professor in 1916. These first twelve years (1910–1922), before he was given the Department of Psychology to build up, were for him still maturational. He was changing from a psychotropic educationalist— the Stanley Hall model—to a sociotropic psychologist. He published three books on health and school hygiene—"if you scratch a health reformer, you will find an invalid," he used to say—but his enduring achievement was the revision of the Binet scale for measuring intelligence.

Up to 1916 Terman's identification had been largely with educators and educational psychologists. He had felt himself to be on, or just beyond, the periphery of the American movement in psychology, as so many of Stanley Hall's men were—the American movement that had its core in experimentation, the new laboratories, and basic fact, the "brass-instrument" psychology, as James called it. Terman at Stanford, disliking the brass instruments which existed across the way in Frank Angell's laboratory, was intellectually and geographically remote from this core of psychology. He was a "mental tester," and the experimentalists looked down on his art, some because it had little to do with consciousness and some because it was applied science. All that was shortly to change.

It was in 1916, the year of the publication of the Stanford Revision of the Binet scale, that Terman went back east to teach in the summer session at New York University. The next summer he taught at Columbia. At that time he actually was not a member of the American Psychological Association, so peripheral did he feel, but he joined in 1917. It was in April, 1917, that the United States declared war on Germany and that the psychologists mobilized themselves to see if they could render aid, especially by testing recruits for intelligence. R. M. Yerkes, because he was then President of the American Psychological Association and also because he was peculiarly well suited to the task, took charge, and late in May a committee of five distinguished "mental testers" met at Vineland, New Jersey, to plan for the psychologists' war effort. Terman, who was one of these five, stayed with the work and finally, in uniform and commissioned as a major, was responsible for the 200,000 words of Part II of the mammoth report that was published in 1921, *Psychological Examining in the United States Army* (Terman, 1921). Hardly had he become a member of the American Psychological Association than he was elected to its Council (1919–1921) and then to its presidency (1923). The psychologists liked Terman and they came—even the conservatives who had contemned mental testing—to respect his ability. Thus the shift of Terman from the periphery of professional American psychology to its core was very rapid in these half dozen years.

In 1922 President Wilbur of Stanford asked Terman to become Executive Head of the Department of Psychology, because of the retirement of Frank Angell, one of Wilhelm Wundt's students, who had been in charge of Stanford's laboratory for thirty years. Terman accepted and his title was changed to Professor of Psychology and Education. This was the sort of challenge to which he would rise with all his drive and energy. The old department had granted only one Ph.D. in the thirty years of its existence. Terman's job was to build it up, and build it up he did. By 1949 three members of his staff, besides himself, had become presidents of the American Psychological Association and members of the National Academy of Sciences: W. R. Miles, C. P. Stone, and E. R. Hilgard. Of the Stanford students who were there during Terman's incumbency, four more became presidents of the American Psychological Association and two members of the Academy (H. F. Harlow and Heinrich Klüver). From the point of view of Academy representation in psychology, Stanford in the Terman period ranks among the five top institutions. From 1922 to 1942 when Terman retired, the Department of Psychology conferred 55 Ph.D.'s. Certainly the scientific contribution of Stanford in psychology passed in this period from little significance to great. The growth could not, indeed, be all Terman's doing. Such developments, once started, are autocatalytic. One good appointment favors others, but Terman's tolerant appreciation of scholarship in any field of psychology, his constant effort to get the best men and then to treat them with a permissive democracy, established a philosophy that made Stanford a very good place to be. He got the process of change going and then steered it until he retired.

Terman took great pride and personal interest in his students and in other students too, for whom he acquired a preceptorial relation, and also in his younger associates on the staff, many of whom had been appointed as the result of his efforts. A list of these students and associates includes many names of great importance in present-day psychology. A score of them we can list here. In 1942, on the occasion of Terman's sixty-fifth birthday, a group of these persons issued a volume, called *Studies in Personality*, to commemorate their debt to Terman for his stimulus and sponsorship. Contributing to the volume from among his graduate students, who wrote their theses under his direction, were Barbara S. Burks, Florence L. Goodenough, Catherine Cox Miles, R. R. Willoughby, and Kimball Young. Contributing from among his other students and protégés, all persons who felt a very real and almost filial debt to him, were R. G. Barker, Franklin Fearing, H. F. Harlow, L. P. Herrington, E. Lowell Kelly, John L. Kennedy, Heinrich Klüver, Ann Magaret (now Garner), F. L. Ruch, R. R. Sears, Eugene Shen, Miles A. Tinker, and Clare Wright (now Thomson). Signing the salutatory preface were, from among his graduate students, R. G. Bernreuter, Quinn McNemar, and Maud A. Merrill, besides Miss Goodenough, Mrs. Miles, and Kimball Young. To these names one ought at the very least to add John W. Gardner, Donald G. Marquis, and Neal E. Miller. An able and distinguished group this, all of whom had felt Lewis Terman's stimulus and stood ready to do him honor.

INTELLIGENCE AND THE GENETIC STUDIES OF GENIUS

Terman's lifework, the persistent core of his scientific contribution, was the study of the nature of exceptionally high ability. He first acquired this interest, so he claimed, in his work with Lindley at Indiana University in 1902. It was, as we have seen, the subject of his thesis in 1905 at Clark University with Stanley Hall. His chief concern was at first with bright children, and in this attack he was driven by his conviction of the falsity of the common belief that brightness in children is undesirable, that the very bright children are apt to be sickly or weak or neurotic or maladjusted. Later, as his research continued to support his conviction, he denounced the conventional thesis and speculated, as had Francis Galton before him, on how to increase the number of gifted children in the community, how to discover them and to make their ability available to society.

When Terman came to Stanford in 1910 he had the opportunity to begin serious work on this topic. Since the Binet-Simon scale of intelligence had appeared in 1908, he now had at hand for the selection of bright children a means that had not been available when he was at Clark. In 1911 he selected from certain schools a group of 31 children with IQ's in excess of 125, described their abilities and characteristics then, and undertook to see what happened to them later. By 1924 one of these children had a Ph.D., another an Sc.D., and a third was studying in Europe.

Terman's own revision of the intelligence scale in 1916 gave him a still better tool for the selection and for charting the development of the tested children as they grew into adulthood. It was becoming plain that it was important not only to show that bright children are not queer and maladjusted but also that they grow up, with IQ fairly constant, into valuable, competent, bright adults. It was in this way that the study of gifted children changed into the *Genetic Studies of Genius,* as Terman called the big volumes, filled with facts, that came out during the last thirty years of his life.

In 1921, just before he became executive head of Stanford's Department of Psychology, Terman secured his initial support from the Commonwealth Fund for the selection and study of a thousand gifted children from the schools of California. Terman and his associates could not test the entire school population of California—about 160,000 pupils—but they had the teachers select the three brightest children in each class, according to the teachers' judgment, and they also took the youngest child in each class. This last criterion turned out to be the best. These selected children were then tested and those with IQ's of 140 and over were retained (and a few in the 130's). Thus the study obtained 661 bright children, the top half of the highest one per cent of the school population. Later the investigators added 365 more to obtain "the thousand." Still later others were added for special reasons, making the total group of gifted children 1,528.

Information was obtained about these children's home life and their school life. They were given medical examinations; anthropological measurements were made on them; school-achievement tests and character tests were given them; their interests, the books they had read, and the games they knew were inventoried. Here was a picture of the whole child, as well as it could be obtained. The description was published in *Genetic Studies of Genius*, I, *Mental and Physical Traits of a Thousand Gifted Children*, in 1925, with Terman as author and fourteen assistants, some of them later to be distinguished psychologists, listed on the title page.

The second volume of the *Studies* was, in a sense, a control for the first. It was called *The Early Mental Traits of Three Hundred Geniuses*, appeared in 1926 (a year after the first volume), was authored by Catherine M. Cox (now Miles) with Terman as one of her assistants, and consisted of 842 pages of analysis of the youth and young manhood of three hundred persons who had attained great distinction because of ability. The biographical facts were studied and an IQ estimated for childhood and another for youth. A measure of reliability was computed, dependent upon the nature and amount of data available for appraisal. These posthumous IQ's for history's great were naturally of much comparative interest—Goethe with an estimated IQ of 210, Descartes at 180, Darwin at 165, and the child who became Napoleon at 145, just barely gifted enough for Terman to add to his group. The real purpose of the control was, however, to compare the childhoods of history's geniuses with especial reference of their IQ performances, with the IQ performances of California's child "geniuses," that is to say, of the children with

IQ's of 140 or more. There was every evidence that history's great were bright as children and that their intellectual performance in childhood fell within the range of Terman's gifted children. The highest IQ's, for both groups, were in the neighborhood of 200.

The third and fourth volumes of the *Studies* were follow-ups. The first resurvey occurred in 1927–28, six years after the initial one. It was published in 1930 under the title *The Promise of Youth* and under the joint authorship of Barbara S. Burks, Dortha W. Jensen, and Terman. Then there were resurveys in 1936, 1940, and 1945. The results of these came out in the fourth volume of the series. *The Gifted Child Grows Up*, by Terman and Melita H. Oden, published in 1947, about twenty-five years after the first study and when the gifted group averaged about thirty-five years of age. Terman retired to become emeritus in 1942, but he kept on at work without interruption. He was in constant correspondence with his gifted "children," as he still liked to call them, and a fifth volume with Mrs. Oden was under way when he died in 1956. She will continue the work. It will show the "gifted group" thirty-five years after the genetic studies began, at about age forty-five. *The Gifted Child at Mid-Life* will round out the enterprise.

The general conclusion as of 1947 was that the gifted group continued to have superior physique and health. Their achievement quotients remained through school as high as their IQ's. They tended to be versatile, not specialized. In school these children had nearly always been placed in classes above their age but below their capacity. They were not more subject to personal maladjustment than normal children, and that statement holds for the very high IQ's above 170 as well as for those between 140 and 170. Vocational achievement rates were high among the group. Marital happiness was normal or a little above normal. Aptitude for marital success was good. There was some little regression of ability toward mediocrity, but only such as should be expected on statistical grounds. The fertility rate at that time was not sufficient to maintain the stock. Many marks of eminence were discovered among the men, and some among the career-minded women.

It is nevertheless clear that a high IQ, though maintained into adulthood, is not a sufficient cause for eminence. Sir Francis Galton believed that genius would emerge even against unfavorable conditions. The truth seems to be that it may not emerge as eminence, even under otherwise favorable conditions, when motivation is lacking. Intelligence alone is not enough. Ambition, career-mindedness, drive may also be necessary to obtain from men and women of ability the maximal contribution to civilization.

Terman suggested that capacity for contentment is also great among gifted persons and that this kind of success must not be overlooked, especially when one is examining the lives of able women who marry. Here lies what must at first have been an unforeseen development in these genetic studies. It is not enough to be able to discover genius by measuring ability and selecting the top persons. Given the material for achievement, it has nevertheless to be energized. There can be, moreover, two kinds of success: society's success that comes through the discontent that drives men of great ability to great achievement and the eminence that marks it, and the individual's success which gives him —or her—the contentment which would make him wish to live the same life over again if he had the choice but does not drive him to notable public accomplishment.

It is clear that these studies represent the taxonomy of genius. Terman's forte was description. It was not a simple naturalist's description. He used statistics to reveal hidden attributes. He was persistently ingenious in thinking up ways to measure new dimensions of ability, inventing tests and scales to support the big descriptive task. These books are crammed full of carefully related facts, systematized and put in order. There is, however, in them very little theory that is more than description, little desire to gain simplicity by the creation of conceptual entities.

The exception is *intelligence.* To that reified construct Terman held vigorously. It was something that could be measured. The different tests might not wholly agree, but it was the tests that were at fault, he thought, as they got differently at the basic thing. Intelligence as a potentiality seemed pretty well fixed in childhood, and probably it was for the most part inherited. That is the way it seemed.

When factor analysis tended to split up "intelligence" into a number of primary abilities, Terman resisted the new thinking. He had too great an investment in intelligence to let it go readily. In the Second World War, however, intelligence tests by that name were abandoned, and the Army General Classification Test was used to measure three of Thurstone's seven primary abilities: verbal ability, numerical ability, and the comprehension of spatial relations. When this biographer remarked in 1955 that the concept of intelligence was on the way out, Terman protested; yet that was also the year of his marginal note about his being less sure than ever that intelligence (at least as the tests test it for Negroes and whites) is inherited.

Along with the scientific study of gifted children goes Terman's great practical achievement, the Stanford Achievement Test, a test for mastery of school subject matter at every school grade from the second to the tenth. The original work was done in collaboration with T. L. Kelley and G. M. Ruch and was put on the market in 1923. As school curricula changed the test was revised in 1929, 1940, and 1953. It has four different forms, which show a very high correlation one with another. The standardization is now based on the performance of 345,736 school children drawn from 363 school systems in 38 states. It is the best known of Terman's tests. Millions of school children have taken them. It would seem that Terman's feeling of financial insecurity disappeared as this test succeeded in the early 1920's, and it is not without interest to note that his drive for achievement did not diminish, so far as a biographer can tell, with the arrival of economic security for him. If compensation for frustration

started the drive in youth—and that theory cannot be proved—
then ambition must have continued from habituation or, as the
psychologists sometimes say, by "functional autonomy."

In the 1930's, when he was about sixty and the gifted children
were being allowed to do some growing up, Terman was responsible for three other important books.

In 1937, with Maud A. Merrill and after ten years of work, he
revised the Stanford Revision of the Binet-Simon scale of intelligence, the 1916 job, publishing the result under the title, *Measuring Intelligence.* They improved the tests greatly, brought the
lower level down to the mental age of two years, adjusted the
tests at three levels for superior adults, arranged the IQ ratings
for adults (the highest IQ obtainable is 152), and made out two
equivalent forms of the scale (124 items each) to permit retest-
ing. Later this improved test became available for testing the
offspring of the "gifted children" now grown up.

While work on the Terman-and-Merrill revision of the Stanford scale was in progress, Terman and Catherine Cox Miles,
with nine other assistants, were working on a scale for measuring masculinity and femininity. The result was the publication
in 1936 of *Sex and Personality: Studies in Masculinity and Femininity.* This project had also occupied about ten years of work.
The scale, as it was finally established, consisted of two equivalent forms of 455 items each, which sought to elicit characteristic
masculine and feminine interests and attitudes by way of word
associations, associations for ink blots, knowledge and information, emotional and ethical responses, interests, opinions, and
position in the extravert-introvert continuum. The scale ran from
+200 at the masculine extreme to −200 at the feminine extreme. The mean male was found to rate at +52 and the mean
female at −70. The means were far apart, but the spread between extreme cases was enormous; nevertheless, the overlap between the two sexes was small (only about 8 per cent). About
1,500 subjects contributed to this study.

The results are characteristic of all of Terman's work, a mass of facts with no simple general theory emerging—a Stanley Hall kind of study, one might almost say. So you find that masculinity —as measured by the scale—increased in males up to the eleventh grade (+70 on the average) and then diminished steadily until old age (0 at age eighty), whereas femininity in females diminished up to the college sophomore level (−60) and then increased a little (to −90 at ages sixty to eighty). The least masculine male group is the old men of all occupations, and the least masculine male group at younger ages is the clergymen, who were still less feminine than the most masculine female group, the women college athletes. (There was one extreme group of women athletes as masculine as the clergymen.) And so on, as education, intelligence, occupation, and interests affect the score on the scale for each sex. There was a special study of homosexuality and another of delinquent girls.

One reviewer of this book remarked that the research "borders perilously on a laborious demonstration of the obvious," but that remark is hardly fair. The quantification was new, the ability to say when there was overlap between the sexes and how much was new, the facts about age in the two sexes were largely new, and some of the findings about homosexuality and about delinquent girls were unexpected. On the other hand, Terman found himself unable to come to a sure conclusion about the basic question as to whether psychological sex differences are due to nature or to nurture. He attacked Margaret Mead's case favoring environmentalism as unproven; he showed his prejudice for hereditarianism here as he had with intelligence; but the data were inappropriate for a decision.

Terman's third report of research in book form in the 1930's was his *Psychological Factors in Marital Happiness,* written with the assistance of four others, published in 1938. It was a survey of the hedonic state of 792 married couples and 109 divorced couples, 1,802 persons altogether. The data consisted in the results of personality tests and the responses to questions. The work led to the establishment of a scale of happiness, which had, as it turned out, a skew toward the more cheery extreme. On this scale it was possible to get scores of happiness and to relate them statistically to various supposed contributors to marital happiness.

What turned out was worth getting. Most of the supposed causes of marital happiness and unhappiness were not valid. Sexual relations mattered much less than had been anticipated. So did differences in age and in education between the spouses. The general conclusion could have been that happy persons make happy pairs. If one goes behind this truism, looking for causes, one can say that happy marriages depend most upon the superior happiness of the couples' parents, on the childhood happiness of the couples themselves, on the strength of attachment to mothers and fathers, and on the infrequency and mildness of childhood punishment.

This was all important information, but it must have fallen short of what Terman had hoped for. Description is not engineering, and you cannot in practice retrieve an unhappy marriage by finding happy parents for each of the unhappy couples. Nor is there yet apparent any good advice for the unhappy, as to whether they should stay unhappily unmarried or become unhappily married. There is this to say, though: An unhappy man or woman may have a happy spouse. The hedonic gift is not dispensed in pairs, and the blame and credit assessed to marriage are perhaps more often a rationalization than a true statement of cause.

Terman, the avid constructer of mental tests, discovered, presumably to his initial surprise, that tests have a commercial value. The poor farm boy, the twelfth of fourteen children, who borrowed money to go to the Central Normal College, to Indiana University, and then to Clark University, who came away from Clark $2,500 in debt and went to poorly paid teaching positions in San Bernardino and Los Angeles—twelve years of relative poverty with a wife and, later, two children—this boy, who became a professor at Stanford University, the author of the

Stanford Revision of the Binet-Simon Tests of Intelligence, and, a little later, of the lucrative Stanford Achievement Test, discovered that the royalties on the tests were no inconsiderable sum when judged by academic standards. Terman's tastes were never extravagant. He continued to lead the life of a somewhat frail academic, but he could not have needed to worry about money after the Stanford Revision became the standard test of intelligence—one might almost say, had become the operational definition of intelligence—throughout the United States. He lived to see America become test conscious. That he profited from the sale of the tests is incidental. We have already noted that his indefatigability was not diminished by his acquisition of an adequate income.

PERSPECTIVE

In 1956 it became the responsibility of the committee of the American Psychological Foundation to decide upon its second annual Gold Medal Award, the award for 1957, "to be given to an American psychologist with a distinguished and protracted history of scientific and scholarly accomplishment." The first Gold Medalist had been Robert S. Woodworth. The committee chose as the second Lewis Terman, but they were not quite in time. Terman died on December 21, 1956, and the award was not to be made until September 2, 1957, at the annual meeting of the American Psychological Association. The committee decided that posthumous awards are not desirable. They announced their intention, and honored Terman by finding for him no substitute, while the assembled members of the Association concurred by remaining silent for a brief interval.

Now let us try to obtain a perspective on the life of this leader of American psychology. Lewis Terman's outstanding characteristics were his drive and his love of learning. It is possible to interpret the drive as compensation for frustration, as original effort to transcend the limitations of a farmer's life, transformed by maturation into the personality pattern of an ambitious adult.

That appeal to the environmentalistic explanation, however plausible, must remain speculative. Terman himself would have looked to heredity for his causation, yet there is no evidence that he was duplicating the pattern of his ancestors or his siblings, even though his son, with a very different youth, has also achieved academic eminence.

It is better, then, to take Terman as a fact, to content ourselves with describing how in fact he did escape from a farmer's life, not because he hated the life—he did not—but because he wanted learning more.

He was a farmer's boy, one of fourteen children. His father owned a few score of books, but there could be no luxuries in that home. He read the books, any book he could get hold of, and determined if possible to acquire an education. In that community the way out of farm life to education was by teaching school. So Lewis Terman took that route.

One sees in his unquenchable avidity for reading and schooling how strong his drive was. He would get through school, and still go on. His parents helped him at first when they could, but that was not much. At each new level he could see the one beyond. At Central Normal College he wanted Indiana University. There, in contact with Bryan, Lindley, and Bergström, he wanted Clark. At Clark the next pattern was set by Stanley Hall. His progress was, however, checked by the emergence of tuberculosis. What happened? Certainly this frustration intensified his determination. He accepted the geographical limitations of climate, but his ambition remained undiminished. San Bernardino was a step to Los Angeles. Always, when the tuberculosis checked him, he refused to surrender, took the minimal means for restoration, and was soon back on the job.

From Los Angeles he went to Stanford. Big ideas were occupying his mind. The revision of the Binet tests was his first big undertaking, and it was successful.

At first he had accepted his isolation as an educationalist, according to the pattern of Stanley Hall, but then he perceived the next level, the new world of scientific psychology, which he had known about at Clark and now was anxious to join. Teaching in the east in the summers, joining the American Psychological Association, being thrown by the psychological work of the First World War into contact with the other psychologists of the country, the growing success of the tests—all these things, plus the financial security that now at last came to him, gave him confidence in his own worth and importance. They gave him confidence, these things, but they did not release the tensions that drove him on.

For twenty years at Stanford as Executive Head of the Department of Psychology, and for fifteen more as an active emeritus, he kept on enthusiastically with the lines of endeavor he had started. The second revision of the Binet tests, the Stanford Achievement Test, the measure of masculinity-femininity, the scale of marital happiness were efforts along the way, efforts that showed what tests could do and also how they might be found limited; but his main undertaking was the *Genetic Studies of Genius*, his work with his "gifted children," with whom he was in correspondence thirty-five years after the work began, an affectionate father figure, as he wanted to be and as many of the "children" regarded him. He kept writing to the "children" and their spouses, asking about the "children's" children and their lives; and they, accepting him as a father figure, replied and gave throughout the years many hours of their time in tests and questionnaires for both themselves and their children.

Terman himself liked to speculate on what would have happened to him if he had not gone to Indiana and met Lindley, if he had chosen Florida instead of California, if the death of Bergström had not led to his being called to Stanford. Such guessing is futile. There are no controls for history, and you cannot state general biographical laws. You can, however, describe what happened, and it is clear that Terman and the times were able to fit each other. Terman was inept with apparatus just when American psychology was becoming brass-instrument conscious, but he found Stanley Hall, an erudite entrepreneur of the mind who was not an apparatus man. Terman fitted the Hall pattern and all his life reflected something of what he learned in Hall's famous vitalizing seminar. Terman wanted to get to the top and did, the top of the particular mountain on which he was.

Lewis Terman was a friendly person. He liked people and wanted them to like him. To avoid a vigorous social life he pleaded habitually his physical frailty, for the tuberculosis had convinced him that he was not physically strong; yet he needed to be liked, he wanted love and affection from many, and his immediate colleagues and the others at a distance warmed to his eager friendliness. Like the gifted children, the graduate students too thought of him as a father figure—especially those who attended his Stanley Hall-like seminar held like Hall's own on a Monday evening, and those few who came beforehand to dinner, where Mrs. Terman always played the gracious hostess.

This need for friendly relations with his associates is consistent with Terman's liberal political philosophy. He believed intensely in freedom of teaching and freedom of thought, in the democratic process, and to some extent in the socialization of education and medicine. He wanted social justice, racial tolerance, equality of opportunity. He believed that the social sciences should set themselves to the task of civilizing man's impulses and emotions so as to make it possible for mankind "to live together in peace, justice and good will" (cf. Hilgard, 1957). This is a philosophy wholly consistent with the reactions of the isolated farm boy who urgently sought success and friends among scientists and scholars.

Some persons, noting that he tended to believe in an hereditary intellectual elite, wonder how such an undemocratic view could be held by this tender-minded, sensitive, ambitious person, but the fact is that Terman thought of the intellectually elite as those who would save civilization for democracy. The gifted were given. You do not choose to have them, for there they are, whether you will or no. You can, however, choose to use them, to separate them from the crowd so that they may be trained to devote their special talents to benefit the crowd from which they have been taken.

That, then, is Lewis Terman, a sensitive man who wished to succeed and was strengthened by difficulty, as able a man as Stanley Hall's seminar ever provided among the many able men that it produced, a widely read man who loved knowledge for its own sake, a clear and felicitous writer with a gift for the popular account that left the scientific values intact, a friendly chap determined to have affection and yet to keep pushing toward the top, the dean of America's premathematical mental testers, a democratic liberal who believed that the intellectual elite, since they are a fact, must be used to promote a peaceful civilization in which new knowledge forever advances the human weal. In addition to his many contributions to modern scientific psychology, this practical demonstration in social philosophy may also in the future come to stand out as of great importance: Lewis Terman, a liberal in his thinking, showed, nevertheless, how democracy cannot avoid stratification as it is given by nature's inevitable division of human material into different levels of ability.

References

Hilgard, E. R. Lewis Madison Terman: 1877–1956. *American Journal of Psychology,* 1957, vol. 70, 472–479.

Sears, R. R. L. M. Terman, pioneer in mental measurement. *Science,* 1957, vol. 125 (New Series), 978 f.

Stern, William. Die psychologischen Methoden der Intelligenzprüfung. *Bericht über den V. Kongress für experimentelle Psychologie,* 1912, vol. 5, 1–109.

Terman, L. M. *The Measurement of Intelligence.* Boston: Houghton Mifflin, 1916.

Terman, L. M. Methods of examining: history, development, and preliminary results. In R. M. Yerkes (Ed.), *Psychological Examining in the United States Army.* (Memoirs of the National Academy of Sciences, vol. 15.) Washington, D.C.: Government Printing Office, 1921. Pp. 293–546.

Terman, L. M. Lewis Madison Terman. In Carl Murchison (Ed.), *A History of Psychology in Autobiography*. Vol. II. Worcester, Mass.: Clark University Press, 1932. Pp. 297–331.

Thurstone, L. L. Primary mental abilities. *Psychometric Monographs*, 1938, no. 1.

When Is Human Behavior Predetermined?
1957

In 1956 my very good friend, Richard M. Elliott, after thirty-eight years of service to the University of Minnesota's Department of Psychology, retired, and the Elliott Lectures were begun in his honor. I was complimented by being asked to give the first of these lectures in November 1956. I chose the ancient topic of freedom and determinism in psychology because B. F. Skinner, himself a former member of the Minnesota Department, had interested me in it by what I thought was his inconsistency. He was—in his *Science and Human Behavior* (1953), for instance —conducting an eager propaganda for the universal belief of educated people (Harvard students) in the predetermination of human behavior. It seemed to me that he was using an essentially voluntaristic language to advocate an unvoluntaristic view of behavior, and I even rewrote one of his eager admonitory paragraphs in sober descriptive language to show how I thought a determinist should talk. Skinner, of course, had his answer: he had to be eager, for how could he escape from nature's necessities?

In giving this talk at Minnesota I also had in mind the fact that Minnesota is the spot when the positivism of psychologists is centered in minds like Herber Feigl's and Paul Meehl's. These positivists did not like my applying the word *antinomy* to the concepts of freedom and determinism and to my four other instances of incompatibles; presumably I erred there—and perhaps Immanuel Kant did too. As I see it now, freedom is not a denial of causation but an ignoring of it.

Reprinted with permission from the *Scientific Monthly*, 1957, vol. 84, 189–196.

A number of persons have liked this lecture, naive though it may be. It has been reprinted in two books of readings.

When is human behavior predetermined? Is man free to choose? sometimes? always? in respect of everything? May he thus by choice control his own individual destiny? This is surely what most men believe most of the time. The scientist, on the other hand—because the business of science is the study of causes and their effects—keeps insisting that any action of man, if we but knew enough, could be referred to its causes; that the explanation of all human behavior lies in the ancestral genes of the behaving person, in his past experience, and in the various accidents that have happened to him since he was conceived. On which side does truth lie? Is man quite free to think as he will or are his beliefs but a reflection of the climate of fact and opinion that envelops him, and of the circumstances that belong to the century, the country, and the family in which he lives?

This problem is not made easier when we realize that man's belief that he is free may itself be predetermined. The belief in freedom could be man's great delusion—nearly, if not quite, immutable. It is conceivable, you see, that there could be a society of talking robots, designed so that they continue to interact one with another in accordance with the principles on which they have been constructed, all of them chattering the while about their behavior in words that imply that each is free to choose whatever he does; that each, choosing freely, thus becomes responsible for his own conduct—a society of robots in which everyone asserts his own freedom for the excellent reason that he is *not* free to deny it.

We keep thinking, representatives of mankind that we are, that the integrity of each of us is so great that our assurances and convictions are at least partially self-validating; that our sense of certainty, even though it may waver, must at the very least tend to point toward truth. But what if delusion has been designed into us? What if the robot residents of some psychologist-designed utopia have been constructed so as to believe in falsehood and never to know it, the truth of their basic determinism being carefully hidden from them behind barriers of rationalizations to which assurance and conviction are firmly fastened? What are we to say in the face of this possibility? Biology offers us no protection against it, for there is always the possibility that survival can be favored by delusion, and that wisdom may on occasion be, if not lethal, at least not maximally helpful. In this respect man finds himself caught in an egocentric predicament, unable to grasp the standard by which he can tell reason from rationalization. What is he to do? What should we do?

This is no new problem, but it has recently received a new importance, because the development of the behavioral sciences has shown how the actions of animals and men can be controlled in greater degree than had formerly been possible, and even more, I should say, because the totalitarian countries, with their brainwashings and their forced self-accusations, have shown that man's integrity—the citadel of his freedom—can be invaded, and man's opinion, faith, and conscience enslaved. Indeed, the sense of freedom could be turning out to be man's great delusion. Is it? How do you answer a question like that?

There is, I believe, an answer, for that is what this paper is about; but first let us see how this dilemma between freedom and determinism keeps turning up as wise men try to understand and cope with human action.

FREEDOM AND DETERMINISM: THE DILEMMA

Just now the universities—all of them—are worrying about what will happen when the new birth rate floods the admissions offices with would-be students. How can academe accommodate them all? This matter came up in a certain faculty of a large university some months ago, and the president expressed his concern and gave his advice on how to meet the coming tidal wave. "But why admit so many?" a professor of government

asked. "Where," he added, "does the area of decision in this matter lie?" The president was able to discern no such area. He
knew that his university, an endowed institution, could still not
remain unconcerned about the applicants it rejects. You might
decide for new dormitories but not for a fixed enrollment. The
professor, of course, was believing in freedom just then. That
is the way governments work: they make decisions. And the two
men, the president and the professor, were representing irrecon-
cilable philosophies. Yet no one remarked that incompatibles
cannot both be true, for this contradition is so commonplace that
people are fully accustomed to ignore it.

Years ago William McDougall, the psychologist, was my colleague at Harvard. He believed in freedom for the human mind
—in at least a little residue of freedom—believed in it and hoped
for as much as he could save from the inroads of scientific determinism (McDougall, 1923, esp. pp. 446–448). To the deter-
minist-psychologists, such a view was scientifically immoral.
John B. Watson (1923), behaviorism's founder, reviewed Mc-
Dougall's textbook of 1923 under the title "Professor McDougall
Returns to Religion," and you may be sure that Watson was not
thinking of himself as a rejoicing father welcoming back a prodi-
gal. I used to wonder about McDougall and determinism, and
then one afternoon in a colloquium—one of those rare occasions
when argument brings insight and does not merely serve to
harden preconceptions—I found out where lay the difference
between us—McDougall, the voluntarist, and me, the determinist. McDougall's freedom was my variance. McDougall hoped
that variance would always be found in specifying the laws of
behavior, for there freedom might still persist. I hoped then—
less wise than I think I am now (it was 31 years ago)—that
science would keep pressing variance toward zero as a limit. At
any rate this general fact emerges from this example: freedom,
when you believe it as operating, always resides in an area of
ignorance. If there is a known law, you do not have freedom.

Then there is Francis Hackett's (1948) assertion that psychoanalysis did not help the novelist after all. The novelists thought at first that Freud had presented them with accurate knowledge of human nature—a knowledge that psychology had hitherto failed to provide. Freud did, of course, but he also gave them determinism. Novelists, however, need heroes, and heroes need freedom. What machine was ever a hero to its owner unless the owner—a child undoubtedly—endowed it with freedom and life? You cannot write a novel about robots, unless they are free. The characters must meet difficulty and overcome it, in face of the possibility that they could have failed (Skinner, 1948). It is the same with an athletic team. A team that won because it was drugged would not be given the trophy. Victory must originate from within the victor, not be rigged in advance.

The Russians—I am relying on Raymond Bauer's (1952) excellent historical account of the development of psychology in the Soviet Union—had occasion to discover this dilemma. In the 1920's they stuck to economic determinism as part of their dialectical materialism—to that and to Pavlov's determinism of conditioning. Then their Five Year Plans got into difficulty and, in the early 1930's, the leaders reversed themselves, abandoning Pavlov, conditioning, mental testing, and everything that seemed to make the individual a consequence of causes outside himself. As a substitute they introduced a voluntaristic dynamic psychology, letting praise and blame, responsibility and guilt, operate instead of conditions external to the individual. The leaders themselves, of course, must still have believed in the predeterminism of behavior, for it was they who were to determine the conduct of the people by making them believe they were free and responsible. That the leaders thought they were free to delude the people into believing they were free is pretty obvious.

And then there is my colleague, B. F. Skinner (1954; 1956), famous for his patterning of the lives of rats and pigeons and now turning his attention to the teaching of children in the grades and to the analysis of psychotic behavior. He preaches a gospel of how psychological knowledge can be used to improve human living (Skinner, 1953), and how, as behavioral science advances, human conduct becomes more and more subject to control (Skinner, 1955). Control by whom, though? Or should one ask, by what? Skinner is saying something more than that behavior is caused, that it is the inevitable consequence of determinable scientific law. He is saying that, because behavior can be controlled, human living can be improved. Not merely that human living will be improved because biological selection promotes human weal willy-nilly, but that it can be and that there is, therefore, a possibility that it may not be, unless the gospel is accepted. This is sheer voluntarism. It is a mixing of languages, a hoping that hoping itself makes no sense except as a sign of the existence of a feeling of desire that contributes to the inevitable. Can one choose to do without choice?

It is in this way that the determinist gets trapped in the egocentric predicament (Perry, 1912, esp. pp. 129–134). He has to be outside the system in order to recommend it. He would be more convincing if he would take up his stand firmly on the outside—the man from Mars viewing human society—and describe what is going on, that and nothing more, just as a human being may describe the behavior of ants, without praise or blame for their conduct, or suggestions for improving their social structure, or even the admonition that ants could be happier if they were controlled by positive reinforcement and not by aversive stimulation. A book by a behavioral determinist ought not so much to advocate the control of behavior as to describe it. Advocacy undermines the argument for determinism because preference belongs to the world of values. You can indeed consider advocacy as a behavioral event with necessary and sufficient antecedents and consequences, but such rigor requires that the author rid himself of preferences and prejudices in his devotion to objective description if his implications are not to subvert his explication.

TRUTH VERSUS POLICY IN SCIENTIFIC THEORY

Perhaps I have now already made my point. It is that fact and value, as surely everyone knows, belong in different worlds, each with its own language, and that the wise man must keep both in his repertoire if he is to get along in the culture in which he lives. To me this view means that the wise man is something more than the scientist, who does indeed need, as scientist, to stick to determinism and thus to description. I am saying that science must be something less than the one way to truth. But is not this exactly the principle that prevails today? In 1907, J. J. Thomson (pp. 1 f.; cf. Conant, 1952, pp. 53 f.) remarked that a scientific theory is a policy, not the truth but a view that, if held, gets us ahead—a view to be held as long as it does get us ahead. Today we hear less about theories and more about models. What is the difference? The theory claims to be true, even though we all know that assurance about the validity of these claims varies greatly from theory to theory and from time to time for the same theory. The theory is an *as*, whereas the model is an *as-if*. The theory is indicative; the model, subjunctive. The model is a pattern to be abandoned easily at the demand of progress. Thus science is less than the whole of wisdom, and the wise teacher of science, being also a human being, will not seek to try to make those other human beings who come under his tutelage less wise or less free than himself.

Now let us examine how this dilemma enters into another field and how it can be met there. Let us consider the great man.

GREAT MEN: FREEDOM AS A NEGATIVE CONCEPT

Long ago the problem of freedom and determinism as it pertains to the conduct of great men came up in the contrasting views of Carlyle and Tolstoy. Carlyle, writing about heroes in 1840, was for freedom. "The history of what man has accomplished in this world," he said, "is at bottom the History of the Great Men who have worked here," Progress is what the great men started. Little is ever said about what started them, for it is conventional to suppose that they are self-starters, creative minds, and it would be derogatory to refer to their causes, if indeed they have any.

Tolstoy—in his *War and Peace* (1869, bk. 9, sect. 1; bk. 10, sect. 1; bk. 11, sect. 1; bk. 13, sect. 11; 1st epilogue, sect. 1; 2nd epilogue; appendix entitled "some words about *War and Peace*") —was, of course, on the other side. "A King is history's slave," he said. "History . . . the unconscious, general, hive-life of mankind, uses every moment of the life of kings as a tool for its own purposes. . . . The higher a man stands on the social ladder, the more people he is connected with and the more power he has over others, the more evident is the predestination and the inevitability of his every action." That is, in part, the *Zeitgeist* theory of history, before Matthew Arnold picked that word out of Goethe's writing and made it important. According to this view the great man becomes merely the agent of history. He is not only the cause of his consequences but also the consequence of his causes. You can regard him, if you wish, as a symptom, an event so conspicuous in an otherwise obscure causal train that it comes to be the sign or label by which the whole train is known—like calling all classical physics *Newtonian*.

Herbert Spencer was on the tough side of this argument with Tolstoy. William James was on the soft side with Carlyle. James was promoting scientific psychology in the days when it was very new, but also he was holding tight to the dignity of man. While he wanted us all to meet the new experimental psychologists, "these new prism, pendulum, and chronograph-philosophers," as he called them, he also wished to save the human mind from destruction by "the spying and scraping, the deadly tenacity and almost diabolic cunning" which the scientific attack in the hands of the meticulous German *Gelehrter* threatened to bring about—as James thought.

There is a proximate solution to this great-man problem, although one that does not go quite far enough. It is that you have freedom only when you are not interested in causal antecedents, in genesis. Everything depends on where you place the boundaries of your universe of discourse. If you are satisfied to consider only great men and their consequences, then, of course, they appear as free, because you have ignored all the conditions that made them great, the conditions that require the great scientist at the moment of discovery (when there is such a moment) to have the insight that puts him into the histories of science. So the great man is found free, freed by the unconcern of all hero worshippers.

Now change your point of view, enlarge your universe of discourse, inquire into the antecedents of the great man's great achievement, find out that he was, at least to some degree, anticipated by others, that another man, a small one, independently made the same discovery later, without knowledge of what the great man had done, and then you begin to transform the great man into a symptom and to believe in the *Zeitgeist* as furnishing the climate necessary for great discovery. Thus you move over from Carlyle to Tolstoy, and from William James to Herbert Spencer. Although you have diminished the dignity of great men, you have, on the other hand, enlarged your vision of the causal web of the universe.

It is possible to visualize a model of this causal nexus. Imagine a diagram, plotted between time, which runs from left to right, and simultaneity, which is up and down. Fill it in with separate little circles, each of which is an event—an event like Max Wertheimer's thought on the train in 1910 about perceived movement's being *ipso facto* a phenomenon, the *phi*-phenomenon, the thought that made him get off at Frankfurt-am-Main, buy a stroboscope at the German equivalent of the dime store, and start, after a few billion other events, the school of *Gestalt* psychology (Newman, 1944). Now on this diagram draw in all the cause-and-effect relations from every event to its consequents at the right. Simultaneous events are above and below each other and are never connected directly. Multiple causes and multiple effects are, of course, the rule. Every event has many causes and many effects. Now select a crucial event, one of the circles: Wertheimer thinking of *phi* on the train. Put in a boundary line that excludes all the antecedents and includes all the consequents. There you have the model for freedom. Wertheimer is seen as an originator. His idea was *sui generis.* When you think of freedom, you think in these terms. But take away the boundary, and you have before you the entire causal nexus. Wertheimer's insight may now be a necessary link in the system, but there are many others. His insight becomes less special, but your universe of understanding is enormously increased.

The main point here is that freedom is a negative conception. It is the absence of causes. The freedom for which men fight and die is also a negative conception, the absence of constraints. Within science the complaint of the intuitionists about the positivists has been that positivism offers constraints upon scientific freedom; that positivism is a police measure insisting that explanation shall be in terms of *nothing but,* as the protesting intuitionists put it, whereas they, the antipositivists, want not exactly *something more,* for they are not prepared to specify the something more, but freedom to let the inquiring mind advance as it will. This is the faith of the artist who resists control or assessment until his job is done and judgment may be passed. Who shall say that artistic expression should be more rigorously constrained?

So the question is: When is *nothing* better than *something?* And the answer is: You can tell *ex post facto,* and freedom—a negative, a faith in a nothing—has justified itself in more contexts than one.

It is true that, in general, men do not like nothings. Scientists will hold on to a disproved theory for long years until there emerges a better theory to replace the wrong one. Belief abhors a vacuum. So, too, men will hypostatize a negative into a positive, as they have done with the concept of freedom and also with the concept of chance. Both *freedom* and *chance* are terms that are used when efficient causes of present events are not known and often appear to be unknowable.

The scientific view of the history of thought is, of course, the deterministic one. You look for causes and believe in their existence even when you cannot specify them. Tolstoy and Herbert

Spencer, not Carlyle and William James. But the scientists' view is often quite different from the scientific view, for a scientist is a human being, required to make value judgments if he is to survive in the milieu in which he has to live. Indeed, there exists what might be called the moral history of science. It deals with the psychological forces that block or misdirect the progress of science and that also drive science forward: the inertias of the scientists, their prejudices, their egoisms, their needs for self-consistency, and also the positives of these negatives—the integrity, the pride, the loyalty of scientists. You might regard these personal characteristics as determining causes which advance or hinder progress, and then you would still be thinking scientifically; but actually this is not the way the business of science runs.

Take enthusiasm, for example. Science runs on enthusiasm, gets its research done by dediciated workers; yet enthusiasm is a prejudice, and science is supposed to eschew prejudice. There is a very real conflict here between objectivity and personal drive, a conflict that has the consequence that you ought not to trust the ego-involved theorist, or at least you ought not to be influenced by the intensity of his conviction. His enthusiasm has pushed the pendulum one way, and a better approximation to fact is reserved for posterity, which will have all the evidence before it and none of the distorting enthusiasms (Boring, 1942, pp. 608–613). Max Planck (1949, p. 33 f.) said that many a wrong theory could not be abandoned until its author died.

So what? You can be too scientific to be successful as a scientist. You need your prejudices. Trust posterity to straighten you out, and posterity's posterity to do even a better job.

This is a psychological antinomy. The scientist's mind must make use of incompatible attitudes. He will have to use now one attitude, now the other. Or the necessary combination of incompatibles may be found in a set of men, or perhaps merely in a pair, say, the enthusiastic researcher and the sober handbook-writer. The basic fact remains, however: the prejudiced mind gets more progress into science than does the mind of the critical assessor.

CAUSES OF BELIEF

In this connection it becomes desirable to inquire into the nature of belief, to ask what use are an organism's beliefs to it, and when, if ever, it is a good thing to believe in error. When is man advantaged by having a great delusion?

There is no need for us to try to distinguish between a belief and a pattern of behavior. The termite believes in a totalitarian society. The life of each termite is devoted to the fulfillment of its role in a complex social organization, which the entomologist, William Morton Wheeler (1920), once compared favorably to the less efficient, more variable, less assured governance under which man survives. The newly hatched gosling follows its mother, real or foster, or rather whatever large, dominating animal or other mobile object has come in those early hours of its life to bear the mother image for it. Lorenz (1935; but see also Beach and Jaynes, 1954; Hinde, Thorpe, and Vince, 1956) calls this fixation *imprinting*. It is the gosling's fifth commandment: Honor thy mother and follow her whither she shall go, that thy days may be long—for it is plain that a good belief has survival value.

Those beliefs survive that help the organism to survive: the termite; the gosling; the spider's web; the lioness springing for the throat of her quarry; man's gregariousness. Nor does a belief have to be in the genes. Man's social institutions persist because they are useful to him: forms of government; forms of religion.

Darwin's (1872, chap. 1) first principle also applies to these beliefs. Harmless but no longer useful remnants of originally useful beliefs survive: the cat circling around before it lies down on the parlor rug, as if treading down its bed in the forest; man, baring his second canine in a sneer, though he will not really bite. With man these remnants of useful habits may, however, gain a secondary use as they become means of communication. Your sneer warns the other fellow that you are ready to attack with teeth other than your biological ones.

Generalization may, moreover, preserve a belief that is actually harmful but not distinguished from the useful beliefs with which it is classed. The classical example is the sweet-tasting poison. But what about appetite? The belief in the goodness of eating is basic to the preservation of life, but it can also induce obesity. America is filled with people today who would be better off with a different adjustment of this habit. In a way the fat man's hunger is his great delusion, for he does not need so much food; and man's belief in his own freedom might turn out to be a similar kind of self-deception. It is doubtful that it would be sensible for a termite to believe in personal freedom. For it the good life is fixed by the state.

These human beliefs are, of course, very complex. For instance, is it ever good for man to believe a superstition? Probably yes, but let us consider ritual. Members of a Jewish family keep a kosher kitchen, not because they believe that any biological harm would follow if the two sets of dishes got mixed, but because they like to preserve ancient customs, to have their children perpetually reminded that they belong to a special group which has these customs. Patriotism is similar. The salute to the flag is good because it is symbiotically reinforcing. It makes you one with your compatriots. Both of these kinds of behavior are examples of good false beliefs—that is to say, false in their manifest content, yet good to have because of the psychological effect of having them.

Certainly the belief in human freedom of action is in one sense a superstition, one that is, however, justified biologically by the fact that it is woven into the fine structure of society. Language itself would have to be eviscerated were this conception to be extirpated from it. Beliefs, you see, can be false as to logical content and good as to use and function. Does not this conclusion settle the problem of freedom? It is a useful superstition.

But no, it does not, for the argument can also be made that causality is another useful superstition. This is what a scientific model is, a useful superstition, for it stands above the observed evidence. So we had better return to our principal inquiry.

CAUSALITY AS A MODEL

Against this background I now have three things to say.

1) The behavioral determinist is not wrong. We do indeed want all the controls for human nature that we can get. To prefer ignorance to knowledge is not best—not in the Western culture of this modern age.

2) The model of human nature in social interaction, which is the natural outcome of scientific thinking about behavior, is nevertheless only a model. It is something to have in your repertoire of usable models, something to use on proper occasions. It is pushing science too far to say that this model is true now, but a model does not have to be true to be useful.

3) The analogy that once recommended this model as something that might be true is classical physics, but physics has changed. Causality is not so simple a relation as it seemed to be to Laplace and to Helmholtz. Physics has become psychological. Operationism says that what you cannot observe does not exist. If you cannot ever observe the position and momentum of an electron simultaneously, then they do not exist simultaneously. Here we are dealing with physical incompatibility, with the physical techniques of observation. In the case we are considering, however, we have only a psychological incompatibility, two attitudes that cannot be assumed simultaneously. The point is that behavioral scientists should not be coerced into too great a simplicity by physical analogy, when physics itself has had to revise its thinking so radically.

SHOULD BEHAVIOR BE CONTROLLED?

Sometimes the humanists raise the question, not whether behavior can be controlled but whether it should be (Krutch, 1953, esp. chap. 3). It is hard for me to take this question seriously. You need all the knowledge of control that you can have. Only then are you prepared to consider how it should be used.

Education and government are instituted for the purpose of

human control, and nearly all discussion and debate of any subject are directed at control. I prepare this paper in the hope that by it I may exercise some small degree of thought-control upon all who read it. Skinner claims to have better and surer methods for the design of behavior than have been available heretofore. You should see his pigeons, taught to earn their livings by the rewarding of their successes (not by punishment of their failures). So it is that he envisages a happy society, in which success and reward are the rule, and frustration has been reduced or eliminated by good social design. No one, of course, ever designs frustration into a machine so that it tries to make the same wheel go in opposite directions at the same moment.

One objection made to the behavioral scientists' development of human control is that their power might get into the hands of evil men. This objection seems to me to miss the point. Surely any elite that undertook to use behavioral science to enslave the world would find beneficence more efficient than maleficence. Slavery would be designed as a happy and desirable state, and, if these successful slaves still felt that they needed variety in their companionship, variety can be designed too. All you need is the specifications for *n* personalities, and the desirable frequency for each of them, to get mass production going.

In any case, you should push knowledge of the means of social control as far as you can. Modern civilization would rather run the risk of being bombed out of existence than return to the complacency of the Middle Ages, when scientific inquiry into natural law was not one of the most important activities of wise men. It is true that the physicists opened a Pandora's box, but what wise man would have stayed them, would have counseled that more safety is to be found in ignorance than in knowledge?

As man alters the world in which he lives, he has to trust that he will be able to adjust it to himself or else adjust himself to it. So far the advance of civilization has consisted of these changes and adjustments, and I see no reason to fear that the behavioral determinists are starting something that will get out of hand.

The attempt to control men's actions and thoughts is as old as history. You cannot have social engineering that does not conscript the individual.

USE OF INCOMPATIBLES

So we come back to the main problem. Do we have to accept incompatibles simultaneously? Perhaps not simultaneously, but certainly alternatively—or so it seems to me. Certainly we all like to believe that nature is uniform and does not admit contradictions. Nevertheless, it seems clear that there may be limits to the resolving power of the understanding mind. Let me remind you of four such instances.

1) First there are the *antinomies* of Immanuel Kant (Watson, 1901, pp. 155–194 *et passim*). The best known is that you cannot conceive of space as finite nor yet as infinite. What do you do? You admit the contradiction as a limitation of the understanding, and the practical man uses one model or the other as suits his thought. Kant also included freedom and determinism among the antinomies (Wheeler, 1956, esp. pp. 372–376).

2) Then there is Ralph Barton Perry's *egocentric predicament*, the dilemma that applies especially to our argument (Perry, 1912). How can the mind that considers other minds include itself? If I am to see all other men as robots, can this seeing be an event in my own robotic nature or have I got to stay outside the system in order to discuss it? Human nature could be viewed whole by the man from Mars. If *n* is the population of the world, then at most you could never knowingly have more than *n*–1 robots, for there has to be the 1 left over to do the viewing. In this way one can get around the difficulty of solipsism, not by reducing all reality to events in the Red King's dream, but by ruling the Red King out of consideration. And this was the reason for Max Meyer's (1921) writing a psychology under the title *The Psychology of the Other One*. Everyone counted but Meyer; he wrote the book.

3) Then there are Sir Arthur Eddington's *Postulates of Impo-*

tence, the *a priori* impossibilities (Whittaker, 1952). The best known is the principle that you cannot detect a uniform translatory motion that is possessed by a system as a whole by means of observations taking place wholly within the system. This is a relativity principle, but it is also a kind of robotic egocentric predicament.

4) And finally there is Bohr's (1934, pp. 9–15, 52–91; also in Schlipp, 1949, pp. 199–241) *Principle of Complementarity,* which includes the Heisenberg *Principle of Uncertainty,* that you cannot know both the position and momentum of an electron for the same instant. This seems to be a physical, not a psychological, incompatibility, but Robert Oppenheimer has told us that Bohr came upon this idea long before he ever formulated it, by thinking about such antinomies as fact and value, the tolerance of pure description as opposed to the intolerance of moral judgment.

So we do not have to be afraid of embracing incompatibles. It happens every day. Thought is polygamous. As a matter of fact, this kind of polygamy has been enormously eased by the present-day tendency to substitute the model for the theory. The theory had truth value. It was a claim upon truth, and it had no right to persist—in spite of the fact that habitually it did—in the face of any single contradictory fact. As I have suggested, the theory is an *as,* whereas the model is but an *as-if.* You can have as many models as you want and use them when you will.

Causal determinism is the scientific model. It works enormously well. There are places in science where it breaks down, but they are not many. On the other hand, there are, in the process of living, all the situations in which values are called for and in which the scientific model itself fails. In such cases we get along best with the truncated causality model which we call freedom.

REITERATION

And that is that. Now that I am done I seem, to myself, to have said very little. Yet when I see the humanist battling the scientific behaviorist, seeking to save human freedom and dignity from the ruthless hands of the invading scientist, I feel that something should be said, and this has been it.

Human dignity is all right. It is not silly to want to save it. Robots do not have it. Science does not preserve it. It is an attribute that lies outside of science. It implies that its possessor is free. Freedom is a negative concept, a truncated causality, but it is part of the warp of language. To get rid of this concept would change the whole of our civilization. Yet we need not attempt that, for causality is only the form of a model, and freedom is also a model, and we can use our models at will without letting them dominate us.

One thing more—my parting shot. Do you want to know where to find a free man, a man who acts as if he were free and thinks of himself as free (and how much freer could he be than that)? Go to him who is earnestly trying to persuade you that all men are robots. He will not claim that his ardor was designed into him and has no necessary connection with the validity of what he is saying. If he calls himself a robot, still he will not act like one, for it takes a free man to start a war on freedom. An IBM machine does not have the dignity to make an argument convincing, and an IBMpty organism is a poor evangelist.

References

Bauer, R. A. *The New Man in Soviet Psychology*. Cambridge, Mass.: Harvard University Press, 1952.

Beach, F. A., and Jaynes, Julian. Effects of early experience upon the behavior of animals. *Psychological Bulletin*, 1954, vol. 51, 239–263.

Bohr, Niels. *Atomic Theory and the Description of Nature*. New York: Macmillan, 1934.

Boring, E. G. *Sensation and Perception in the History of Experimental Psychology*. New York: Appleton-Century, 1942.

Carlyle, Thomas. *On Heroes, Hero Worship and the Heroic in History*. London: Chapman and Hall, 1840.

Conant, J. B. *Modern Science and Modern Man*. New York: Columbia University Press, 1952.

Darwin, Charles. *The Expression of the Emotions in Man and Animals*. London: Murray, 1872.

Hackett, Francis. The novel and human personality. *New York Times Book Review*, 15 Aug. 1948, 1, 15.

Hinde, R. A., Thorpe, W. H., and Vince, M. A. The following response of young coots and moorhens. *Behaviour*, 1956, vol. 9, 214–242.

Krutch, J. W. *The Measure of Man*. Indianapolis: Bobbs-Merrill, 1953.

Lorenz, K. Z. Der Kumpan in der Umwelt des Vogels. *Journal für Ornithologie*, 1935, vol. 83, 137–213, 289–413.

McDougall, William. *Outline of Psychology*. New York: Charles Scribner's, 1923.

Meyer, Max. *Psychology of the Other One*. Columbia: Missouri Book Company, 1921.

Newman, E. B. Max Wertheimer: 1880–1943. *American Journal of Psychology*, 1944, vol. 57, 428–435.

Perry, R. B. *Present Philosophical Tendencies*. New York: Longmans, Green, 1912.

Planck, Max. *Scientific Autobiography and Other Papers*. (Trans. by Frank Gaynor.) New York: Philosophical Library, 1949.

Schlipp, P. A. *Albert Einstein: Philosopher-Scientist*. Evanston, Ill.: Library of Living Philosophers, 1949.

Skinner, B. F. *Walden Two*. New York: Macmillan, 1948.

Skinner, B. F. *Science and Human Behavior*. New York: Macmillan, 1953.

Skinner, B. F. The science of learning and the art of teaching. *Harvard Educational Review*, 1954, vol. 24, 86–97.

Skinner, B. F. Freedom and the control of men. *American Scholar*, 1955, vol. 25, 47–65.

Skinner, B. F. What is psychotic behavior? In *Theory and Treatment of the Psychoses*. (Papers presented at the dedication of the Renard Hospital, St. Louis, Oct. 1955.) St. Louis: Washington University Studies, 1956. Pp. 77–99.

Thompson, J. J. *The Corpuscular Theory of Matter*. New York: Charles Scribner's, 1907.

Tolstoy, L. N. (1869). *War and Peace*. (Trans. by Leo Wiener.) Boston: Dana Estes, 1904. 4 vols.

Watson, J. B. Professor McDougall returns to religion. *New Republic*, 11 Apr. 1923, vol. 34 (Spring Book Section), 11–14.

Watson, John. *Selections from Kant*. Edinburgh: Maclehose, 1901.

Wheeler, J. A. A septet of sibyls: aids in the search for truth. *American Scientist*, 1956, vol. 44, 360–377.

Wheeler, W. M. The Termitodoxa, or biology and society. *Scientific Monthly*, 1920, vol. 10, 113–124.

Whittaker, E. T. Eddington's principle in the philosophy of science. *American Scientist*, 1952, vol. 40, 45–60.

Psychological Factors in the Scientific Process
1954

My concern with the history of psychology made me become interested in the psychology of history. In my presidential address before the American Psychological Association in 1928 I dealt with the psychology of controversy and how egoism, since it blinds scientists, hinders progress. Later I came to see that there is a "motivational predicament" in that egoism hinders by blinding and helps by energizing the productive drive. With these problems in mind and also the matter of how thinking is helped and hindered by the current *Zeitgeist* (see the next paper), I wrote this summary of how scientific activity operates perpetually under the intellectual and motivational psychodynamics of the scientists—the very human scientists.

The scientific process is partly observation and partly logic. You observe particular relations and then by induction you arrive at such a generalization as a fact, a function, a law, or a theory. Or, having formed a generalization by logic, insight, or hunch, you deduce from it a testable relationship and submit that to observation. There are other formulations that describe the scientific process, but my point here is nothing more than that science is a human activity and that you have, therefore, to take into account the properties of human beings when you are assessing facts and theories. This thought is not new. Errors of observation, both instrumental and human, have long been matters of

Reprinted with permission from the *American Scientist*, 1954, vol. 42, 639–645.

scientific concern, and the discussion of how to treat them mathematically goes back to Daniel Bernoulli and Lagrange in the eighteenth century and, as almost everyone knows, to Laplace and Gauss in the nineteenth. It was in 1820 that the astronomers discovered, in the observation of the times of stellar transits, the personal equation, and this technical term has now come to be used for any individual bias that affects human judgment or action.

For all their antiquity, personal equations receive within science much less attention than their importance deserves. One exception to this general neglect has been the suggestion of C. W. Morris (1938) that we should recognize a field of study to be called *pragmatics,* a branch of the theory of signs that deals "with all the psychological, biological, and sociological phenomena which occur in the functioning of signs." Much less esoteric than this plan of Morris' is the program of Kubie (1953; 1954) for the study of certain problems that affect scientific careers, problems that arise from unrecognized neurotic forces and socioeconomic forces. You do not have to go very far toward neurosis, however, to find the personal equation making trouble in science. You have to go only far enough to find egoism, which would seem to be no distance at all. What is it that creates scientific controversy? Ego-involvement. Ego-bias. Never do you find two scientists in bitter controversy because each believes the other is right and he himself wrong. I used to think that psychologists at least, knowing so much about emotion and ego-involvement, should be incapable of vanity in their professional controversies, but the record shows that I was wrong (Boring, 1929). When his own precious past achievement is involved, even the psychologist has pride.

Ego-involvement is not, however, the only or even the chief source of bias in the scientific process. A subtler and sometimes more sinister prejudicial force is to be found in the intellectual atmosphere that envelops the thinking of the scientist. It is commonplace to say that science depends on communication, that the invention of printing eventually advanced science enormously, that the publication of results is always essential, that the iron curtain and the secret classification of data are bad for science. All such obvious statements are concerned with whether or not the normal overt mechanisms of communications are working or blocked. On the other hand, there are covert influences that make up what has been called the climate of opinion, and by Goethe the *Zeitgeist*—the conventions of thought and the unquestioned assumptions that are implicit in the culture in general and in science in particular. These forces act as *vires inertiae*. They constrain originality and reinforce tradition, as well as limiting the irresponsibility of the cranks who, excelling in originality, are deficient in critical wisdom. Conant (1947, pp. 88–90, 98–109, esp. pp. 88, 103) has remarked that "a scientific discovery must fit the times. . . . A well-established concept may prove a barrier to the acceptance of a new one. If a conceptual scheme is highly satisfactory to those who use it, neither a few old facts which cannot be reconciled nor a few new ones will cause the concept to be abandoned. . . . Old concepts may be retained in spite of alleged facts to the contrary." The *horror vacui* that science cannot deny is the scientist's fear of being left without any theory at all. "It takes a new conceptual scheme to cause the abandonment of an old."

It is obvious that there is a complementarity about the effects of both ego-involvement and the *Zeitgeist*. Each is both good and bad for progress. Out of egoism are derived the drive and enthusiasm that lead men to undertake research, to keep at it, to publish the results, to keep promoting the knowledge and use of these results. Also out of egoism is derived the emotional support for the cranks, for Velikovsky's collision of two worlds, for Hubbard's dianetics, for every scientist who still holds on to a theory after the weight of evidence no longer justifies it (Cohen, 1952; Boring, 1952). "New scientific truth does not triumph by convincing its opponents and making them see the light," said

Max Planck (1949, pp. 33 f.), "but rather because its opponents eventually die."

The complementarity of the *Zeitgeist* as intellectual inertia is equally clear. It makes progress slower but also surer, for it favors the caution and judiciousness that take time. That statement can be made of the climate of opinion as it pervades the culture of any period and of any geographically communicating region. It can also be applied to the intellectual atmosphere of any scientific in-group like a scientific school or the disciples of some leader. Their loyalty, enthusiasm, and egoism all promote research and encourage effort and thoroughness, while also increasing inflexibility and narrowing the perspective. At the moment when new thought is being formed, these complementarities are genuine and inescapable; you cannot eat your cake and have it too. Nevertheless such psychological incompatibilities need not affect posterity who, free from past commitments, egoism, loyalties, and enthusiasm, see more clearly, remaining limited only by the unrecognized biases that always pervade the atmosphere of thinking (Boring, 1955).

The history of science shows how the explicit communication of fact and opinion influences research and promotes progress, and it may touch also upon the manner in which the inertia of accepted belief opposes the promotion of what is novel and original and upon the way in which presumably discarded beliefs keep returning to confuse and hamper later thinking. Seldom, however, does the history of science explain how the *Zeitgeist* works, how implicit views covertly distort thinking, without the thinker himself being aware of this influence or of its effect upon him. Nor may the psychologist conjure up the past and be certain that, even if Newton did discover the calculus independently of Leibnitz, he was not influenced by the lectures of his old teacher, Isaac Barrow at Trinity College, Cambridge; or that Johannes Müller conceived the idea of five specific nerve energies in ignorance of the fact that John Locke and Thomas Young and

Charles Bell had each, although in very different ways, already made it clear that the properties of the sensory nerves are interposed between the mind and the objects that it perceives. What the psychologist does understand is how such influences can be effective without being "conscious"—in one of the two senses of that term. In a different sense, you are indeed aware of an idea if it influences you; its influence upon your thought is the sign of your awareness. But still you may not be at all aware of your awareness. You may be like an animal perceiving an object without perceiving that he is perceiving. The greater part of consciousness in man, and presumably almost all of the consciousness in animals, must be of this unself-conscious kind. Nor did it require Freud to make us believe in this kind of unconscious sensitivity, for the new conception was a gradual growth. Freud had scarcely had his new thought in Vienna before Külpe had a comparable inspiration in Würzburg, and I doubt if Külpe had heard of Freud in 1905. If he had, he would not have been impressed (Boring, 1950).

In fact, the argument for the unconscious and semiconscious effects of generally accepted views—of the *Zeitgeist*—upon thought arises from the many anticipations and synchronities noted in connection with scientific discoveries which have been recorded as original achievements. To discover anticipations of important theories—somtimes vague anticipations or early statements made on insufficient evidence—is a commonplace of the history of science. What is noteworthy is the way that such anticipations multiply as simultaneity is approached and how many discoveries, inventions, and new ideas occur so close together in time as practically to exclude direct cross-communication, thus making it appear that the coincidence is the consequence of some pre-established harmony that is maturing in the intellectual social climate, a *Zeitgeist* indeed.

In 1921, explicating this view, Ogburn and Thomas (pp. 83–93) printed a list of 148 synchronous or nearly synchronous, seemingly independent discoveries and inventions. While this list contains some errors (for Helmholtz definitely based his color theory on Thomas Young's suggestion, and, besides, those two bits of originality were fifty-one years apart), the total effect of it is convincing. On the other hand, the investigator may not know the origin of his brilliant insight. That fact accords with a common maxim of psychology which, however, is not very often mentioned in the history of science. When men are sure of their own motives, as often as not they are apt to be clinging to rationalizations and are ignorant of the true reasons.

Since Freudian platitudes are apt to convince only those who have already accepted them, let me set down here what I can say about a recent case of two poets who were simultaneously inspired to write practically the same poem. Or were they? It is my conviction that on publication neither author believed he had borrowed from the other, but that one of them did actually borrow, having at one time known all about the other poem and having since forgotten it—perhaps because forgetting was convenient or perhaps not. The poets are Miss Victoria Sackville-West (VSW) and Mr. Clifford Dyment (CD), both of whom have generously given me permission to reprint their so nearly synchronous inspirations, in the interest of promoting further general knowledge of what sometimes makes inspiration happen. I shall use their initials because we are interested in a principle, not in persons, and note merely that this coincidence is already a matter of public record (Editor, 1950).

These two persons are poets of considerable importance, both with a distinguished list of publications to their credit. VSW, twenty-two years older than CD, belongs to a family distinguished for public service throughout three centuries of British history, and being older, may be said at the moment to have achieved somewhat greater recognition as a writer. In 1949 CD published in a volume of his collected poems a poem called "Saint Augustine at 32." At almost the same time VSW published in *The Poetry Review* a poem which she called "The Novice to Her Lover." Here they are:

ST. AUGUSTINE AT 32	THE NOVICE TO HER LOVER

Girl, why do you follow me
When I come to the threshold of
   the holy place?
My resolution falters: it seems a
   death to enter
When, turning back, I look into
   your face.
	Why must you follow me
	When I come to the threshold of
	   this holy place?
	My resolution falters and it seems
	   death to enter
	When, turning back, I look upon
	   your face.

I saw you when I lay alone
 	
And ran from you as from a
   searching light
Into the gentle, acquiescent
 	
Obscurity of the night.
	I could renounce you when I lay
	   alone;
	I ran from you as from a
	   hungry light
	Into the gentle, the infinite, the
	   healing
	Clemency of the night.

I crave communion that is not
   words
And life fulfilled in my cell
   alone—
And you, you come with your lips
   and your gold hair
And at your feet is a leaf that
   the wind has blown.
	I crave an eloquence that is not
	   words,
	I seek fulfillment in the kiss of
	   stone—
	But you, you come with your mouth
	   and your dark hair
	And at your feet a leaf that
	   the wind has blown.

What happened? The two poems are almost identical, although each poet has given his own sex to the central figure in the poem. Does the *Zeitgeist* deal in ready-made poetry, or was there some unconscious communication that explains away this bit of pre-established harmony? What is true of poetry in this instance can also be true of scientific theory.

The editor (1950) of the magazine that first published the two poems in juxtaposition, having written to CD and VSW, printed their replies. CD said he had published his poem in a magazine in January 1943, then included it in a volume of his collected poems in 1944, and then again published it later in a larger collection of his poems that appeared in 1949. He was a gentleman; he made no suggestion as to the nature of VSW's inspiration. VSW said, in late 1949, that she had written the poem in 1942 or early in 1943, when she was writing about Ste. Thérèse of Lisieux, that she did not, however, publish it then, but copied it into a letter to a Catholic friend who was interested in Ste. Thérèse. The friend now says that she never copied the poem out of the letter nor showed it to anyone. VSW goes on to say that in 1949 she was asked by *The Poetry Review* for some unpublished poem to print in a special issue. She then hunted in her Manuscripts book and found this one which she sent in to the magazine where it was published in the summer of 1949. When in November she read CD's poem in his 1949 volume, she recognized it at once as practically her own; so she wrote to CD about the matter, and he replied, reminding her that after he had published this poem in his 1944 volume, she had written him of her special admiration for it. Thus VSW, having by 1949 identified this particular poem with herself, forgot what had actually happened in 1944, and might in the same way have remembered what did not happen in 1942 or 1943.

It is not for us to say what really happened, but let us spin a plausible account which, if true, would surprise no psychologist. CD, we may suppose, did just exactly what he said he did: he published the poem early in 1943, and again in 1944 and 1949. In 1942 and early in 1943 VSW was writing about Ste. Thérèse and she published a book about her in 1943. Sometime in 1943 or 1944 she saw CD's poem and liked it. It is certain she saw it in the 1944 book, if not earlier, for at that time she wrote CD of her admiration for it. Presumably she had read CD's poem when she was still under the spell of enthusiasm for Ste. Thérèse, and the poem caught her fancy. She copied the poem, reversing the sexes to make it apply to Ste. Thérèse, made other small changes and improvements to suit both her taste and the reversal of the sexes, admired the result, and, wanting to preserve it, tucked the poem away in her MSS book. It does not matter whether she wrote to CD before or after she wrote out her own version. VSW would not have mentioned her parody, which was not yet near to becoming a plagiarism, to CD at that time. Then she forgot about what she had done, and, when she was asked five years later in 1949 to find some of her unpublished verse, she turned up this one among the odds and ends of her MSS. Her feeling about Ste. Thérèse and her liking for the poem revived, but there was no recall of the circumstances under which she had "written" the poem. Only a few months later VSW found CD's version in his 1949 book. She must have recognized the similarity at once but continued to suppress her memory of 1944 until CD reminded her of the letter she had written to him. It was a convenient suppression, for it saved VSW from embarrassment, and as such the phenomenon was not one to surprise a psychologist. That is the way this thing we call the mind works.

Others, commenting on this interesting case, have offered psychological explanations similar to mine (Various, 1950), and one writer has noted that Hilaire Belloc had written a quatrain almost identical in thought and development with a quatrain of Voltaire's, although different in meter, rhyme scheme, and language (English *vs.* French). When Belloc had this similarity pointed out to him, he replied that he had never heard this epigram of Voltaire's, but that he was not surprised; nor was he ever disturbed when accused of appropriation of "other people's ideas or even lines of verse," for that merely put him in company with Shakespeare, Marlowe, Catullus, and Homer (Hamilton, 1950).

Now let no reader misunderstand my meaning. I have no thought that most or even many of the synchronous discoveries and inventions that occur are unconscious plagiarisms, except as we all of us plagiarize the *Zeitgeist* again and again. When I was a ten-year-old I had a philosophy of life, picked up partly from my mother and partly from other vague sources, a philosophy that included items of thought from Descartes, Jeremy Bentham, and Herbert Spencer. I doubt if I had ever heard of any of these philosophers; certainly I had read about none of them at the age of ten. My point is that, if it is possible unconsciously to steal a specific poem, it is also possible unconsciously to appropriate thought from the common domain and from particular thinkers who cultivate some portion of that domain. The culture, the atmosphere of opinion, the *Zeitgeist* are the reservoirs from which the originator gets his materials and sometimes his elaborately prefabricated parts. He can perceive and select what he wants without perceiving his perceiving—like a bird building a nest.

These then are some of the ways in which personal equations enter into the content of science. Enthusiasm, loyalty, egoism— it is always some personal need that drives you to research and to publication, and perhaps beyond, so that you are impelled to advertise your results or to enter into controversy about them. The urge gets the work done, but it may also blind you to the defects and shortcomings of the work itself. Ultimately, instead of pushing progress on, the same need may lead to pushing it backwards, and the truth of objectivity may be left for others to perceive, or even reserved for posterity. You get your original ideas in part from your own insight, your skill, or good fortune in seeing novel relationships where no relations had been perceived before. You are helped to such insight when the new thought fits in with the current trend of thinking, and conversely you may be blocked from originality if the trend of the times is against the correct new thought that never became quite explicit enough to stick in your conscious mind.

Much of your dependence upon the thought of others is explicit, clear, and overt, coming about by way of normal verbal communication in speech and print. A great deal of conventional thinking, on the other hand, is implicit, obscure, and covert, being carried in the unexpressed assumptions and value judgments of current common sense. You know all these common values and beliefs, but you do not assess them because you are apt not to be occupied with doing any knowing *about* your knowing. The habitual modes of thought that belong to a particular time and culture may help you to help these modes to advance further in the direction in which they already tend, but such modes of thought may also prevent you from having an insight that is inconsistent with the cultural background. Again and again scientific progress halts because the correct next step contravenes some firmly rooted theory or belief. The *Zeitgeist* may help or it may hinder, but always it is with us, and experiment and theory are inevitably formed under its influence.

References

Boring, E. G. The psychology of controversy. *Psychological Review,* 1929, vol. 36, 97–121.

Boring, E. G. Great men and scientific progress. *Proceedings of the American Philosophical Society,* 1950, vol. 94, 339–351.

Boring, E. G. The validation of scientific belief. *Proceedings of the American Philosophical Society,* 1952, vol. 96, 535–539.

Boring, E. G. The dual role of the *Zeitgeist* in scientific creativity. *Scientific Monthly,* 1955, vol. 80, 101–106.

Cohen, I. B. Orthodoxy and scientific progress. *Proceedings of the American Philosophical Society,* 1952, vol. 96, 505–512.

Conant, J. B. *On Understanding Science.* New Haven: Yale University Press, 1947.

Editor. A question of inspiration. *New Statesman and Nation,* 1950, vol. 39, 62.

Hamilton, G. R. A question of inspiration. *New Statesman and Nation,* 1950, vol. 39, 133.

Kubie, L. S. Some unsolved problems of the Scientific career. Part I: Problems arising from unrecognized neurotic forces. *American Scientist,* 1953, vol. 41, 596–613.

Kubie, L. S. Some unsolved problems of the scientific career. Part II: Problems arising from socio-economic forces. *American Scientist,* 1954, vol. 42, 104–112.

Morris, C. W. Foundations of the theory of signs. *International Encyclopedia of Unified Science,* 1939, vol. 1 (no. 2), 29–42.

Ogburn, W. F., and Thomas, Dorothy. Are inventions inevitable? A note on social evolution. *Political Science Quarterly,* 1922, vol. 37, 83–93.

Planck, Max. *Scientific Autobiography and Other Papers.* (Trans. by Frank Gaynor.) New York: Philosophical Library, 1949.

Various. A question of inspiration. *New Statesman and Nation,* 1950, vol. 39, 100. 4 letters.

Dual Role of the Zeitgeist
in Scientific Creativity
1955

This paper, like the preceding one, also deals with the psychology of scientific activity, this time more with the intellectual reinforcements and inhibitions of the *Zeitgeist* than the motivational effects of the ego. The term *Zeitgeist* is useful and is coming now to find a limited employment, but inevitably it is being altered from meaning the way in which the climate of opinion affects thinking at a given time to the way in which the climate and its effects keep continuously changing. The *Zeitgeist* is no longer an atmosphere but a steadily changing current of common belief.

This "magic" term *Zeitgeist* means at any one time the climate of opinion as it affects thinking, yet it is also more than that, for the *Zeitgeist* is forever being altered, as if the thinker whom it affects were shifting latitude and longitude over sea and land so that his climate keeps changing in unpredictable ways. Goethe, who in 1827 (p. 78) may have been the first to use this word with explicit connotation, limited it to the unconscious, covert, and implicit effects of the climate of opinion, at the same time ruling out thought control by such explicit processes as persuasion and education.

Such a concept proves useful in those cases where plagiarism is

Reprinted with permission from the *Scientific Monthly*, 1955, vol. 80, 101–106.

clearly unconscious, as so often it is. No man clearly understands the sources of his own creativity, and it is only since Freud that we have begun to have an inkling of how general is this lack of understanding of one's own motives and of the sources of one's own ideas. On the other hand, this conception long antedates Freud, for it was the essence of Tolstoy's argument in 1869 that "a king is history's slave" whose conscious reasons for action are trivial and unimportant. Charles Darwin, Herbert Spencer, and Francis Galton all supported Tolstoy's view of the unconscious determination of the actions of great men, against the more voluntaristic views of Thomas Carlyle, William James, and some lesser writers.

Later the historians of science and of thought in general found themselves faced with the essential continuity of originality and discovery. Not only is a new discovery seldom made until the times are ready for it, but again and again it turns out to have been anticipated, inadequately perhaps but nevertheless explicitly, as the times were beginning to get ready for it. Thus the concept of a gradually changing *Zeitgeist* has been used to explain the historical continuity of thought and the observation that the novelty of a discovery, after the history of its anticipations has been worked out, appears often to be only a historian's artifact.

In addition to these anticipations there are, however, also the near-simultaneities and near-synchronisms that are clearly not plagiarisms: Napier and Briggs on logarithms, Leibnitz and Newton on the calculus, Boyle and Mariotte on the gas law, D'Alibard and Franklin on electricity. The sociologists Ogburn and Thomas have published a list of 148 contemporaneous but independent discoveries or inventions. Since you cannot in these pairs assume that one man got the crucial idea from the other, you are forced to assume that each had his novel insight independently by his ordinary processes of thought, except that each was doing his thinking in the same climate of opinion. Some such appeal to a maturing *Zeitgeist* is necessary to explain the coincidence (Boring, 1950b; Ogburn and Thomas, 1922).

Now how, we may ask, does the *Zeitgeist* of the present time interpret the generic concept of the *Zeitgeist?* Today the *Zeitgeist* is certainly *not* a superorganic soul, an immortal consciousness undergoing maturation with the centuries, an unextended substance interpenetrating the social structure. The *Zeitgeist* must be regarded simply as the sum total of social interaction as it is common to a particular period and a particular locale. One can say it is thought being affected by culture, and one would mean then that the thinking of every man is affected by the thinking of other men in so far as their thinking is communicated to him. Hence the importance of communication in science, which both helps and hinders progress. That is the thesis of this paper.

It is always hard to be original, to make progress in a minority thinking that goes against the majority. In science, moreover, even the dead help to make up the majority, for they communicate by the printed word and by the transmitted conventions of thought. Thus the majority, living and dead, may slow up originality. On the other hand, the chief effect of scientific communication and of the availability of past thought is facilitative. We all know how the invention of printing advanced science.

We shall not be far wrong—being prejudiced, of course, by the *Zeitgeist* of the present—if we regard the scientist as a nervous system, influenced by what it reads and hears as well as by what it observes in nature and in the conduct of other men—the smile of approbation, the sneer of contempt—and affected also by its own past experience, for the scientist is forever instructing himself as he proceeds toward discovery and is also forever being instructed by other men, both living and dead.

The single investigator works pretty much like a rat in a maze —by insight, hypothesis, trial, and then error or success. I am not trying to say that rats are known to prefer deduction to induction because they use hypotheses in learning a maze. The maze is set up to require learning by trial and error, which is to say, by hypothesis and test. The rat's insight, as it learns, may indeed be false: the rat looks down the alley, sees it is not immediately blind but later finds it is blind after all. An error for the rat. And its trial may be vicarious. The rat looks tentatively down an alley, entertains it as hypothesis, rejects it, chooses to go the other way. Anybody's hypothesis can come as the brilliant perception of an unexpected relationship and yet be wrong. It may be a hunch. Rodent hypotheses begin as hunches—and by this I mean merely that the rat does not understand the ground of its motives.

The human investigator, on the other hand, may consciously base his new hypothesis on his own earlier experiment, or on something other persons did. For this reason erudition is important, and communication is vital in modern science. Nevertheless it remains possible to regard the single scientist as an organic system, as a discovery machine, with a certain input from the literature and from other forms of social communication and also —let the essential empiricism of science not be forgotten—from nature, which comes through to insights and a conclusion by that method of concomitant variation which is experiment. There we have the individual investigator, who, as he grows older, gains in erudition and wisdom and becomes more mature, with his past discoveries now available as part of his knowledge.

A broader and more interesting question, however, concerns, not the individual, but the maturation of scientific thought itself. The mechanics of one person applies to too small a system to throw much light on the history of science. The larger view substitutes social interaction and communication for an individual's input, thus exposing the whole dynamic process as it undergoes maturation down the years, the centuries, and the ages. This interaction *is* the *Zeitgeist*, which is not unlike a stream. It is bounded on its sides by the limits of communication, but it goes on forever unless, of course, some great cataclysm, one that would make Hitler's effect on German science seem tiny and trivial, should some day stall it.

Here we have a physicalistic conception of the *Zeitgeist*. The *Zeitgeist*, of course, inevitably influences the conception of the *Zeitgeist*. And the *Zeitgeist* ought to be the property of psychologists, for the psychologists have a proprietary right in all the *Geister*. Now the psychology of the nineteenth century was dualistic, mentalistic, spiritualistic. In those days the *Zeitgeist* would certainly have had to be the maturing superconsciousness of science, something comparable to the immediate private experience that everyone then believed he had. The twentieth century, on the other hand, at least since 1925, is physicalistic and behavioristic. Nowadays the term *behavioral sciences* is on everyone's lips and there is no English equivalent for *Geisteswissenschaften*.

Between 1910 and 1930 the *Zeitgeist* changed. Mind gave way to behavior. This transition was eased by the positivists who supplied the transformation equations from the old to the new, transformations by way of the operational definitions of experience; but only a few bother to use these equations. It is enough for most persons that they are using the convenient language of the great majority. And truth in science, as S. S. Stevens (1935a; 1935b; Boring, 1952) has pointed out, is simply what competent opinion at the time in question does not dissent from. In a physicalistic era, we, physicalistically minded scientists, choose a physicalistic definition of the *Zeitgeist*. Our predecessors in 1900 would not so easily have accepted such nonchalance toward Cartesian dualism.

We are wise thus to accept the wisdom of the age. Nor is my personal history without interest in this respect, for I was brought up in the introspective school of E. B. Titchener and for twenty years believed firmly in the existence of my own private immediate consciousness. Then, about 1930, en route to Damascus, as it were, I had a great insight. I knew that I was unconscious and never had been conscious in the sense that to have experience is to know instantaneously that you have it. Introspection always takes time, and the most immediate conscious datum is, therefore, obtained retrospectively. Once this basic truth is assimilated, once one realizes that no system can include the report of itself and that to one's own introspection one's own consciousness is as much the consciousness of some "Other One" as is the

consciousness of a different person, then it becomes clear that
consciousness is not in any sense immediate, and then—just
exactly then—the introspectionist gladly and sincerely joins the
behavioristic school (Meyer, 1921; Stevens, 1935a; Boring, 1953).

THE ZEITGEIST'S DUAL ROLE

The *Zeitgeist* has a dual role in scientific progress, sometimes
helping and sometimes hindering. There can be nothing surprising
in such a statement. Forces in themselves are not good or bad.
Their effects can be, depending on what it is you want. Inevitably
by definition the *Zeitgeist* favors conventionality, but conventionality itself keeps developing under the constant pressures of
discoveries and novel insights. So the *Zeitgeist* works against
originality; but is not originality, one asks quite properly, a good
thing, something that promotes scientific progress? In the cases
of Copernicus, Galileo, Newton, and other comparably great
men of science, originality was good—good for what posterity
has called progress. These are the men to emulate. The indubitably original people are, however, the cranks, and close to them
are the paranoid enthusiasts. Velikovsky's conception of the collision of two worlds is original. Does science advance under his
stimulus? Hubbard's dianetics is original. Is it good? Most of us
right now think not, yet these men point in self-defense to Galileo
who also resisted the *Zeitgeist* (Boring, 1952). This dilemma
arises because it is well to know and respect the wisdom of the
ages and also to correct it when the evidence for change is adequate. If men were logical machines and evidence could be
weighed in balances, we should not be mentioning the *Zeitgeist*
at all. The *Zeitgeist* comes into consideration because it can on
occasion work irrationally to distort the weight of the evidence.

When does the *Zeitgeist* help and when does it hinder the
progress of science?

1) It is plain that knowledge helps research, and knowledge,
whether it be explicit on the printed page of a handbook or implicit in the unrecognized premises of a theory, is in the *Zeitgeist*.

There is no use trying to limit the *Zeitgeist* to that knowledge which you have without knowing it, for the line simply cannot be kept. One discovery leads to another, or one experiment leads to a theory that leads to another experiment, and the history of science tells the story. The law of multiple proportions, for instance, validates the atomic theory, and then the atomic theory leads off to all sorts of chemical research and discovery.

On the other hand, the *Zeistgeist* does not always help, for there is bad knowledge as well as good, and it takes good knowledge to get science ahead. It is useful to be ignorant of bad knowledge.

The idea that white is a simple color was a bit of bad knowledge that was in the *Zeistgeist* in the middle of the seventeenth century. It was not a silly idea. It was empirically based. You can see colors, can you not? And white is a color. And you can see that it is simple and not a mixture, can you not? It is not clear whether Newton was lucky enough not to have absorbed this bit of false knowledge from the *Zeitgeist* or whether he was just stubborn, when, having bought his prism at the Stourbridge Fair, he concluded that white is a mixture of other colors. He was probably consciously flouting the *Zeitgeist*, for he sent his paper up to the Royal Society with the remark that it was in his "judgment the oddest if not the most considerable detection which hath hitherto been made into the operations of nature." But Robert Hooke and the others at the Royal Society would have none of it. They were restrained from belief by the *Zeitgeist*. White is obviously not colored, not a mixture. There was bitter controversy before the conventional scientists gave in, before the truth shifted over to Newton's side (Boring, 1942, pp. 101 f.).

Helmholtz ran into a similar difficulty when in 1850 he measured the velocity of the nervous impulse. The *Zeitgeist* said: The soul is unitary; an act of will is not spread out over a period of time; you move your finger; you do not will first that the finger move with the finger not moving until the message gets to it. Thus Helmholtz' father had religious scruples against accepting his son's discovery. And Johannes Müller, then the dean of experimental physiology, doubted that the conduction times could be so slow. At the very least, he thought, the rate of the impulse must approximate the speed of light (Boring, 1950a, pp. 41 f., 47 f.).

The persistence of the belief in phlogiston is still another example of the inertia that the *Zeitgeist* imposes on progress in thought. Here both Lavoisier and Priestley broke away from convention enough to discover oxygen, but Lavoisier, with the more negativistic temperament, made the greater break and came farther along toward the truth, wheras Priestley could not quite transcend his old habits of thought. His theory was a compromise, whereas we know now—insofar as we ever know truth in science—that that compromise was not the way to push science ahead then (Conant, 1950).

So it is. Good knowledge promotes progress, bad knowledge hinders, and both kinds make up the *Zeitgeist*. Ignorance of good knowledge and awareness of bad hinder; awareness of good and ignorance of bad help. The history of science is full of instances of all four.

2) Not only do the discovery of fact and the invention of theory help progress when fact and theory are valid, but also comparable principles apply to the discovery and invention of new scientific techniques. The telescope seems to have come out of the *Zeitgeist*, for it was invented independently by half a dozen different persons in 1608, although lenses had been made and used for magnification for at least three hundred years. But then Galileo's discovery of Jupiter's moons the next year created, as it were, a new phase in the *Zeitgeist*, one that promoted astronomical discovery. So it was with the invention of the simple microscope, the compound microscope, the voltaic pile, the galvanic battery, the galvanometer, the electromagnet, and recently the electron tube—the possibilities opened up by the availability of a new important instrument change the atmosphere within a field of science and lead quickly to a mass of

valid research. Within psychology the experimental training of a rat in a maze in 1903 in order to measure its learning capacity led at once to a long series of studies in the evolution of animal intelligence with the maze as the observational instrument.

It is true that the negative instances of this aspect of the *Zeitgeist* are not so frequent or obvious; yet they occur. For years the Galton whistle, used for the determination of the upper limit of hearing, was miscalibrated, because its second harmonic had been mistaken for its first. The highest audible pitch was thought to occur at about 40,000 cycles per second, whereas the correct figure is about 20,000. Did this error of an octave hold back science? Not much, but a little. For a couple of decades investigators reported facts about the octave above 20,000 cycles per second, an octave that is really inaudible. One experimenter even found a special vowel quality for it to resemble. Thus bad knowledge about the whistle led to confusion and hindered the advance of science.

3) The *Zeitgeist* acts as inertia in human thinking. It makes thought slow but also surer. As a rule scientific thinking does not suddenly depart widely from contemporary opinion. In civilization, as in the individual, the progress of thought is sensibly continuous. Consider, for example, the history of the theory of sensory quality.

Empedocles believed that eidola of objects are transmitted by the nerves to the mind so that it may perceive the objects by their images. Later there arose the notion that there are animal spirits in the nerves to conduct the eidola. Then, under the influence of materialism, the animal spirits came to be regarded as a *vis viva* and presently a *vis nervosa*. Next Johannes Müller, seeing that every sensory nerve always produces its own quality, substituted for the *vis nervosa* five specific nerve energies, using the word *energy*, in the days before the theory of conservation of energy, as equivalent to *force* or *vis*. He said that the mind, being locked away in the skull, cannot perceive the objects themselves, or their images, but only the states of the nerves that the objects affect, and he fought a battle against the Empedoclean theory—as indeed had John Locke and Thomas Young and Charles Bell before him, and as still others were to do after him. After a while it was seen, however, that the specificity of the five kinds of nerves lies not in the peculiar energies that they conduct to the brain but in where they terminate in the brain. Thus there arose the concept of sensory centers in the cerebrum. Nowadays we see that a cerebral center is nothing more than a place where connections are made and that sensory quality must be understood in terms of the discriminatory response in which stimulation eventuates—or at least many of us see this fact while we fight a *Zeitgeist* that still supports a theory of centers (Boring, 1942, pp. 68–83, 93–95).

Is there any reason why Galen in A.D. 180 or Albrecht von Haller in 1766 should not have invented the modern theory of sensory quality? None, except that most of the supporting evidence was lacking and, being contrary to the accepted notions of the time, it would have sounded silly. Yet each contributor to this strand of scientific maturation was original, and several contributors had to fight again the battle against the notion that the mind perceives an object by embracing it, or, if it cannot get at the object itself, by getting itself impressed by the object's eidolon or simulacrum. Nor has the *Zeitgeit* even yet been thoroughly disciplined in this affair, as you can tell whenever you hear the remark: "If the lens of the eye inverts the image of the external world on the retina, why do we not see upside down?"

The *Zeitgeist* was hindering progress in this piece of history. It made originality difficult and it made it necessary to repeat the same arguments in 1690 (John Locke) and in 1826 (Johannes Müller) and, if one may believe current advertisements of a scientific film, nowadays too. Yet let us remember that this *Zeitgeist* also helped progress. The continuity of development lay always within the *Zeitgeist*. It was a conservative force that demanded that originality remain responsible, that it be grounded on evidence and available knowledge. Had Galen espoused a connectionist's view of sensory quality in the second century, he would have been irresponsibly original, a second-century crank, disloyal to the truth as it existed then. Loyalty may be prejudice and sometimes it may be wrong, but it is nevertheless the stuff of which responsible continuous effort is made. Science needs responsibility as well as freedom, and the *Zeitgeist* supports the one virtue even though it may impede the other.

4) What may be said of the big *Zeitgeist* may also be said of the little *Zeitgeister* of schools and of the leaders of schools and of the egoist who has no following. They have their inflexible attitudes and beliefs, their loyalties that are prejudices, and their prejudices that are loyalties. Every scientific in-group with strong faith in a theory or a method is a microcosm, mirroring the macrocosm which is the larger world of science.

Take egoism. Is it bad? It accounts for a large part of the drive that produces research, for the dogged persistence that is so often the necessary condition of scientific success. So egoism yields truth. It accounts also for the hyperbole and exaggeration of the investigating enthusiast, and then it may yield untruth.

When two incompatible egoisms come together, they account for the wasted time of scientific warfare, for the dethronement of reason by rationalization. Egoism is both good and bad.

Take loyalty. Think how it cements a group together and promotes hard work. Yet such in-groups tend to shut themselves off from other out-groups, to build up their special vocabularies, and so, while strengthening their own drives, to lessen communication with the outside, the communication that advances science. Loyalty is both good and bad, and with loyalty a person sometimes has to choose whether he will eat his cake or will keep it.

This dilemma posed by the little *Zeitgeister* of the in-groups and the scientific evangelists has its root in basic psychological law. Attention to this is inevitably inattention to that. Enthusiasm is the friend of action but the enemy of wisdom. Science needs to be both concentrated and diffuse, both narrow and broad, both thorough and inclusive. The individual investigator solves this problem as best he can, each according to his own values, as to when to sell breadth in order to purchase depth and when to reverse the transaction. He, the individual, has limited funds and he has to sell in order to buy, and he may never know whether he made the best investment. But posterity will know, at least better than he, provided that it troubles to assess the matter at all, for posterity, having only to understand without hard labor, can assess the effect of prejudice and loyalty and enthusiam, of tolerance and intolerance, as no man ever can in himself.

CODA

This is a broad meaning for the word *Zeitgeist*—the total body of knowledge and opinion available at any time to a person living within a given culture. There is, certainly, no rigorous way of distinguishing between what is explicit to a scientist and what is implicit in the forms and patterns of communication, between what is clear conclusion and what is uncritically accepted premise. Available knowledge is communicated whenever it becomes effective, and this is the *Zeitgeist* working.

The *Zeitgeist* is a term from the language of dualism, while its definition is formally physicalistic. That paradox is for the sake of convenience in the present communication and is allowable because every statement can be transformed into physicalistic language when necessary. Dualism has the disadvantage of implying a mystery, the existence of a *Zeitgeist* as a vague supersoul pervading and controlling the immortal body of society. We need no such nonsense, even though this abstinence from mystery reduces us to so ordinary a concept as a *Zeitgeist* inclusive of all available knowledge that affects a thinker's thinking.

That such a *Zeitgeist* sometimes helps progress and sometimes hinders it should be clear by now. As a matter of fact, the distinction between help and hindrance can never be absolute but remains relative to some specific goal. The *Zeitgeist* hindered

Copernicus, who, resisting it, helped scientific thought onward and presently changed the *Zeitgeist* on this matter to what it was in Newton's day. Did the *Zeitgeist* that Newton knew help relativity theory? No; relativity had to make its way against that *Zeitgeist*. The newest *Zeitgeist*, which will include the principles of relativity and uncertainty and complementarity, presumably exists today within the in-group of theoretical physicists. It will become general eventually, and then it will reinforce progress, and after that, much later, perhaps our posterity will find today's truth tomorrow's error. The one sure thing is that science needs all the communication it can get. The harm communication does to progress never nearly equals the good.

References

Boring, E. G. *Sensation and Perception in the History of Experimental Psychology*. New York: Appleton-Century, 1942.

Boring, E. G. *A History of Experimental Psychology*. (2nd ed.) Appleton-Century-Crofts, 1950. (a)

Boring, E. G. Great men and scientific progress. *Proceedings of the American Philosophical Society*, 1950, vol. 94, 339–351. (b)

Boring, E. G. The validation of scientific belief. *Proceedings of the American Philosophical Society*, 1952, vol. 96, 535–539.

Boring, E. G. A history of introspection. *Psychological Bulletin*, 1953, vol. 50, 169–189.

Conant, J. B. *The Overthrow of the Phlogiston Theory*. Cambridge, Mass.: Harvard University Press, 1950.

Goethe, J. W. v. (1827). Homer noch einmal. In *Goethes sämtliche Werke*. Vol. XXXVIII. Berlin: I. J. Cotta, 1902–1907. Pp. 77 f.

Meyer, Max. *Psychology of the Other One*. Columbia: Missouri Book Company, 1921.

Ogburn, W. F., and Thomas, Dorothy. Are inventions inevitable? A note on social evolution. *Political Science Quarterly*, 1922, vol. 37, 83–93.

Stevens, S. S. The operational basis of psychology. *American Journal of Psychology*, 1935, vol. 47, 323–330. (a)

Stevens, S. S. The operational definition of psychological concepts. *Psychological Review*, 1935, vol. 42, 517–527. (b)

CP Speaks

When *"CP"* (*Contemporary Psychology*) began in 1956, the Editor hoped that he might egg his writers on into being interesting and his readers into being interested. There needed to be for the American psychologists, he thought, a personal touch of the kind that was all ready to be borrowed from the *New Yorker* and the *Saturday Review,* and he did his best to move his colleagues toward a more attractive literary style than was their wont and into writing with a touch of gaiety and humor. How can a psychologist look upon the paradoxes of human motivation without being amused at man's sober egoism and his certainty that his own assurance is self-validating? *CP* tried to interdict the bitter *ad hominems*—not always successfully—but it also undertook to introduce editorials that would suggest to its readers and even more to its writers that criticism, being idiosyncratic, is not to be given personally nor taken bitterly. Such, thought *CP,* is the mature view of the educated man, and properly the scientific view, and very especially the view of him who understands human nature, the psychologist.

At any rate *CP* wished to talk with its readers, and it could through an editorial page called *CP* SPEAKS. Here it explained its aspirations to its readers. It asked them questions about what they wanted. It apologized when it recognized its own failure. It joked with them. But most especially, when it had a serious idea about writing or books or words or printing or about the kinds of thinking that make psychological books what they are, it would speak seriously and yet tentatively, without bluster or certainty or cockiness, always wishing it might turn this trick as neatly as does E. B. White with his demure humor and his persuasive charm. Here follow two of the longer CP Speakses. Long and short, there will have been nearly three hundred of them when the Editor retires after six years. He has loved writing them and thinks the doing has helped to keep him young.

Good Writing

1957

Good writing! How do you manage it? What is it? Are there any rules for it? Every now and then some editor comes out with his set of principles and *CP*, reading them, finds them stuffy. "That's the way *he* edits," *CP* thinks. Yet there are both good writing and bad, and ought not a psychologist to be able to analyze each and specify the difference?

CP suggests that the difficulty here may lie in the fact that good writing is relative, relative to its purpose. Writing is as good as its achievement of its purpose. What is intelligible may not be beautiful, and writing can stimulate without being understood. The editor-poet, John Ciardi, defends the obscurity of modern poetry on the ground that, although obscure, it is not unintelligible but "open to interpretation and the self-rewarding labor of understanding" (*Saturday Review*, 20 July 1957, 9 ff.). And the same goes, he says, for the Bible. Obscurity happens when the reader is insufficiently prepared for what the writer is doing, unintelligibility when the writer himself is insufficiently prepared for what he is undertaking. Do not rob the sufficiently prepared reader of the fun of figuring out what the author was trying to convey, or the insufficiently prepared reader of the fun of becoming prepared.

Is there a lesson for psychologist-writers here? Should they cultivate an intelligible obscurity so that understanding them becomes an achievement for the reader? Active participation is

Reprinted with permission from *Contemporary Psychology*, Nov. 1957, vol. 2, 279.

one of the most important conditions of learning. Should not the writers of textbooks try to be obscure—though intelligible— so that the student, having finally figured out the meaning, will never forget it? It would be the project method in a new form— deciphering the author, growing meanings from a book consisting of its seeds.

CP is not opposed to this view. If an ingenious author can find a way of teaching psychology by double crostics, he will have shown how communication is more than input, how it is reaction. Perhaps the reader should properly hope for obscurity and a chance at "the self-rewarding labor of understanding"; but for what, then, should the writer be hoping? For readers, plainly— and then for understanding.

CP thinks that for any writing the product of numbers of readers by their individual understandings will be maximal when the writer tries to be clear and interesting. You do not have to frustrate people to interest them. Bewilderment is not the only condition of attention. You can charm readers into attention or stimulate them into it, and you will get ahead fastest if you do not distract them with irrelevancies. So *CP* believes that the author who takes for his goal the greatest understanding by the greatest number will be he who has his audience clearly in mind—an audience that is real to him whether it matches the actual eventual one or not—and who has himself out of mind. His own ego, for this kind of writing, is almost always an intrusive irrelevancy. The reader—this kind of reader—wants to be led along the course of the author's thought without thinking of the author as person. In other words—so *CP* thinks—egoistic writing is generally less than maximally clear when the reader, coming up against the author's idiosyncrasies, notices them, is distracted to them.

For instance, how does the author refer to himself? Does he say *the writer, the reviewer,* or *I* and *me* if there is but one of him? He'll almost surely say *we* if there are two of him, but dare he say *we* if he is alone? The only rule, *CP* thinks, is for the writer to write so that the reader will not notice what the writer does in this respect. The "benevolent" writer, the nonegotistic writer, who is thinking about his reader and not about himself, can use either form or mix the two and still not distract the reader. He will not use self-reference often, because he is telling the reader about facts and ideas and is not talking about himself and his own opinions.

For the same reason he will not apologize for what he says, for apology is egoistic, an attempt to say something without accepting full responsibility for it.

Mixed metaphors become distractions to the visually minded and not to the readers who do not visualize. *Above the threshold* is a psychologist's mixed metaphor since thresholds exist in vertical doorways, not in trap doors, but in this case the interference with thought is little because usage has killed the visual context for even the habitual visualizers. *In the evening when we use our toothbrush* distracts a visual reader with the irrelevant thought about hygiene, but the auditory-kinesthetic reader trips gaily past this clause with never a puzzlement. *We,* when it refers to a single author—not to joint authors, or to the single author plus his readers—is a mixed figure that bothers the visually minded readers more than the others. Surely it is better to avoid mixing figures and distract no one.

The same rule applies to that pet problem of pedants, the split infinitive. When splitting makes the meaning clearer, then the thing to do is to split, but *CP* has yet to find such a case. Even the instances in Fowler are not convincing. Otherwise the best practice is not to split, for splitting distracts the non-splitter, whereas non-splitting never distracts the splitter. So the benevolent writer never splits until splitting has a certain use. Then he splits and writes at once about it to *CP* which is waiting, waiting for a valid instance.

So there you are. Is *CP* getting stuffy with rules like everybody else? No, it is not stuffy to tell authors that, if they write with ready comprehension by their readers as their goal, it is a good thing for them (*a*) to be clear and (*b*) not to distract readers with the irrelevances of self-conscious writing. This is what *CP* calls "benevolent writing" and *CP* wants this kind of English in its own pages. It is not the intelligibly obscure writing of which John Ciardi likes the challenge in modern poetry, but science is not poetry any more, perhaps not since Erasmus Darwin's poetical *Botanic Garden* back in the 1790's.

Humanizing Psychology

1958

The great and current American dilemma: Whether to pour money, enthusiasm, and prestige into scientific and technological education so as to keep up with the Soviets, preserving some of our liberties by sacrificing others, or whether to attempt to reinforce the humanities as well as science, amplifying at once both the endeavors of our cloven scholarship. Can America afford both, or even one? Perhaps it might if it could bring itself to exchange rewards, surrendering material comfort for spiritual exhilaration; yet could it ever do that? Meanwhile the American predicament is real.

For this problem *CP* has no miraculous remedy all ready for revelation; yet, because it thinks of its own effort as directed in a sense toward the humanizing of psychology, *CP* feels that its comment on America's plight is not inappropriate, at least as far as it concerns American psychology.

If the world's most prosperous nation cannot, by an act of sheer power, treble the intensity of its educational effort in both science and the humanities—it is the American delusion that the will to success needs only to be strong enough in order to prevail —then surely a first step is to look out a way to amalgamate the

Reprinted with permission from *Contemporary Psychology*, Dec. 1958, vol. 3, 361 f.

sciences and the humanities so that they may prosper together and not at each other's expense. With this aim in mind a committee of the American Council of Learned Societies worked for five years to uncover and describe the humanistic aspects of science, and recently they published a volume about their findings, calling it *Science and the Creative Spirit* (K. V. Deutsch, F. E. L. Priestley, Harcourt Brown, and David Hawkins, Univ. Toronto Press, 1958, pp. xxvii + 165, $4.50). It is a good book but it does not render much aid in the present predicament. In it we see again how knowledge as such is one, though the individual be forced to specialize. There are and always have been cross-currents between the sciences and the humanities, and it is indeed scarcely more than a century since natural philosophy counted as literature. John Turner, writing editorially in *Science* (30 May 1958, 127, 1267) has, however, a word of practical advice: Teach science humanistically. Go not only broad but also deep. He quotes Alfred Whitehead on how depth is right for general education, how vertical penetration means more for the cultivated man than horizontal spread.

So here *CP* raises the basic question. Are there ways in which modern psychology, that social institution known for the past hundred years as *Psychology*, ways in which it can, in spite of its ardent and vocal dedication to science and its aggressive repudiation of whatever argument is not experimental in origin, are there ways in which Psychology can edge itself over toward humanism, strengthening, not weakening, its proficiency the while? Here is what *CP* thinks.

(*a*) *Scope.* Breadth is good. So is depth, and the two work against each other. Just the same, breadth is good, and the wise man knows more than his own *Fach*. *CP* has correspondents who write that they battle constantly against complete ignorance of any considerable segment of psychology, and it has other correspondents, young men, who say that they were never sure as to just what is this Psychology in which they got their PhDs until *CP* began handing them its sample packages. It is *CP*'s

packaging, of course, dear old idiosyncratic *CP;* yet the selection
is a lot more definitive than a Ph.D. examination, and maybe—
CP heard this whisper—the American Psychological Association
would stay married and not break up again if only every half
knew how the other half thinks. Being a liberal in psychology
is a step toward humanization, and arrogance, while it is often
the additive that dynamizes research, may at other times be the
prejudice that stops progress in its tracks.

(*b*) *Xenophilia* is geographical scope. The cultivated psychologist knows, besides other subjects, the psychology and psychologists of other lands. Twice *CP* has been wistful about Americans'
not knowing the other languages in which psychology is being
thought (*CP,* Nov. 1956, 1, 331 f.; Apr. 1957, 2, 105). Your dedicated experimentalist says: Substitute statistics and electronics
for the languages; they are more important tools. Others say:
Russian has now made the idea of learning the "essential" languages impracticable; what we need are translation services—as
well as computing centers and commercially designed black
boxes. True, but how are psychologists to think wisely except in
the atmosphere of other men's thinking? The social institution
that is Psychology is international. Do we not need wisdom as
well as skill and competence?

(*c*) *History* is temporal scope. You need to know of other
times as well as other lands. Why? Because, says the dedicated
researcher, you want not to be caught doing over an experiment
that has already been done. Nonsense. No historically sophisticated psychologist knows for relevant citation the 328,690 articles
cited merely since 1894 in the *Psychological Index* and the *Psychological Abstracts.* One gets from a knowledge of the history
of psychology not facts but wisdom. One see how thought works
itself out, how human nature operates in the social institution to
generate discovery and also sometimes to prevent it. One acquires knowledge in learning history, but the purpose of the
learning is not the acquisition of facts but cultivation of wisdom.

(*d*) *Objectivity* is a humanizing attribute. The wise man sees whole. Here we come up against a dilemma within science, the motivational predicament. "Enthusiasm is the friend of action and the enemy of wisdom." Current enthusiasm—prejudices, if you like—get the discoveries made and the theories laid out, and then posterity, sober, wiser, and more objective, assesses the work, accepts some and discards some. You have to have both attitudes, and the good scientist oscillates between the two, now checking his enthusiasm with criticism, now bursting restraints in a flight of fancy. Spread of knowledge, both into the past and across the broad sweep of the present, supports this critical wisdom. Objectivity is good, yet the predicament is real, for enthusiasm is needed too. The dilemma is met by fluctuation of attitude from moment to moment in the individual investigator, from person to person within the science.

(e) *Depth* is what Whitehead recommended for general education. It is also what President Lowell of Harvard put into undergraduate education at Harvard College nearly fifty years ago, when he made the AB into "the little Ph.D.," as some called it. The evidence was that the successful college graduates, assessed twenty-five years after their ABs, tended to be those men who had in college gone deep into a subject, not those who spread broad by taking many elementary courses in different subjects. So here is a paradox or perhaps another predicament. Depth or scope? Obviously both, as much as you can. If not in the same man, then in different men associated in the same endeavor. The pursuit of knowledge is, moreover, like mining; you go deep but you also go where the ore lies. There is an isolated kind of concentration that ignores the side veins. Depth goes broad underground. It is not wholly incompatible with scope.

(f) *Diversification* is the way to eat your cake and have it too, the way to succeed in spite of predicaments. The individual gets a balance by fluctuation. The science gets it by the distribution of attitudes and endeavors among individuals and the maintenance of communication among them. Let the science itself be wisely mature, though it depend for existence on the adolescent enthusiasm of its workers.

Does all this talk get us anywhere? *CP* feels, as it views the steady stream of psychology's books and the reviews of them, that the psychologists resist the humanizing deviations that would bring their science over toward scholarship and wisdom and understanding, resist them sometimes because they are dedicated to a narrow empiricism and sometimes because they have accepted a model for rigid theorizing. Their science could go deeper and broader, becoming more objective as a consequence, and so gain strength and importance and significance. True, it would not be much of a step toward the humanities, but it would be a move in that direction; and the new psychologists who grew up in this altered atmosphere, being better educated, wiser, and no less proficient, would throw America less out of balance as it seeks to multiply its scientific competence.

Bibliography

Principal Publications of Edwin G. Boring: 1912–1960

The following list of 176 items omits 202 editorials from the first five volumes of *Contemporary Psychology* (1956–1960); 49 book reviews, all of the book reviews within the limiting dates; 45 brief notes about everything under the sun, none so much as two pages, many quite short; 17 minor scientific contributions ghosted for undergraduates in 1917–1926 but not later; 10 committee and conference reports and proceedings; 4 abstracts and general reviews; and 3 letters to the editor. That seems to give us an *omnium gatherum* of 505 items, which must be just about the least interesting dimension of a man that could possibly be polled.

1912

Note on the negative reaction under light-adaptation in the planarian. *Journal of Animal Behavior*, vol. 2, 229–248.
With Bentley, M. and Ruckmick, C. A. New apparatus for acoustical experiments. *American Journal of Psychology*, vol. 23, 509–516.

1913

The course and character of learning in dementia precox. *Bulletin of the Government Hospital for the Insane*, vol. 5, 51–79.
Introspection in dementia precox. *American Journal of Psychology*, vol. 24, 145–170.
Learning in dementia precox. Princeton, N.J.: Psychological Monographs, vol. 15, no. 2. iv + 101 pp.

1914

The marking system in theory. *Pedagogical Seminary,* vol. 21, 269–277.
Method in the investigation of sensibility after the section of a cutaneous nerve: preliminary communication. *Proceedings of the Society for Experimental Biology and Medicine,* vol. 11, 69–71.

1915

Processes referred to the alimentary tract: a qualitative analysis. *Psychological Review,* vol. 22, 306–331.
The sensations of the alimentary canal. *American Journal of Psychology,* vol. 26, 1–57.
The thermal sensitivity of the stomach. *American Journal of Psychology,* vol. 26, 485–494.

1916

Capacity to report upon moving pictures as conditioned by sex and age: a contribution to the psychology of testimony. *Journal of Criminal Law and Criminology,* vol. 6, 820–834.
Cutaneous sensation after nerve-division. *Quarterly Journal of Experimental Physiology and Cognate Medical Sciences,* vol. 10, 1–95.
The number of observations upon which a limen may be based. *American Journal of Psychology,* vol. 27, 315–319.

1917

A chart of the psychometric function. *American Journal of Psychology,* vol. 28, 465–470.
On the computation of the probable correctness of differences. *American Journal of Psychology,* vol. 28, 454–459.
Urban's tables and the method of constant stimuli. *American Journal of Psychology,* vol. 28, 280–293.
With Boring, Lucy D. Temporal judgments after sleep. In *Studies in Psychology: Titchener Commemorative Volume.* Worcester, Mass.: private publication. Pp. 255–279.
With Luce, Amy. The psychological basis of appetite. *American Journal of Psychology,* vol. 28, 443–453.

1919

Mathematical *vs.* scientific significance. *Psychological Bulletin,* vol. 16, 335–338.
Psychology (general article). *Nelson's Loose-Leaf Encyclopedia.*

1920

A priori use of the Gaussian law. *Science,* vol. 52, 129 f.

The control of attitude in psychophysical experiments. *Psychological Review,* vol. 27, 440–452.

Intelligence (article). *Nelson's Loose-Leaf Encyclopedia.*

The logic of the normal law of error in mental measurement. *American Journal of Psychology,* vol. 31, 1–33.

Predilection and sampling of human heights. *Science,* vol. 52, 464–466.

Statistics of the American Psychological Association in 1920. *Psychological Bulletin,* vol. 17, 271–278.

With Titchener, E. B. Sir Thomas Wrightson's theory of hearing. *American Journal of Psychology,* vol. 31, 101–113.

1921

The stimulus-error. *American Journal of Psychology,* vol. 32, 449–471.

Joint editor and author. Psychological examining in the United States Army. *Memoirs of the National Academy of Sciences,* vol. 15, 547–875.

1922

Urban's tables again. *American Journal of Psychology,* vol. 33, 303 f., 450.

1923

Intelligence as the tests test it. *New Republic,* vol. 34, 34–37.

With Titchener, E. B. A model for the demonstration of facial expression. *American Journal of Psychology,* vol. 45, 471–485.

1924

Attribute and sensation. *American Journal of Psychology,* vol. 35, 301–304.

Is there a generalized psychometric function? *American Journal of Psychology,* vol. 35, 75–78.

Relation of the limen of dual impression to Head's theory of cutaneous sensibility. *Proceedings of the VII International Congress of Psychology,* 57–62.

1926

Anger (article). *Nelson's Loose-Leaf Encyclopedia.*

Auditory theory with special reference to intensity, volume and localization. *American Journal of Psychology,* vol. 37, 157–188.

The paradox of psychic research (Science and mediumship, with special reference to Margery). *Atlantic Monthly,* vol. 137, 81–87.

Scientific induction and statistics. *American Journal of Psychology,* vol. 37, 303–307.

With Peak, Helen. The factor of speed in intelligence. *Journal of Experimental Psychology,* vol. 9, 71–94.

1927

Construction and calibration of Koenig cylinders. *American Journal of Psychology*, vol. 38, 125–127.

Edward Bradford Titchener. *American Journal of Psychology*, vol. 38, 489–506.

Empirical psychology. *American Journal of Psychology*, vol. 38, 475–477.

The intensity of sensation. *Proceedings of the VIII International Congress of Psychology*, 71–78.

The problem of originality in science. *American Journal of Psychology*, vol. 39, 70–90.

1928

Demonstrational experiments in memory. *American Journal of Psychology*, vol. 40, 513 f.

Did Fechner measure sensation? *Psychological Review*, vol. 35, 443–445.

Do American psychologists read European psychology? *American Journal of Psychology*, vol. 40, 647 f.

A new system for the classification of odors. *American Journal of Psychology*, vol. 40, 345–349.

Psychological necrology (1903–1927). *Psychological Bulletin*, vol. 25, 302–305, 621–625.

1929

Discrimination; Organic sensations; Psychophysics; Titchener (Edward Bradford); Visceral sensations (articles). *Encyclopaedia Britannica*.

A History of Experimental Psychology. New York: Century. xvi + 699 pp.

The psychology of controversy. *Psychological Review*, vol. 36, 97–121.

1930

The gestalt psychology and the gestalt movement. *American Journal of Psychology*, vol. 42, 308–315.

A new ambiguous figure. *American Journal of Psychology*, vol. 42, 444f.

Psychology for eclectics. In C. Murchison (Ed.), *Psychologies of 1930*. Worcester, Mass.: Clark University Press. Pp. 115–127.

The two-point limen and the error of localization. *American Journal of Psychology*, vol. 42, 446–449.

1931

Behaviorism (article). *Nelson's Loose-Leaf Encyclopedia*.

The psychologist's circle. *Psychological Review*, vol. 38, 177–182.

1932

Gestalt psychology (article). *Nelson's Loose-Leaf Encyclopedia*.

Max von Frey: 1852–1932. *American Journal of Psychology*, vol. 44, 584–586.

The physiology of consciousness. *Science*, vol. 75, 32–39.

1933

Amerikan Ruhiyati (American Psychology). M. Sherif (Turkish trans.). Istanbul: Remzi Kitaphanesi. (Translation of pp. 493–563, 580–589 of *History of Experimental Psychology*, 1929.)

The Physical Dimensions of Consciousness. New York: Century. xii + 251 pp.

1934

Edward Bradford Titchener (article). *Encyclopedia of the Social Sciences*, vol. 14, 639 f.

With Ekdahl, A. G. The pitch of tonal masses. *American Journal of Psychology*, vol. 46, 452–455.

1935

Georg Elias Müller: 1850–1934. *American Journal of Psychology*, vol. 47, 344–348.

The relation of the attributes of sensation to the dimensions of the stimulus. *Philosophy of Science*, vol. 2, 236–245.

With Langfeld, H. S. and Weld, H. P. (Eds.). *Psychology: a Factual Textbook*. New York: Wiley. xviii + 555 pp.

1936

Another note on scientific writing. *Science*, vol. 84, 457–459.

Georg Elias Müller (1850–1934). *Proceedings of the American Academy of Arts and Sciences*, vol. 70, 558 f.

Psychophysiological systems and isomorphic relations. *Psychological Review*, vol. 43, 565–587.

Temporal perception and operationism. *American Journal of Psychology*, vol. 48, 519–522.

With Stevens, S. S. The nature of tonal brightness. *Proceedings of the National Academy of Sciences*, vol. 22, 514–521.

1937

Isochromatic contours. *American Journal of Psychology*, vol. 49, 130–134.

The lag of publication in journals of psychology. *American Journal of Psychology*, vol. 49, 137–139.

A psychological function is the relation of successive differentiations of events in the organism. *Psychological Review*, vol. 44, 445–461.

Titchener and the existential. *American Journal of Psychology*, vol. 50, 470–483.

With Langfeld, H. S. and Weld, H. P. (Eds.). *A Manual of Psychological Experiments.* New York: Wiley. ix + 198 pp.

1938

The Society of Experimental Psychologists: 1904–1938. *American Journal of Psychology,* vol. 51, 410–423.

Titchener on meaning. *Psychological Review,* vol. 45, 92–96.

1939

The psychophysics of color tolerance. *American Journal of Psychology,* vol. 52, 384–394.

With Langfeld, H. S. and Weld, H. P. (Eds.). *Introduction to Psychology.* New York: Wiley. xii + 652 pp.

1940

Size constancy and Emmert's law. *American Journal of Psychology,* vol. 53, 293–295.

The size of the differential limen for pitch. *American Journal of Psychology,* vol. 53, 450–455.

With Holway, A. H. The moon illusion and the angle of regard. *American Journal of Psychology,* vol. 53, 109–116.

With Holway, A. H. The apparent size of the moon as a function of the angle of regard: further experiments. *American Journal of Psychology,* vol. 53, 537–553.

With Holway, A. H. The dependence of apparent visual size upon illumination. *American Journal of Psychology,* vol. 53, 587–589.

With Sachs, H. Was this analysis a success? *Journal of Abnormal and Social Psychology,* vol. 35, 4–16.

1941

Communality in relation to proaction and retroaction. *American Journal of Psychology,* vol. 54, 280–283.

An operational restatement of G. E. Müller's psychophysical axioms. *Psychological Review,* vol. 48, 459–464.

Statistical frequencies as dynamic equilibria. *Psychological Review,* vol. 48, 279–300.

With Holway, A. H. Determinants of apparent visual size with distance variant. *American Journal of Psychology,* vol. 54, 21–37.

With Scheerer, M. and Goldstein, K. A demonstration of insight: the horse-and-rider puzzle. *American Journal of Psychology,* vol. 54, 437 f.

1942

Human nature *vs.* sensation: William James and the psychology of the present. *American Journal of Psychology,* vol. 55, 310–327.

The psychology of perception: its importance in the war effort. *American Journal of Psychology*, vol. 55, 423–435.

Sensation and Perception in the History of Experimental Psychology. New York: Appleton-Century. xv + 644 pp.

With Bentley, M. and Dallenbach, K. M. William James: 1842–1910. *American Journal of Psychology*, vol. 55, 309f.

With Taylor, D. W. Apparent visual size as a function of distance for monocular observers. *American Journal of Psychology*, vol. 55, 102–105.

With Taylor, D. W. The moon illusion as a function of binocular regard. *American Journal of Psychology*, vol. 55, 189–201.

1943

The celebrations of the American Psychological Association. *Psychological Review*, vol. 50, 1–4.

The growth of psychological journals in America. *Psychological Review*, vol. 50, 80.

The moon illusion. *American Journal of Physics*, vol. 11, 55–60.

Psychology for the Fighting Man: report of the subcommittee on a textbook of military psychology. *Psychological Bulletin*, vol. 40, 591–594.

With Van de Water, M., *et al. Psychology for the Fighting Man*. Washington, D.C.: Infantry Journal. 456 pp.

1944

The use of operational definitions in science. *Psychological Review*, vol. 52, 243–245, 278–281.

With Alper, T. G. Intelligence test scores of northern and southern white and Negro recruits in 1918. *Journal of Abnormal and Social Psychology*, vol. 39, 471–474.

With Bryan, A. I. Women in American psychology: Prolegomenon. *Psychological Bulletin*, vol. 41, 447–454.

With collaborators. *Psychology for the Armed Services*. Washington, D.C.: Infantry Journal. xvii + 533 pp.

1946

Mind and mechanism. *American Journal of Psychology*, vol. 59, 173–192.

Perception of objects. *American Journal of Physics*, vol. 14, 99–107.

With Allport, G. W. Psychology and social relations at Harvard University. *American Psychologist*, vol. 1, 119–122.

With Bryan, A. I. Women in American psychology: factors affecting their professional careers. *Pi Lambda Theta Journal*, vol. 25, 92–95. (Vita, p. 113.)

With Bryan, A. I. Women in American psychology: factors affecting their careers. *Transactions of the New York Academy of Sciences*, Ser. II, vol. 9, 19–23.

With Bryan, A. I. Women in American psychology: statistics from the
OPP questionnaire. *American Psychologist*, vol. 1, 71–79.

1947

With Bryan, A. I. Women in American psychology: factors affecting their
professional careers. *American Psychologist*, vol. 2, 3–20.

With Stevens, S. S. The new Harvard Psychological Laboratories. *American
Psychologist*, vol. 2, 239–243.

1948

Current trends in psychology (special review). *Psychological Bulletin*, vol.
45, 75–84.

With Boring, M. D. Masters and pupils among the American psychologists.
American Journal of Psychology, vol. 61, 527–534.

With Harper, R. S. Cues. *American Journal of Psychology*, vol. 61, 119–123.

With Langfeld, H. S. and Weld, H. P. (Eds.). *Foundations of Psychology.*
New York: Wiley. xv + 632 pp.

1950

Great men and scientific progress. *Proceedings of the American Philosophical
Society*, vol. 94, 339–351.

A History of Experimental Psychology. (2nd ed.) New York: Appleton-
Century-Crofts. xxi + 777 pp.

The influence of evolutionary theory upon American psychological thought.
In Stow Persons (Ed.), *Evolutionary Thought in America.* New Haven:
Yale University Press. Pp. 268–298.

Learning *vs.* training for graduate students. *American Psychologist*, vol. 5,
162 f.

1951

The book review. *American Journal of Psychology*, vol. 64, 281–283.

A color solid in four dimensions. *L'Année pychologique*, vol. 50, 293–304.

Consciousness; Psychology; Psychology (History of) (articles). *Encyclopaedia Britannica.*

The woman problem. *American Psychologist*, vol. 6, 679–682.

With Edwards, Ward. What is Emmert's law? *American Journal of Psychology*, vol. 64, 416–422.

1952

Edwin Garrigues Boring. In *A History of Psychology in Autobiography*,
vol. IV. Worcester, Mass.: Clark University Press. Pp. 27–52.

Foreword. In J. D. Hardy, H. G. Wolff, and H. Goodell, *Pain Sensations
and Reactions.* Baltimore: Williams & Wilkins. Pp. v–x.

The Gibsonian visual field. *Psychological Review*, vol. 59, 246 f.

Bibliography   355

Organic sensations (rev.); Psychophysics (rev.); Visceral sensations (rev.) (articles). *Encyclopaedia Britannica.*

The validation of scientific belief: a conspectus of the symposium. *Proceedings of the American Philosophical Society,* vol. 96, 535–539.

Visual perception as invariance. *Psychological Review,* vol. 59, 141–148.

With Dennis, Wayne. The founding of the APA. *American Psychologist,* vol. 7, 95–97.

With Werner, H., Yerkes, R. M., and Langfeld, H. S. Preface. In *A History of Psychology in Autobiography,* vol. IV. Worcester, Mass.: Clark University Press. Pp. v f.

1953

A history of introspection. *Psychological Bulletin,* vol. 50, 169–189.

John Dewey: 1859–1952. *American Journal of Psychology,* vol. 66, 145–147.

Life membership. *American Psychologist,* vol. 8, 86–88.

Psychological museum. *American Psychologist,* vol. 8, 166f.

The role of theory in experimental psychology. *American Journal of Psychology,* vol. 66, 169–184.

1954

The nature and history of experimental control. *American Journal of Psychology,* vol. 67, 573–589.

Psychological factors in the scientific process. *American Scientist,* vol. 42, 639–645, 624.

Science and faith: a foreword. In H. Misiak and V. M. Staudt, *Catholics in Psychology: a historical survey.* New York: McGraw-Hill. Pp. ix–xi.

With Bennett, Suzanne. Psychological necrology (1928–1952). *Psychological Bulletin,* vol. 51, 75–81.

1955

Dual role of the *Zeitgeist* in scientific creativity. *Scientific Monthly,* vol. 80, 101–106.

Introspection (article). *Encyclopaedia Britannica.*

The present status of parapsychology. *American Scientist,* vol. 43, 108–117.

Psychology. In James R. Newman (Ed.), *What Is Science?* New York: Simon and Schuster. Pp. 291–314.

1956

Gustav Theodor Fechner. (Reprinted from *History of Experimental Psychology,* 1950.) In James R. Newman (Ed.), *The World of Mathematics.* New York: Simon and Schuster. Vol. II, pp. 1145–1166.

1957

Robert Mearns Yerkes (1876–1956). *Year Book of the American Philosophical Society,* 1956. Pp. 133–140.
When is human behavior predetermined? *Scientific Monthly,* vol. 84, 189–196.

1958

Karl M. Dallenbach. *American Journal of Psychology,* vol. 71, 1–40.
Introductory statement. In E. H. Jacobson and H. C. J. Duijker (Eds.), *International Directory of Psychologists.* Assen, Netherlands: Royal Van Gorcum. Pp. ix f.
When is behavior predetermined? (Reprinted from 1957.) In D. E. Dulany, R. L. Valois, D. C. Beardslee, and M. R. Winterbottom (Eds.), *Contributions to Modern Psychology.* New York: Oxford University Press. Pp. 201–215.
With Langfeld, H. S. and Weld, H. P. (Eds.). *Foundations of Psychology.* Soon Duk Koh (Japanese trans.). Tokyo: Education Ministry.

1959

Foundations of Psychology. Japanese photographic reproduction of 1948 edition.
John Gilbert Beebe-Center: 1897–1958. *American Journal of Psychology,* vol. 72, 311–315.
Lewis Madison Terman: 1877–1956. *Biographical Memoirs of the National Academy of Sciences,* vol. 33, 413–461.
On eschewing teleology. *Science,* vol. 129, 608–610.
Science and the meaning of its history. *Key Reporter,* vol. 24, no. 4, 2f.
When is behavior predetermined? (Reprinted from 1957.) In R. S. Daniel (Ed.), *Contemporary Readings in General Psychology.* Boston: Houghton Mifflin. Pp. 336–345.
With Cobb, S., Hisaw, F. L., and Stevens, S. S. Karl Spencer Lashley. *Harvard University Gazette,* vol. 54, 115f.

1960

Lashley and cortical integration. In F. A. Beach, D. O. Hebb, C. T. Morgan, and H. W. Nissen (Eds.). *The Neurophysiology of Lashley.* New York: McGraw-Hill, pp. xi–xvi.
The pattern of modern psychology: the psychodynamics of the history of discovery. *Bulletin of the British Psychological Society,* no. 40, 16–19.
The psychologists' concept of mind. *Journal of Psychological Researches* (Madras), vol. IV, no. 3, 7 pp.

Index of Names

The important items are keyed by subject and given first. Less important items and incidental mentions of a name are labeled *inc.*, and given next. Citations of the literature are labeled *ref.*, and given last. No *inc.* item is included when there is an important subject item or a *ref.* item for the same page.

Index of Subjects

American and British psychology, 94–98; and Titchener, 254 f.
American Journal of Psychology, sale of, 42; Titchener crisis and, 42 f.
American Psychological Association, 50; reorganization of, 64 f.
American Psychological Foundation, Gold Medal Award, 80 f., 289
amnesia, retroactive, 40
ancestors, Boring, 5–7; Garrigues, 5–9, 11 f.; Moravian, 6, 8, 12; Quaker, 5–9; Truman, 7 f.
animal consciousness, 232–235; Titchener on, 234; Washburn on, 233 f.; Watson on, 234 f.
anthropomorphism, 233
anti-intellectualism, American, 79
antinomies, 310 f.
attributes, of psychophysics, 231

behavior, as belief, 306 f.; and consciousness, 232–235; control of, 308–310; and Watson, 234 f.; when predetermined, 295–313 (*see also* verbal behavior)
belief, causes of, 306 f.
Bethlehem Steel Co., 17, 19 f.
bibliography, E.G.B., 347–356
biography, of Boring, 3–83; of Dallenbach, 77 f.; E.G.B.,

perspective of, 80–83; Lashley's research, 78; the nature-nurture dilemma, 267–271, 292 f.; of Terman, 77, 266–294; of Titchener, 246–265; of Yerkes, 77
"BLW" texts, 57 f.
Britain, contributions to psychology, 94–98
Boyhood attitudes, 8–13

Call, from Cornell, 43; from Harvard, 32 f., 38 f., 50; from Minnesota, 32 f.; from Princeton, 40 f.; from Stanford, 39
causality, as model, 308
childhood, 8–11
Clark University, 32–39; call from, 33 f.; controversy at, 35–39; honorary degree from, 39; laboratory at, 34 f.; reappointment to, 32 f.; Terman's account of, 275
clinical psychology *vs.* experimental psychology, 180–182
cogent reason, principle of, 146–151
committee dynamics, 58
complementarity, Bohr's principle of, 311
concussion, cerebral, 39 f.
Congress of Psychology, at New Haven, 51; at Oxford, 41
Contemporary Psychology (*CP*), 74–76, 338 f.